The Cunningham Lectures for 1904

ST PAUL'S CONCEPTIONS OF THE LAST THINGS

ST PAUL'S CONCEPTIONS OF THE LAST THINGS

BY

THE REV. H. A. A. KENNEDY

M.A., D.Sc.

SECOND EDITION

WIPF & STOCK · Eugene, Oregon

Wipf and Stock Publishers
199 W 8th Ave, Suite 3
Eugene, OR 97401

St Pauls's Conceptions of the Last Things
By Kennedy, H. A. A.
ISBN 13: 978-1-5326-1881-9
Publication date 3/10/2017
Previously published by Hodder and Stoughton, 1904

TO

DR MARCUS DODS

WITH

GRATITUDE AND AFFECTION

PREFACE

THE following chapters are a study in the history of early Christian thought. This description fixes the method and the limits of the investigation.

When I had the honour of being appointed to the Cunningham Lectureship, I chose the subject here discussed, for reasons which may be briefly summarised. In an investigation of Paulinism, undertaken for another purpose, I had been growingly impressed by the vital bearing of St Paul's eschatological outlook upon his theology as a whole. His conceptions of the Last Things were manifestly factors of supreme importance in the organisation of his religious thought. Yet there seemed to be no department in which greater confusion prevailed as to the precise interpretation of his statements. Evidences of this were patent even in the works of well-equipped students of New Testament theology. Further, one was well aware that in the innumerable publications of modern times having the Last Things for their theme, all sorts of arguments in support of the most conflicting theories had been founded on passages selected from the writings of St Paul.

Such considerations as these suggested the propriety of a fresh investigation of the sources, an investigation which should keep in close touch with the genesis of the apostle's thought. From this standpoint, large use has been made of the prophetic books and the later apocalyptic literature, while the developments of the Synagogue-theology have also been kept in view.

Two features, pre-eminently, have emerged into prominence for my own mind as the result of the inquiry. The one is the necessity of grasping the great religious conceptions of the Old Testament in their original setting, if we are to penetrate into the texture of the Pauline theology. For the apostle clearly reveals himself as "an Hebrew of the Hebrews," and carries forward in a larger atmosphere the most splendid traditions of the prophets. His new Christian experience, indeed, seems to have quickened within him a finer sensitiveness to the deeper elements in the earlier revelation.

The other feature which impresses one most powerfully is the decisiveness with which St Paul has laid the foundation of the Christian hope of Eternal Life, not in any vague speculations concerning human personality in the abstract, but in the relation of the individual soul to the risen Lord, Jesus Christ. He attains his end without any of those theoretical surmises as to *existence* which have brought confusion into so many modern discussions. Life in Christ is for him something larger than existence. It is existence raised to its highest power—the supreme, unsurpassable reality.

If these pages contribute in any measure to a clearer vision of the inspiring prospect which the apostle reached through knowing "the power of Christ's resurrection," the labour spent upon them will not have been in vain.

In view of what has been said above as to the intimacy of St Paul's relation to the Old Testament, there will be nothing surprising in the acknowledgment that I owe more than I can tell to the class lectures of my late revered teacher, Dr A. B. Davidson. The published literature to which I am under obligations is referred to throughout.[1] I must also express my deep indebtedness to my friend, the Rev. H. R. Mackintosh, D.Phil., Aberdeen, who was good enough to read the proofs, for many valuable suggestions and criticisms.

H. A. A. KENNEDY.

CALLANDER, *March* 1904.

[1] My MS. was in the press before Sokolowski's recently-published monograph, *Die Begriffe Geist und Leben bei Paulus in ihren Beziehungen zu einander* (Gött., 1903), came into my hands.

CONTENTS

CHAPTER I

THE PLACE OF ESCHATOLOGY IN ST PAUL'S RELIGIOUS THOUGHT

CHAPTER II

FORMATIVE INFLUENCES IN ST PAUL'S CONCEPTIONS OF THE LAST THINGS

CHAPTER III

St Paul's Conceptions of Life and Death

CHAPTER IV

St Paul's Conceptions of the Parousia and the Judgment

CHAPTER V

St Paul's Conception of the Resurrection

CHAPTER VI

St Paul's Conception of the Consummation of the Kingdom of God

ADDITIONAL NOTE TO CHAPTER II

The Pauline Eschatology and Hellenism

INDEX

CHAPTER I

THE PLACE OF ESCHATOLOGY IN ST PAUL'S RELIGIOUS THOUGHT

FEW provinces of religious thought have possessed a more perennial interest for the average man than that which is concerned with conceptions of the Last Things. The religious ritual of primitive races is pre-eminently associated with the events which follow the cessation of earthly existence. The sacred books of ancient peoples are peculiarly rich in eschatological speculations. We have only to recall the Egyptian *Book of the Dead*, the Babylonian epic of the *Descent of Istar*, the *Bundehesh* of the Persian Avesta, to realise the remarkable fascination of the unseen world and its experiences for the naïve theologians of antiquity. The *Nekyia* of the *Odyssey* and the Sixth Book of Vergil's *Æneid* no doubt reflect the popular beliefs, and also, in their turn, react upon them. The quaint *Apocalypses* of post-canonical Judaism are almost wholly engrossed with the events of the End. And as the history of religion is traced down the centuries, those periods are rare which do not give evidence of the absorbing attraction with which Eschatology is invested for human thought

A

and imagination.[1] The Christian faith has not been exempt from this inherent bias of religious speculation. The New Testament gives no scanty space to conceptions of the Last Things. And in so doing, it serves itself heir to the spirit of Old Testament prophecy. It is natural to expect that a man like St Paul, so deeply imbued by nature and training with the traditions of his nation, and so earnestly absorbed in its Messianic hope,[2] would continue even from his Christian standpoint to assign a peculiar prominence to the occurrences of the final epoch. In any case, as we shall presently discover, his course was marked out for him by the evangelic tradition. The teaching of Jesus Himself had contained a remarkable eschatological strain. This reappears in most of the New Testament writings. But perhaps nowhere is it found so closely woven into the texture of the primitive theology as in the Letters of St Paul. Accordingly, a study of his conceptions of the Last Things is of fundamental importance for his whole Christian outlook. In them is most fully revealed the transformation which Christianity produced in this region of thought.

[1] Dr Fairbairn probably does not exaggerate when he says: "To the thinker, the theological is the distinctive side of a religion; but to the multitude, the eschatological . . . Christianity has exercised a greater command over peoples, though not over individual minds, by its Eschatology than by its Theology."—*Studies in the Philosophy of Religion and History*, p. 154.

[2] The fact of his devotion to the Law is evidence of this. For the meaning of zeal for the Law in Judaism lay in its conception of the covenant between God and His people. Devoted observance of the Torah on their part was the condition of God's fulfilment of His promises, notably the inauguration of the Messianic epoch (see especially Marti, *Geschichte d. Israelit. Religion*, p. 289).

We can trace the workings of the apostle's religious experience as he starts from the inherited beliefs of Judaism, modifies these under the influence of his new relation to the risen Christ, and transfers the emphasis and the accent from the letter to the spirit. But St Paul has also laid the foundation for the Eschatology of the Christian Church. That has in some important respects deviated from its Pauline basis. It is therefore of value to reach as accurate and comprehensive a view as possible of the form in which his conceptions of the Last Things took shape. Thereby we shall be able to check the accretions of subsequent ecclesiastical theories. And at a time when discussions of the Future State and kindred topics appear to possess a growing fascination for the public mind, it should help towards sanity of judgment and a due respect for the limits of human knowledge, to aim at a closer acquaintance with the eschatological teaching of one who did not shrink from the frank confession, "At present we see in a mirror only dim outlines, but then face to face. At present my knowledge is a fragment, but then shall I know as completely as I have been known."[1]

[1] The objection may be brought against our inquiry that it is illegitimate to speak of a specially *Pauline* Eschatology. Thus, *e.g.*, Wrede: "There is a Pauline doctrine of redemption, a Pauline doctrine of justification, but there is—to speak *cum grano salis*—no Pauline angelology and eschatology, but only a Jewish or primitive-Christian" (*Aufgabe u. Methode d. sogenannten Neutestamentlichen Theologie*, p. 66). Even granting the general accuracy of this assertion, we should consider it well worth while to make a careful examination of the Pauline conceptions as representing the best type of primitive-Christian Eschatology. We will readily admit that the apostle has much

Perhaps no more important contribution has been made within recent years to the interpretation of the New Testament than the accentuation of the eschatological strain which runs throughout its literature. The dream of that little group of disciples who formed the nucleus of the Christian Church was a purified theocracy. In this they were true to the highest expectations of Jewish Apocalyptic. When their Master preached the Kingdom of God, a willing echo responded from their hearts. For prophets and psalmists had seen glorious visions of a time when God's purpose for His people should be fulfilled: when the genuine Israel should rejoice beneath the Divine sway: when the holy nation should be a light to lighten the Gentiles. The Baptist had announced that the Kingdom was at hand. When the disciples had reached the point of confessing that Jesus was the Christ, they thereby virtually acknowledged that the rule of God had already begun: the coming age (*αἰὼν μέλλων*, עוֹלָם הַבָּא) was casting its shadow upon the course of the present. Their conviction was for ever established by their experience of the risen Lord. A momentous problem which pressed upon their minds was the reckoning of the time when the new Æon should break in. The mysterious hints concerning the future which their Lord had given them were hard to comprehend and adjust. The main impression they had gained was

in common with the average beliefs of the earliest Christian communities. But it is precisely the points at which he deviates from these, not only in details and definite representations, but still more in general breadth of outlook and caution of judgment, which appear to us of primary importance in the history of Christianity.

the expectation of His speedy return and the accompanying world-judgment. Perhaps they foreshortened the perspective. Perhaps the wonder of the new Christian movement, with all its amazing experiences, seemed to demand a rapid development of events up to the great consummation of the Parousia. Just as the Old Testament prophets, when they felt the currents of Providence quickening in any direction, looked for the immediate entrance of Jehovah into the world-history, and saw the fortunes of the nations ripening for a final decision, so the phenomena of the dispensation of the Spirit seemed to promise to the ardent hearts of the first Christians the immediate close of the earthly and secular era, and the ultimate separation for glorious ends of the community of believers. Thus an eager upward gaze characterises the New Testament epoch. It will be modified by its immediate environment. When worldly opposition to the Gospel is most stubborn, when the persecution of the saints rages most fiercely, the cry, "Come quickly, Lord Jesus," will rise with more piercing intensity. When the wrath of man is restrained, and the Christian society is suffered to expand and flourish, the yearning for the Parousia will take the form of a heightened activity in preparing the way of the Lord. St Paul shares to the full in the dominant mood of his age. It is evident that the burden of his early missionary preaching was a Christian version of the Baptist's older message: "Repent, for the Kingdom of heaven is at hand." For he reminds the Thessalonians of their response to his Gospel in these words: "Ye turned to God from idols to serve the living and true God, and to await His Son from heaven, whom He raised from the dead, even Jesus, who delivers us from the coming wrath" (1 Thess. i. 9, 10).[1]

In subsequent chapters the several conceptions of the Last Things which bulk most largely in the pages of the apostle must be dealt with. For the present we shall briefly examine the eschatological implications which lie deep in his view of religion.

It might be difficult, in the case of so many-sided a religious nature as that of St Paul, to attempt to sum up in a single conception that which he regarded as the supreme blessing of the Christian calling. Some might identify it with the forgiveness of sins, some with the condition of the justified person. Some might describe it under the vague term salvation, others might find it in fellowship with Christ, and others still in eternal life.[2] All these statements

[1] Of course this conviction of a speedy fulfilment is a commonplace of eschatological expectation, *cf.* Apoc. Bar., xx. 6, "For they (*i.e.* the times) will come, and will not tarry"; Rev. i. 1, "Things which must shortly come to pass"; and Smend (*Z.A.T.W.*, 1885, p. 236), "The essence of Apocalyptic is the certainty of the immediate nearness of the Messianic future." See also Volz, *Jüdische Eschatologie*, p. 164.

[2] Thus Steffen: "At least as strong as, indeed, even more powerful than the experience of the forgiveness of sins, is his joy regarding the certainty of an eternal life . . . He sighed, as scarcely any other has done, beneath the curse of the transiency of all that is earthly" (*Z.N.T.W.*, 1901, ii. p. 124). So also Titius: "Since (for Paul) the conception of life is the decisive one for religion as contrasted with that of righteousness, and since, accordingly, the conception of resurrection has, in the representation of salvation, preference to that of judgment, the view of the pneumatic life in Christ has preference to the conception of justification, while at the same time, in this latter, attention to the ethical nature of the new life falls into the background" (*Paulinismus unter d. Gesichtspunkt d. Seligkeit*, p. 270).

are certainly justifiable, as expressing each a side of the truth in which the mind of the apostle can rest with perfect satisfaction. They are all, moreover, consistent with one another, for they are all closely linked with his personal Christian experience. The forgiveness of sin, justification, salvation—these represent one primary aspect of it. The possession of the Spirit, fellowship with Christ, eternal life, set forth another of equal value. The result of his meeting with the risen Jesus was the creating within him of a new life. "If any man be in Christ, he is a new creature" (2 Cor. v. 17). He shares in the eternal life of his Lord. He possesses the Spirit of Christ. "If any man have not the Spirit of Christ, he is none of His" (Rom. viii. 9). But this wonderful relationship in which his soul recognises an immediate contact with the Divine has nothing arbitrary about it. It is God's response to his faith, faith in Jesus Christ as the Propitiation for sin, as the Mediator of forgiveness, as the Saviour in whom men may be reconciled to God. Without pursuing for the present the discussion of the organic connection between these two normative aspects of Christianity, according to St Paul,[1] we have to inquire how far they imply, in their content, a forward gaze. We may select Justification as typical of the one side of the relationship, and the Life in the Spirit as representing the other. Now Justification and the New Life may be so accurately described as the two *foci* of the Pauline system, that if we discover an

[1] See an instructive discussion by Steffen, of "The relation of Spirit and Faith in Paul" (*Z.N.T.W.*, 1901, H. ii. pp. 115 ff., 234 ff). Steffen distinguishes too sharply between the "mystical" and the "ethical" aspects of St Paul's religious consciousness.

eschatological bias in them, we may safely postulate such a background for the whole world of his religious thought.[1]

In the first place, let us briefly sum up St Paul's teaching on Justification. We are justified freely by the grace of God through the redemption which is in Christ Jesus (Rom. iii. 24). God has manifested His grace (ἐχαρίτωσεν) to us in the Beloved, in whom we have redemption through His blood, the forgiveness of transgressions (Eph. i. 6, 7). This new relation to God, this new standing which we have in His sight, is His response to our faith. He looks upon us, not as we are in ourselves, but as we are in Jesus Christ, His dear Son, who died in our stead (2 Cor. v. 14-21). What we could not do, that Christ *has* done, done *for us* (Rom. viii. 3, 4). Therefore in the boldness of faith we can claim the saving benefits of His death for ourselves. Thus, having been justified as the result of (ἐκ) faith, we have peace with God through our Lord Jesus Christ (Rom. v. 1). In Him we are made heirs of God, assured of His fatherly love. These are the first stages in our new relation of reconciliation to God: the first stages, and not the consummation. There is still a race to be run: there is still an inward conflict to be faced: there is still a goal to be reached, the prize of God's high calling in Christ Jesus (Phil. iii. 14). "If, when we were enemies, we were reconciled to God through the

[1] Wrede's caution is thoroughly to the point: "In proving that Paul always looks to the future, it is not enough to emphasise certain passages. It must be shown that all the chief conceptions of his doctrine of salvation, and especially those which one would like to interpret otherwise, *bear in themselves* a reference to the future, or are definitely determined by expectations of the future" (*Th. L.Z.*, 1894, Sp. 131).

death of His Son, much more, having been reconciled, we shall be saved by His life" (Rom. v. 10: *cf.* ver. 9, "Much more, having been justified now (νῦν) by His blood, we shall be saved through Him from the wrath"). The apostle rejoices, indeed, in the assurance of God's forgiveness for Christ's sake. He is confident that there is now (νῦν) no condemnation for those that are in Christ Jesus (Rom. viii. 1). But the passages which have been quoted, the crucial passages for this conception, clearly show that, in the midst of his joy, he looks forward with yearning to the completion of salvation which awaits the believer in the day of God's final decision. Justification may truly be called the anticipation of salvation, the anticipation of the final judgment. But St Paul —who, for all his Christian idealism, is too sadly acquainted with the struggles of the life in the flesh— craves the realisation of that blissful future, when sin and death and judgment are no more to be reckoned with. There is no real inconsistency between the two positions. His outlook is absolutely true to religious experience. The joy of God's favour in the present earthbound life is at best a broken joy. "We were saved by hope; but hope that is seen is not hope; for what one sees, why does he hope for? But if we hope for that which we do not see, by patient endurance we eagerly expect it" (Rom. viii. 24-25). The believing soul dare not trust itself. It has staked its all upon the grace of God made manifest in Christ. It remains conscious of its extraordinary debt to that grace. Thus, in the tremulousness of such self-distrust, and keeping in view the lofty heights of spiritual excellence to which he is summoned in the knowledge of the power of Christ's resurrection and the fellowship of His sufferings, St Paul speaks with humble caution: "If haply I shall attain to the resurrection from the dead. Not that I have attained already, or have been already perfected, but I follow after, in the hope that I shall indeed grasp that for which I was grasped by Christ Jesus" (Phil. iii. 11, 12). Quite plainly, then, from the standpoint of a justified man, the apostle's gaze is turned eagerly towards the future. He knows himself to belong to the σωζόμενοι, but the salvation (σωτηρία) is a process which culminates when the exalted Christ shall return in glory, and both the dead and the living shall be transformed into perfect fitness for His fellowship. Probably it is stating the truth too strongly to say, with Titius, that in Paul's "hope, not in his present possession of salvation, lies the crucial point for his personal feeling" (p. 21)[1]. The man who can exclaim with exultation, "Who shall separate us from the love of Christ," and then, after weighing all his perils, can triumphantly affirm, "Nay, in all these things we are more than conquerors through Him that loved us," is surely sufficiently aware of the surpassing worth of the salvation which has already been brought near to him. Yet the statement points in the true direction. "This present evil age" (Gal. i. 4) hampers the fulfilment of God's saving purpose. The coming era,[2] the era

[1] The opposite tendency is found in the assertion of Beyschlag, that "hope . . . does not, in the case of Paul, as in the case of Peter and the other original apostles, form the centre of gravity of subjective Christianity: he finds that in a belief in the salvation that has appeared in the fact of the Cross" (*N.T. Theol.*, E. Tr., ii. p. 254). But that salvation, as St Paul conceives it, has hope in the very heart of it.

[2] It is a one-sided view of Pauline Christology which would

of the perfected Divine order, which will be inaugurated by the Parousia of Christ, the Resurrection, and the Judgment, will be the entire vindication of the believer. The full meaning of his justification will appear when he is openly acknowledged by the Judge. The eschatological element in Justification is fully borne out by St Paul's use of the terms *σωτηρία* and *σώζεσθαι*. The noun does not occur very frequently in his writings, but its usage is unmistakable. In 2 Cor. vii. 10 it is contrasted with *θάνατος*, in Phil. i. 28 with *ἀπώλεια*. In Rom. xiii. 11, the eschatological character of the conception appears with decisive clearness: "It is time for you now to be roused from sleep; for now is our *salvation* nearer than when we believed. The night has advanced, the day (*i.e.* of the Lord) is at hand." The same thought lies behind his exhortation to the Philippians: "Work out your own salvation to the end" (*σωτηρίαν κατεργάζεσθε*, Phil. ii. 12). Here the main emphasis falls on the final issue. Salvation is only accomplished, is only, in the complete sense, realised, when Christ shall appear. It seems to us by no means accidental that in the Pauline Epistles the word appears most commonly in the phrase *εἰς σωτηρίαν*, in which the idea of a goal to be reached is quite obvious. An instructive instance is 1 Thess. v. 9: "For God did not appoint us with a view to wrath (*εἰς ὀργήν*), but with a view to the obtaining of salvation." Noteworthy, and fully corroborating this position, is the

affirm that "the entire function of the Son of God, who has appeared in the flesh, consists in the introduction of this close of the world which leads to the final death of the flesh" (so Holtzmann, *N.T. Theol.*, ii. p. 196). But the side which is here exaggerated has too often been ignored by expositors of the New Testament.

antithesis of salvation to wrath. For ὀργή is an eschatological term, and, in the Epistles, invariably denotes the condemnation of the judgment day.[1] Another example worthy of notice is 2 Thess. ii. 13: "God chose you from the beginning with a view to salvation." The phrase εἰς σωτηρίαν is explained or supplemented, a few clauses further on, by the words, "with a view to the obtaining of the glory of our Lord Jesus Christ." Here again our contention is amply verified, for "glory," as we shall see afterwards, is one of what may be called the technical terms of New Testament Eschatology. It is needless to refer to the contrast several times drawn between *οἱ σωζόμενοι* and *οἱ ἀπολλύμενοι*, a contrast which points self-evidently to the final issues of human character. But it is worth while to lay stress on the remarkable expressions in Rom. v. 9, 10, which have been already quoted: "We shall be saved through Him from the wrath," and "we shall be saved by his life." These statements, which occupy a fundamental place in the apostle's argument, can have nothing in view but the experience of the redeemed believer at the Parousia of Jesus Christ. A further illustration of the position we are emphasising is to be found in the term ἀπολύτρωσις, which is a kind of synonym for σωτηρία.[2] Justification is effected "through the

[1] The term has already come to have this application in Judaistic literature. *Cf.* Jub., xxiv. 30; Slav. Enoch, xliv. 2.

[2] Titius describes σωτηρία and ἀπολύτρωσις as being merely negative expressions for equipment with life (p. 54). It is so far true that St Paul regards eternal life as the supreme blessing of the End for believers. The terms, however, may be just as strictly taken as positive expressions for deliverance from sin. And it is easy to trace the connection between the two sides of the conception, when we remember the apostle's

redemption which is in Christ Jesus" (Rom. iii. 24). When we investigate the full content of "redemption," according to St Paul, we discover that it includes certain remarkable elements. Thus, from Rom. viii. 23, "We also ourselves groan within ourselves, eagerly expecting (our) sonship, the redemption of our body," the true scope of ἀπολύτρωσις may be ascertained. It is not exhausted in the forgiveness of sins, and the deliverance from their guilt and dominion. It stretches into the future, and embraces the transformation of the bodily nature which Christ shall accomplish by changing it "into the likeness of the body of His glory" at the Parousia (Phil. iii. 21). The same idea meets us in Eph. i. 14, where St Paul speaks of the Spirit as "the pledge of our inheritance with a view to the redemption of the purchased possession" (*i.e.*, the entire life and constitution of the believer). This is repeated in Eph. iv. 30, where again he describes believers as being sealed by the Spirit, "with a view to the day of redemption" (εἰς ἡμέραν ἀπολυτρώσεως), the day, of course, when Christ shall be revealed.[1]

statement in Rom. vi. 23, that "the wages of sin is death."

[1] On the eschatological aspect of Justification, see especially Kölbing, *S.K.*, 1895, pp. 1 ff.; Pfleiderer, *Paulinism*, i. pp. 227, 228; Wernle, *Der Christ u. die Sünde bei Paulus*, pp. 22, 100 ff. This last suggestive discussion is marred here and there by unqualified statements. Thus, *e.g.*, "The Christian receives through justification the right to all the blessings of the Messianic community, without an ethical transformation being derived from it," as if the faith in Christ which justifies is not ethical from its very *raison d'être*. The same paradoxical character is found in the author's main contention, as *e.g.*, p. 112: "The doctrine of the walk in the Spirit is so enthusiastically set forth, and so completely regulated by the hope of

It might be felt, however, that the conception of Justification was one which, from its very essence, possessed eschatological bearings.[1] The idea of acquittal or condemnation presupposes a judgment. And from the apostolic standpoint, that judgment takes place at the end of the present era, and constitutes the inauguration of the future Kingdom of God. It is otherwise when we turn to the second focal conception of St Paul's religious thought, the Life in the Spirit. At the first glance it appears as if there were little room here for a relation to the Last Things. "In Paul," says J. Weiss, "the eschatological tension is strongly counterbalanced by his Christ-mysticism. He who, through the Spirit, is united with Christ and lives in Him, has surmounted space and time" (*Die Predigt Jesu vom Reiche Gottes*, p. 61). Nevertheless, in this province also, we discover the very same trend. The Life in the Spirit is the direct result of St Paul's first contact with Christian realities. The revelation to him of the risen Jesus was necessarily the revelation of the Messiah. The hope of his fathers was actually realised. The ends of the world had come. He was now living in the last time. But this revelation was not merely *to* him. It was also *in* him (Gal. i. 16: ἀποκαλύψαι τὸν υἱὸν αὐτοῦ ἐν ἐμοί, "to reveal His Son in me"). He had not only been convinced of the existence of that Jesus whom he persecuted. The living Lord had laid hold on his life (Phil. iii. 12: κατελήμφθην ὑπὸ Χριστοῦ Ἰησοῦ). He had become its energising principle. It was no

the Parousia, that no place is left for sin in the life of Christians."

[1] "Righteousness, Judgment, Parousia, are indissolubly connected" (Cremer, *Rechtfertigungslehre*, p. 350).

longer he that lived, but Christ that lived in him (Gal. ii. 20). It was so amazing a transformation for a human experience, that he could, in all soberness, call it a new creation. But this transfigured life, with all its potency, with all its victorious energy, was, of necessity, grievously hampered. Its medium for the present was a fleshly nature, liable to sin and weakness and decay. Ideally, indeed, the flesh was crucified: annulled through fellowship with the death of Christ (Rom. vi. 6, 11; Gal. v. 24). That was its ultimate fate—a fate as to which there could be no question. As a matter of real experience, the flesh still warred against the spirit, thwarting its impulses and often defeating its strivings (Gal. v. 16, 17). The law of sin and death had been abolished for those who were in Christ Jesus. The law of the Spirit of life in Him had taken its place (Rom. viii. 2). But that new law, the law of liberty (*cf.* Gal. v. 1) could not have free scope for its workings under present earthly conditions. It was the spirit of sonship which Christians had received, for God had sent forth the Spirit of His Son into their hearts, crying, Abba, Father. So that they were now heirs of God, joint-heirs with Christ (Gal. iv. 6, 7; Rom. viii. 15-17). Yet that Spirit was only the first-fruits (ἀπαρχή, Rom. viii. 23) of the glorious heritage one day to be possessed. Even for the children of God (Rom. viii. 16) it was a time of waiting, of sighing, of groaning: they must still yearn for the perfected sonship (viii. 23). This relation to God, when consummated, involved a transformation of the whole man, not only of spirit, but of body. And the redemption of the body, which meant its conformity to the glorified body of Christ (Phil. iii. 21), would be the final stage of the Spirit's operation. For the present, the life-giving Spirit was possessed only as pledge (ἀρραβών, Eph. i. 14). Such an earnest pointed continually forward. Even the mute creation sympathised with the craving of believers for their future inheritance of bliss (Rom. viii. 22). They were linked together by the ardent yearning to be delivered from the bondage of corruption (φθορά, Rom. viii. 21), and to attain to indissoluble life. At this point we can clearly perceive the eschatological bearing of St Paul's idea of the possession of the Spirit. The peculiar function of the Spirit is to impart life (ζωοποιεῖν, *e.g.*, 2 Cor. iii. 6, τὸ δὲ πνεῦμα ζωοποιεῖ, "the Spirit makes alive"; *cf.* 1 Cor. xv. 45, ὁ ἔσχατος Ἀδὰμ εἰς πνεῦμα ζωοποιοῦν, "a life-creating Spirit"). That gift fortifies its possessor against the doom of death. For, "the gift of God is eternal life (ζωὴ αἰώνιος) in Christ Jesus our Lord" (Rom. vi. 23). Its true significance is revealed in the words of Rom. viii. 11: "If the Spirit of Him who raised Jesus from the dead dwell in you, He that raised Christ Jesus from the dead shall quicken (ζωοποιήσει) also your mortal bodies through His Spirit, which dwelleth in you." Plainly, the full realisation of this life belongs to the events of the End, is finally attained in the Resurrection.

We have briefly considered the eschatological trend in the two primary conceptions of St Paul's religious thought. But his wistful yearning for the future, blissful consummation is everywhere visible. The hope that lies in front of him is in very truth the anchor of his soul. It is no casual thought which he expresses in the words, "By hope we were saved" (Rom. viii. 24). When tribulation presses on him, he contrasts "the light affliction which is for a moment" with "the exceeding and eternal weight of glory" which is its issue (2 Cor. iv. 17). When he reflects on his own experience, he comes to the conclusion that "the sufferings of the present time are not worthy to be compared with the glory which is to be revealed in us" (Rom. viii. 18). If the Christians' confidence in Christ belongs only to *this* life, then are they of all men most miserable. The present is the time of imperfection. "We know in part and we prophesy in part, but when the consummation (τὸ τέλειον) shall have come, then that which is fragmentary (τὸ ἐκ μέρους) shall be abolished" (1 Cor. xiii. 9, 10). The principle of his life, in a word, is to look, not at the things which are seen, but at the things which are not seen. "For the things which are seen are temporal, but the things which are not seen are eternal" (2 Cor. iv. 18).

Before proceeding to examine St Paul's conceptions of the Last Things, so far as that is possible, in detail, it will be of advantage to observe the form in which these conceptions are presented, and the limits within which the apostle has chosen to move. Such an inquiry will provide us with cautions for our further investigation. It will place us on our guard against illegitimate inferences from the statements of the Epistles. It will supply us with certain regulating principles for our estimate of St Paul's positions. It will suggest to us the kind of questions we have a right to put, and the lines on which we may expect to be answered.

The whole treatment of the Last Things in the New Testament is noteworthy for its freedom from exaggeration, its habit of abstaining from precise definition, its tacit acknowledgment of the mystery of the unseen world and the future life. This can only be realised after a careful study of the parallel Eschatologies in other sacred literatures, and the curious cross-questionings of the future which meet us in modern times.[1] The contrast is decisive, when we place, for example, the teaching of Jesus side by side with the speculations of the Jewish Apocalypses. In the former, details are conspicuously absent. There is no elaborate delineation of the events which belong to the consummation of all things. There is no highly-coloured portrayal of the bliss of Paradise, or of the doleful gloom of Gehenna. The grotesque pictures of the renewal of nature are altogether lacking: so is the vivid scenery which forms the background of the Judgment and God's final victory over evil.[2] A similar antithesis reveals itself if we compare St Paul's conceptions with, say, the Persian

[1] "The spirit of man coveteth divination" (Lord Bacon).

[2] We fail to see any ground for Holtzmann's sharp polemic against Haupt for laying emphasis on the lack of highly-coloured pictures in the Eschatology of Jesus (*N.T. Theol.*, i. p. 335, note 3). Haupt would, of course, admit the use of figurative descriptions. This is all that can be asserted of the "great feast," "eating of bread," "thrones of judgment," etc., which Holtzmann quotes as examples of "colours." Haupt's statement does not seem to us one-sided: "The conception of ζωή in its full meaning—the supra-earthly Divine life—is the central thing for Jesus, which He always keeps in view. He who has that has all, and there is no advantage in laying stress on the peripheral features. So we find in Him no answer to all the questions which are usually treated in connection with the Resurrection. When this ἀνάστασις is to come, how the body of the consummation will be related to the present body, how to the condition in Hades . . . all these are questions which do not exist for Him. He believes in the power of God (Mark xii. 12), which can establish life in all directions, and it is enough for Him that this life will be a heavenly one, analogous

Eschatology, which some scholars regard as an influential factor in Jewish beliefs. Here, side by side with remarkable spiritual intuitions, there appears a crude realism. Thus the restraint and caution of St Paul's idea of the life after death are thrown into relief by the minute delineation of the journey of the soul, *e.g.*, in *Vendîdâd*, xix. 27-33, where we read that the pious soul, after he has departed, is met by a beautiful virgin, the incarnation of his own good deeds. She conducts him over the Hara-Berezaiti (the sacred mountain, now Elburz): she bears him upwards from the bridge Çinvat into the road of the spiritual divinities. Vohu-manô, the good spirit, rises to greet him; then with joy the soul of the faithful passes into the presence of Ahura-Mazda (see Söderblom, *La Vie Future d'après le Mazdéisme*, pp. 88-91). Doubtless the explanation of this contrast which we have been emphasising lies in the fact that the normative element of New Testament Eschatology (Gospels and Epistles) is to be found in the religious consciousness of those who gave it shape. The careful and sensitive reader has always the impression that Jesus and His apostles, in dealing with the Last Things, are perfectly well aware that they must use imagery derived from human life, as lived under its ordinary earthly conditions, to body forth processes which belong altogether to the suprasensible world.[1] To interpret the picture of judgment

to that of the angels and of God Himself" (*Eschatolog. Aussagen Jesu*, p. 92).

[1] One of the chief flaws in Kabisch's *Eschatologie des Paulus* is the persistently literalistic treatment of metaphorical language. At the same time, it must be remembered that for New Testament writers the boundary lines between fact and symbol were far less rigid than for modern minds.

in Matt. xxv. by a crass literalism, is to ignore the most valuable instrument of the preacher, the use of impressive figure, to say nothing of the fact that our Lord, as a true man, must constantly have thought in pictures.[1] We need only reflect upon our own conceptions of the events of the End, in order to discover how large a place must be given to metaphor, if we are to deal with that region of religious thought at all.[2]

Further, the writers of the New Testament must employ language which will find some point of contact with the minds of their hearers or readers. And so they are content to move more or less among the conceptions of the Last Things current with their audience, modifying these when it is needful to bring into prominence some spiritual aspect of the question which is, as yet, unfamiliar. In the light of this fact, it is almost ludicrous to find St Paul's eschatological ideas discussed at times in a tone of disparagement, because they so frequently harmonise with the teachings of Judaism. The conceptions of the Parousia and the Judgment must have constituted, as we shall see, a most powerful element in the missionary preaching of the apostle. Then, as now, the solemn *issues* of life possessed a unique force of appeal to the

[1] *Cf.* Haupt, *op. cit.*, p. 159: "The designedly pictorial character of His utterances, which are only the individualising and plastic expression of religious and ethical ideas, is, in this department, entirely analogous to the manner in which He is wont to express Himself in other provinces."

[2] See *Paradise Lost*, bk. v. 571-577 :—

"What surmounts the reach
Of human sense, I shall delineate so,
By lik'ning spiritual to corporal forms,
As may express them best, though what if Earth
Be but the shadow of Heaven, and things therein
Each to other like, more than on earth is thought."

conscience. Would not that force have vanished if St Paul had been led to approach his hearers from a more theoretical or philosophical standpoint? We know that he found his most ready converts in the God-fearers (οἱ σεβόμενοι τὸν θεόν) who were already acquainted with the Old Testament and the doctrines of the Synagogue. It was in accord with the remarkable preparation of the Diaspora for the Christian Gospel that the apostle's affirmations concerning the Last Things should follow the general outlines laid down by the Scriptures and the teaching of post-canonical Judaism. More noteworthy, as we shall discover, is the freedom with which he deviates from traditional views, or rather transforms them for use in the service of the faith of Christ.[1]

It may be said without exaggeration that St Paul has no Eschatology. By that we mean that he has never approached the subject in a systematic fashion.[2] A man of his speculative cast of mind, and one whose supreme hope was bound up with the glorious, unseen future, must often have been borne along in flights of ardent search, if by any means he might pierce the darkness lying round the borders of the world where Christ now ruled. But while he delights to dwell on certain sides of the eschatological problem, and seems, at first sight, to give these a disproportionate place, he does not even supply the materials for constructing anything in the nature of a scheme, far less does he

[1] See especially, Titius, pp. 47-49; Reuss, *Histoire de la Théologie Chrétienne*, ii. p. 211.

[2] *Cf.* Deissmann (*Th. L.Z.*, 1898, Sp. 14): "What is called the 'Eschatology' of Paul has little that is 'eschatological' about it . . . Paul did not write *de novissimis* . . . One must be prepared for a surging hither and thither of great thoughts, feelings, expectations."

attempt to reach such a construction for himself.[1] It is difficult, in examining the religious thought of a born theologian like St Paul, to refrain from attempting to classify it within the confines of a dogmatic plan. And when an investigator, of set purpose, refuses to deal with his teaching on these lines, he is supposed to be doing an injustice to the apostle. It is surely no discredit to St Paul that he did not attempt to bind himself down to a logical sequence in his views of Christian truth.[2] He is

[1] This is in harmony with his general theological method, which is aptly described by Prof. Ramsay (*Expos.*, vi. 6, p. 86): "Paul sees like a man. He sees one side at a time. He emphasises that—not indeed more than it deserves—but in a way that provokes misconception, because he expresses one side of the case and leaves the audience to catch his meaning, to sympathise with his point of view, to supply for themselves the qualifications and the conditions and the reservations which are necessary in the concrete facts of actual life." *Cf.* A.B Davidson on Heb. xii. 1: "Even a writer of Scripture may be allowed to throw out a brilliant ideal conception without our tying him down to having uttered a formal doctrine." In this avoidance of rounded-off system the apostle is true to the traditions of his nation. "You can make a digest and system of their (*i.e.* the Rabbinic) law, but a system of their *theology* you can only make with the utmost caution and many reservations" (Montefiore, *J.Q.R.*, xiii. p. 171). From this point of view, Weber's well-known work, *Die Lehren des Talmud*, must be checked by Bacher's admirable collections, *Die Agada der Tannaiten*, 2 vols., 1884-1890.

[2] *Cf.* Fairbairn, *Philosophy of the Christian Religion*, p. 440: "Paul, as he lives before us in his Epistles, is a man who holds many men within him—so many . . . that we may describe him as the most unintelligible of men to the analytical reason of a critic who has never warmed to the passion or been moved by the enthusiasm of humanity; but the most intelligible of men to the man who has heard within himself the sound of all the voices that speak in man."

logical enough when his spiritual experience demands it, but a large part of his affirmations regarding the religious life and destiny of men is thrown off, as occasion prompts, in vague hints, in outbursts of intense spiritual emotion, in pictures set within the framework of his inherited training, in arguments devised to meet the needs of a particular church or a particular group of converts. As Professor Gardner finely expresses it, "His writings do not constitute a philosophic system, because they are not purposefully hammered out, but fused by an intense heat from within. . . . His basis is not only certain principles worked out to their logical results, but also experiences, like flashes of lightning, which lit up the cave of consciousness, and melted its contents into new and sometimes irregular forms" (*Historic View of Christianity*, pp. 217, 218). Obviously, therefore, we need never be surprised to find gaps in the hypothetical system for which our minds crave.[1] Especially, in a

[1] See a most instructive paragraph in Drummond's *Philo*, i. p. 186: "While a system of thought is still growing, its successive stages and ultimate logical results disclose themselves only by degrees. For a time an explanation may be deemed sufficient which contains, unperceived and unresolved, a variety of problems destined to try the skill of future inquirers: we are not justified in forcing on one of its earliest exponents its implicit contents, which may never have become explicit in his consciousness. The critical historian is apt to be impatient of vagueness, and in a question which appears to him inevitable, and did in fact arise inevitably in the course of the development, he will have it that each writer must have had an opinion one way or the other: whereas to many thinkers the question may never have occurred, and were we able to propound it to them, we should find them unprovided with an answer." Pfleiderer, *Paulinism*, i. p. 259 ff. (E. Tr.), greatly exaggerates the lack of cohesion in Pauline Eschatology.

department like Eschatology, in which words and images derived from prosaic earthly experiences have to translate for human minds the mysterious events and processes of a life raised above material limitations, we may expect to move among half-truths, dim symbols of realities, paradoxical statements which refuse to be harmonised.[1] We believe, indeed, that St Paul's eschatological conceptions have a far greater mutual congruity than some recent investigators have been willing to recognise. But in an age when the notion of development is regarded as the key to all problems, it is perhaps natural that scholars should use it in explaining certain phenomena which look like antinomies in the Pauline Epistles. This view has been worked to its furthest limit by Sabatier, Pfleiderer, Teichmann, and others. Such a possibility must, of course, be admitted; but when we consider the very brief space of time within which all the extant letters of the apostle were written, we may well be on our guard against straining this line of argument.[2] If at any point there appears to be a

[1] That perplexities of this kind belong to the very nature of Biblical Eschatology, is well brought out by Laidlaw (*Bible Doctrine of Man*, p. 223): "There are two distinct lines on which . . . these disclosures (*i.e.* of eschatological truth) are set forth. The first is that which we may call "personal," for in it the future is spoken of as part of the development of an individual human being. . . . The other is that which we may call "dispensational," when these last events are spoken of on the public scale as moments in the development of the kingdom of heaven, or of the dispensation of redemption in the hand of the Lord Jesus Christ. Thoroughly to connect these two in a complete system of eschatology, is a task for which our theology is confessedly incompetent. . . . The Scripture itself does not give us a complete view of these connections."

[2] *Cf.* Denney (*Death of Christ*, p. 115): "To suppose that a

change of view or a modification of statement, it is safer to look for the cause in the immediate occasion of the writing, or in some marked crisis in St Paul's experience which has led him to recast his earlier conclusion. An alteration of standpoint, for example, regarding the state entered immediately after death, is often supposed to have taken place in the apostle's mind in the interval between the writing of the First and Second Epistles to the Corinthians.[1] This is held by some expositors to be the result of theological development. By others it is regarded simply as a more or less arbitrary modification of view. While others still attribute it to the terrible perils through which St Paul had passed during his sojourn at Ephesus.[2] If there be any such change of conception, a question which must be examined in detail in a subsequent chapter, the last-named hypothesis is certainly the most satisfying. But after all, it must be borne in mind that, as a distinguished theologian once said in our hearing, a man may have several Eschatologies. That is putting the matter summarily, but the remark is abundantly true to experience. Probably most of us are conscious of the fact in our own religious thought.[3] Its real

great expansion of his (Paul's) thoughts took place between the letters to the Thessalonians and those to the Corinthians, is to ignore at once the chronology, the nature of letters, and the nature of the human mind."

[1] So, *e.g.*, Holtzmann, *N.T. Theol.*, ii. p. 193; Teichmann, *Die paulinischen Vorstellungen von Auferstehung u. Gericht*, p. 39. *Cf.* also Beyschlag, *N.T. Theol.*, ii. pp. 270, 271.

[2] See 2 Cor. i. 8.

[3] Account should certainly be taken of the peculiar habit of the Semitic mind. See a luminous statement by Dr E. Caird (*Newspaper Report of Gifford Lectures*, Glasgow, 1902): "It

explanation lies in the nature of the problem with which we are dealing. Our Lord Himself, as we have seen, in place of setting forth any definite instruction as to the unseen world and the future destiny of men, spoke at all times in pictures, only making clear the spiritual side of the mystery, namely, the certainty for the believer of unbroken fellowship after death with the eternally-living God. It was the same with the apostles. They also confine themselves, as a rule, to hints and illustrations. In their missionary preaching they emphasise one aspect or group of aspects of the Last Things. When they come to detailed arguments, dealing with particular difficulties, a different phase of the subject gains a momentary prominence. It is no concern to them if some of the details do not admit of inclusion in a general scheme. Indeed we need never expect entirely harmonious pictures in this province of thought. For the profoundest imagination is soon baffled when it attempts to depict the inexpressible realities of the heavenly world in terms of earthly experiences.[1] No perfect definiteness is attainable; rather a distant adumbration which must be estimated as nothing more. If we should be confronted at any points in St Paul's eschatological thought by conceptions which seem to overlap each other, or

(*i.e.* the Hebrew mind) lived . . . in the consciousness of an unanalysed whole of experience, and represented it now in one aspect and now in another, as one might stand before a sea that was illuminated from moment to moment by flashes of lightning." This seems to us as truly as it is strikingly expressed. It contains the key to many problems of New Testament thought.

[1] See Schleiermacher, *Der christliche Glaube*, iv. pp. 209, 220; Orr, *Christian View of God and the World*, pp. 334-336

images which, if expanded to their furthest limits, appear to leave an unresolved residuum, we must not only bear in mind the cautions already laid down, but we must also endeavour to realise by the use of the philosophical imagination that ideas, which from our standpoint present an aspect of mutual exclusiveness, might seem far more consistent if we could take up our position in that world of thought to which the first Christian writers belonged.[1]

Further, in attempting to grasp St Paul's conceptions of the Last Things, we must not begin by putting certain definite questions to which *we* demand an answer. The function of New Testament theology is to understand the statements of the apostolic writers "from within their ideas and experiences." We must be prepared to recognise that some of those eschatological problems which press most heavily upon us, did not appeal to the apostle at all. Others, on which we care for nothing but a definite decision, St Paul is content to leave on a borderland of mystery. While, occasionally, he takes considerable pains with matters which have come to be more or less remote from our religious interest. These facts are fully explained by the long interval which separates our time from the Apostolic Age. It is a false conception of inspiration which would expect St Paul to satisfy all our questionings even within his own sphere. The inspiration of the apostle is an equipment of

[1] See an admirable treatment of assumed contradictions in Pauline Eschatology in Bornemann's edition of Meyer on *Thessalonians* (*Meyer*, 5-6 1894), pp. 186, 534-536. *Cf.* Jülicher, *Einleitung in d. N.T.*, p. 27. Deissmann, in an instructive review of Teichmann's *Paulinische Vorstellungen von Auferstehung u. Gericht* (*Th. L.Z.*, 1898, Sp. 14), points out the danger of mixing up *Nebeneinander* with *Nacheinander*.

the Spirit for the work he has immediately to do. Certainly much of that work was to be for all time, but its conditions were determined by given historical facts. And one of the fundamental truths of God's operation in history is a gradual change in the mental perspective of nations and individuals.

Enough has been said to show that it is impossible to discover anything in the nature of a system of Eschatology, a group of logically related and wholly coherent conceptions of the Last Things, in the Pauline Epistles. We find, indeed, many distinct and momentous affirmations, many fragments of doctrines, respecting certain facts and events of the End. Some of these are an echo of popular ideas, some remain fixed beliefs, fundamental data for the apostle, whenever he chances to deal with eschatological questions. But however unsystematic they may be in their nature and form, we are not for that reason to imagine that they were only of secondary importance in the judgment of St Paul. The attempt has been made in the earlier part of this chapter to prove that an eschatological element lies in the very centre of his religious thought. But he lays no stress on those scenic features which are so prominent in most speculations on the Last Things. It is extremely suggestive to observe that in the Imprisonment-Epistles, written apart from the heat of controversy, written when their author has leisure to survey the complete bearings of his Christian knowledge, and is plainly rejoicing with a serene gladness in the solidity and majesty of the Christian certainties, he delights to sum up his forecasts of the Last Things under the general designation of Hope. Undoubtedly this aspect of his thought is prominent throughout the Epistles. As early as his letter to the *Galatians*, we come upon the remarkable affirmation of his Christian position in these words: "We through the Spirit by faith eagerly expect the hope of righteousness" (ἐλπίδα δικαιοσύνης, *i.e.*, the hope which righteousness brings or guarantees, chap. v. 5). In *Romans*, side by side with more detailed conceptions of the End, the idea of Hope stands in the foreground. Apart from the classical passage in chap. viii., which we quoted at the outset in dealing with the eschatological strain in his doctrine of Justification, we find the apostle asserting in chap. v. 5 that "the (*i.e.* Christian) hope does not put to shame, because the love of God has been poured out in our hearts through the Holy Spirit given to us." The only definition of this Christian hope is that it rests on the assurance of the love of God imparted by the Holy Spirit.[1] In the Imprisonment-Epistles he leaves his conception of Hope still more undefined. "The hope laid up for you in heaven" (Col. i. 5), "the hope of glory" (Col. i. 27), "the hope of His calling" (Eph. i. 18), "one hope of your calling" (Eph. iv. 4)—these are typical descriptions of the blissful consummation which awaits the believer.[2] It might be an

[1] *Cf.* the hope of enduring life in several Psalms, a hope which was also based on the assurance of God's faithfulness (virtually = His love). A striking parallel is Wisd. iii. 4: ἡ ἐλπὶς αὐτῶν ἀθανασίας πλήρης. J. Weiss suggestively observes that the fundamental note of the preaching of Jesus was hope, "undoubtedly a hope certain of its end, but still always hope" (*Die Predigt Jesu v. Reiche G.*, p. 71).

[2] This conception, like all those which are normative for St Paul, has its roots in the Old Testament. "One can see how closely the meaning which *life* has in the sum of religious thoughts in the Old Testament, coheres with the character of

exaggeration to say that at this stage in his Christian career the apostle prefers to turn aside from all statements of detail, and to rest in a blessed certainty around which he leaves a margin of mystery. Yet one feels that such a view lies at least in the direction of the truth. Certainly, in those letters which form the climax of his religious thinking, he deals very slightly with the pictorial elements of Eschatology, choosing rather to select and emphasise those aspects of it which have a directly spiritual value. This is in genuine harmony with the teaching of our Lord Himself. He varies His imagery, He changes the picture, but underlying every metaphor and every illustration are to be found certain commanding spiritual affirmations which bear with immediate force upon the central issues of human destiny. And the apostle has unquestionably transformed the prophetic-apocalyptic traditions of Judaism from which he started, in the spirit of Jesus, and under the influence of His teaching. It is not, of course, to be supposed that St Paul has wholly renounced the original framework of his conceptions. Statements, for example, in *Philippians*, which is probably the latest of the Imprisonment-Epistles, remind us vividly of his earlier eschatological utterances. But, as the result of advancing Christian experience, and a more complete surrender to the power of the Spirit, he has discovered where to place the *accent* in his teaching on the Last Things. He is more concerned about the essential realities, and less about their temporary

hope, which pre-eminently determines the stamp of this religion. It is not the *beginning* of things which the Old Testament emphasises: everything stretches into the future. On this is founded the healthiness of their religion" (Kleinert, *S.K.*, 1895, p. 711).

expression. May we not suppose that the apostle's experience is a picture in miniature of the experience of the Christian Church in this dimly-lit and mysterious province of her thinking? May we not believe that, in the purpose of her Divine Guide, she also is led forward from the material vestments of eschatological conceptions to the great spiritual certainties which they enwrap? In this historical process the teaching of St Paul must prove of permanent value, since, by reason of his Divinely-trained instinct, he remains a master in the delicate and precarious operation of discerning between the letter and the spirit.[1]

[1] *Cf.* Titius, p. 289: "The expectation of the Parousia continues, and is still, for a whole century, a powerful guarantee for the self-realisation of the Church and a stimulus to more ardent effort, but the distressing effect of its delay has disappeared. They can look forward to it with calmness. And this altered mood is above all else the life-work of the apostle Paul . . . It is his life-work, in spite of the fact that he himself, as regards his personal feeling, is rooted in the eschatological-enthusiastic condition of mind, and abides by that." Mr Myers' beautiful lines are scarcely true to the apostle's outlook :—

"Oh that thy steps among the stars would quicken!
Oh that thine ears would hear when we are dumb!
Many the hearts from which the hope shall sicken,
Many shall faint before thy kingdom come."—*St Paul*, p. 24.

They bear the impress of a wearier age.

CHAPTER II

FORMATIVE INFLUENCES IN ST PAUL'S CONCEPTIONS OF THE LAST THINGS

In the preceding chapter we have attempted to show that St Paul does not possess anything in the nature of a balanced or well-defined system of eschatological beliefs. But from the necessity of his Christian standpoint, as one who holds an ethical view of the world and human life, and as a firm believer in the future of the Kingdom of God, that Kingdom which has already begun to take shape, he will often have to deal with the Last Things. For the moral order and purpose of the universe, which have been illumined by the revelation of Jesus Christ, must be clearly vindicated to the Christian consciousness. Hence, although his conceptions of events and processes in this obscure realm find an utterance simply as the occasion prompts, and although no questions as to the due proportions or the respective prominence of separate subdivisions of Eschatology ever concern the apostle, we may be prepared to discover certain fundamental lines of thought which usually regulate his eschatological discussions. Thus we are not dealing with *casual* statements which St Paul has thrown off without reflection, statements to which he would not assign the weight of firm conviction. Eschatological considerations, as we have seen, occupy a foremost place within his mental horizon. They must have been constantly emphasised in his missionary preaching, as may be gathered from the letters to the Thessalonians and Corinthians. Probably the *lacunæ*, which sometimes puzzle us as we read these discussions, could often be filled up by his readers from their recollection of his oral instructions.[1] Famous passages like 1 Cor. xv. and 2 Cor. v. 1-10 are sufficient proof that St Paul had devoted careful thought to the events of the End. Accordingly, there are certain clear landmarks which serve to guide us through the domain of his Eschatology. These may come into view, at times, in the most isolated fashion. The apostle may never have occasion, at least in his extant Epistles, to follow out his main positions to their logical conclusions. But there is a group of crucial certainties among the "Things to Come," round which his thought invariably revolves.[2] They may be roughly classified as the Parousia or Final Advent of Christ, the Resurrection from the dead, and the Consummation of a redeemed and glorified humanity, in which the universe reaches the goal of the Divine purpose. Obviously these great conceptions will draw others in their train. Death and Eternal Life, the State after death, Judgment and Retribution, the Inheritance of the Saints—all are implicated in the data with which he starts, although we cannot forecast, from

[1] *Cf.* Bornemann on *Thessalonians* (*Meyer*, [5-6]), p. 534.

[2] Titius remarks with justice that St Paul selects for special treatment the two aspects of Eschatology to which a *saving interest* belongs, the Resurrection and the Judgment (involving, of course, the Parousia). In each of these he can sum up salvation as a whole (pp. 50, 51).

their relative importance to *our* minds, the proportions which they will assume in the discussions of the apostle.

As soon as the primary conceptions of which he treats are stated, we recognise that some of them at least are common to all systems of religion.[1] In one shape or other, eschatological beliefs belong to primitive man. In several ancient faiths they occupy the forefront. In all they are necessarily interwoven with men's fundamental religious ideas. And they will usually be linked to these in their cruder forms.[2] Accordingly, we ought to mark the essential difference in origin between them and other prominent factors in St Paul's theology. Justification may be taken as an instance in point. No doubt it would be true to say that we find the roots of this epoch-making doctrine to some extent in the Old Testament, and to a greater still in Judaism. The righteousness of God and His demand for righteous-

[1] "Eschatological conceptions seem generally, in all religions, to belong to the most ancient animistic group of ideas" (Schwally, *Leben nach d. Tode*, p. 6).

[2] *Cf.* Jeremias (*Babylon.-Assyr. Vorstellungen v. Leben nach d. Tode*, p. 107): "In no province of religious thought has the original Semitic popular tradition so lastingly endured in the Old Testament as in the ideas of the fortunes of man after death." See also Davidson on the Old Testament idea of death: "This idea is not strictly the teaching of revelation . . . it is the popular idea from which revelation starts; and revelation on the question rather consists in exhibiting to us how the pious soul struggled with this popular conception and strove to overcome it, and how faith demanded and realised . . . its demand that the communion with God enjoyed in this life should not be interrupted in death" (on Job xiv. 13-15). This general consideration is largely normative for the methods of Pauline Eschatology.

ness in men are paramount ideas in prophets and psalmists. And to the Hebrew mind, righteousness "is not so much a moral quality as a legal status" (W. R. Smith, *Prophets of Israel*, p. 72), a judgment of God that we are right with Him. In the later extra-canonical literature, righteousness according to the law is the chief aim of every devout Jew. His deeds of obedience procure merit for him with God. God weighs his actions in the balances, and one side or other prevails. He is accepted or he is condemned.[1] It is easy to discover that in these ideas we have the mental atmosphere in which St Paul's great doctrine originates. But its centre of gravity is wholly changed. So many new factors intervene, that the transformation of the conception is far more conspicuous than its connections with pre-existing Jewish thought. Faith in Jesus Christ as the sole ground of justification alters so completely the older views of the soul's relation to God, that we are ushered into a new world of spiritual phenomena. The very terms employed have been filled with a fresh content. In essential respects, the doctrine has become the converse of its counterpart in Judaism. It is natural that it should be otherwise with the data of St Paul's Eschatology. While a truly recreating power has entered that domain also, we may still expect to deal largely with current beliefs and current imagery. An Eschatology will not call so quickly for change as a Theology or a

[1] See, *e.g.*, 4 Ezra iii. 34: "Now, therefore, weigh our sins and those of the inhabitants of the world on the balance, that it may be discovered to which side the turn of the scale inclines"; Enoch xli. 1, lxi. 8. *Cf.* Weber, *Lehren d. Talmud*, pp. 272, 273 *et al.*; Volz, *Jüdische Eschatologie*, p. 95.

Soteriology. It will adapt itself but slowly to the higher stages of spirituality which may have been reached in the doctrines of God or salvation. The reasons are obvious. Men represent the Last Things to their minds by means of pictures. They possess a kind of eschatological scenery. This stamps itself upon their imagination from childhood. By degrees they may fully recognise that it is crude and imperfect. But it serves as a rough, working instrument of thought. Meanwhile the more central truths within their spiritual vista may have been undergoing a silent but essential modification. It may be long before it is borne in upon them that they must readjust the various positions of their tacitly-held theological system for the sake of congruity. For imagery, unlike abstract thought, is exceedingly flexible. And we unconsciously read into the familiar pictures the new spiritual significance which has been independently attained. In the case of St Paul, we cannot, indeed, overestimate the remoulding power of his Christian experience in the province of Eschatology. But we shall be better able to appreciate the range and depth of the transformation if we endeavour to realise, in brief outline, first, the heritage of belief he carried with him from the Old Testament, and second, the Judaistic background which must, to some extent, have affected his conceptions of the Last Things.

Before making this attempt (and it can only be done within narrow limits), let us guard against the prejudice which often attaches itself to such methods of investigation. We have no sympathy with those who reduce great factors in the spiritual or intellectual history of the race to mere bundles of influences which can be discovered and classified by minute analysis. This is dull pedantry. The transcending personality is immeasurably greater than all those forces which have fostered his development. The secret of his mastery among his fellows is just that elusive and yet commanding individuality which refuses to be tracked, which welds together in itself all that is of worth in its environment, repelling, attracting, selecting, transfiguring, impressing upon the whole mass of its experience the stamp of its own unique power. Yet, on the other hand, it is no disparagement, even to a master in the science of the Divine like St Paul, to take account of the intellectual habits amidst which his mind received its bent, to try to discover how he dealt with the beliefs and convictions which he found existing, to trace his relation to contemporary thought, in order that we may more accurately estimate the influence of his personal Christian experience. Obviously, the attempt has to be made with delicacy and caution, for the workings of spiritual forces are not mechanical processes. "The wind bloweth where it listeth, and thou hearest the sound thereof, but canst not tell whence it cometh, and whither it goeth : so is every one that is born of the Spirit." Moreover, it has to be remembered that no stage in the religious or ethical development of a people is accidental or unimportant. Some investigators, for example, seem to assume that when they have referred a particular view or speculation to later Judaism or to the Rabbis, they have thereby proved its worthlessness as a normative element in Christian theology. It appears to us that this is an utterly unscientific procedure. If we believe in any Divine purpose leading on humanity to purer and higher apprehensions of spiritual truth, we must assign no secondary place to that movement of thought which was the immediate precursor of the religion of the New Testament.

In attempting to estimate the influence of the Old Testament on St Paul's Eschatology, we shall begin by noticing more generally the lines along which such influences may be traced.

The Old Testament contains chiefly an Eschatology of the *nation*. In this is revealed the organic connection of its Eschatology with its *theology*. Jehovah is the God of Israel rather than of the individual Israelite. His covenant is made with His people. In the Old Testament, the solidarity of the nation stands always in the forefront. *It* is the unit with which Jehovah enters into relations. Hence the fulfilment of the Divine purpose, the realising of the Divine order, must be looked for on national rather than on individual lines.[1] Such facts largely account for the absence of any clear or well-defined utterances on those problems of the End which have a paramount interest for us. The favourite ideal of the prophets is a purified Israel, which, according to some of them, shall be the centre of light for the whole world.[2] This regenerated kingdom absorbs their thoughts on the consummation of all things. Israel

[1] Probably Prof. Charles does not overstate the truth in asserting, that "never in Palestinian Judaism, down to the Christian era, did the doctrine of a merely individual immortality appeal to any but a few isolated thinkers" (*Encycl. Biblica*, ii. col. 1347).

[2] This is the view of Micah iv. 1, 2; Isaiah ii. 2-4; xi. 9, 10. On the other hand, Amos, Hosea, and Joel seem to restrict the future blessedness to their own people. See Drummond, *Jewish Messiah*, pp. 186 ff.

shall become in the fullest sense God's people, and He will be their God. The scene of the perfected theocracy is this earth, often conceived as renewed and glorified (Isa. lxv. 17, lxvi. 22).[1] An era of unbroken felicity fills up the horizon. Probably to their minds it is eternal. For, as Dr Davidson was wont to express it, the events they ascribed to the Messianic age were equivalent to those which we assign to the time following the Second Advent. There is no *terminus ad quem* in that epoch. From another point of view, the kingdom is really synonymous with heaven. For God's presence is enjoyed in it without let or hindrance.

Different writers present varying pictures of the events which lead up to the establishment of the Divine order. In some the figure of the Messianic King occupies a prominent place. This is true, *e.g.*, of Isaiah (xi. 1), Micah (v. 2), and Zechariah (ix. 9). In the second part of Isaiah, the Servant of the Lord is the great instrument of Jehovah's operations. But most of the prophetic writers agree in ushering in the crisis of transformation by a definite event, the Day of the Lord. For Jehovah's own presence and working are the most inspiring of all Messianic hopes (so Dr Davidson). This is a day of judgment, and also of vindication. Its character, like all manifestations of Jehovah, is ethical. It comes laden with terror and destruction for the enemies of God: it marks out for favour and salvation His chosen people. It is

[1] Such a conception is true to a typical dogma of Apocalyptic which affirms that the end is to be like the beginning. *Cf.* Barn. vi. 3; ἰδού, ποιῶ τὰ ἔσχατα ὡς τὰ πρῶτα. See Gunkel on 4 Ezra vii. 11 (in *Kautzsch*), and *cf.* Enoch xlv. 5; Jub. iv. 26; 4 Ezra vii. 75 *et al.;* and Volz, *op. cit.*, pp. 296, 297.

the day when the Divine purposes, which have been slowly ripening, come to maturity. From that time forward the new reign of righteousness is firmly established, whether God, or His vicegerent, the Messiah, be directly conceived as Ruler. (On the parallel existence of these two conceptions in O.T., see Davidson, *Old Testament Prophecy*, pp. 311, 312.) Old Testament writers depict this epoch in glowing colours, but the details are vague, and the outlines more or less fluctuating. It is obvious that we need not expect to find any coherent forecasts of the *time* when these decisive occurrences shall break in upon the common order of human life. It is characteristic of the prophetic vision, to compress great moments within a brief space (so Dr Davidson). But the prophets had their expectations heightened when they saw rapid and crucial movements shaping themselves in the history of their nation. Sudden revolutions and catastrophes, overwhelming disasters like the Babylonian invasion and conquest, seemed to portend a speedy intervention of the Divine arm. At such times, when the bulk of their fellow-countrymen had already begun to recognise the punishment of their stubborn sinfulness, the hopes of the prophets were bound up with the righteous remnant (*e.g.* Isa. vi. 13), the holy kernel of the nation, of whose existence they were assured, and who must ultimately form the nucleus of the realised Kingdom of God. Now, however nationalistic their conception of the Kingdom might be in its earlier stages, such a limitation was bound to be ultimately transcended. Their contact with the great empires of Assyria and Babylon must have immensely widened their conception of the world. And already the germ of universalism was to be found in the intimate relation between their Eschatology and their Theology. The great spiritual fact, which was the basis of their faith, the *unity* of God, must finally lead them to its corollary, the unity of mankind. And the rule of God being, necessarily, a righteous rule, there must follow the idea of a moral renovation of humanity.[1] We can see, therefore, how all along their conceptions of the Last Things contained the potentiality of a world-wide application: how the way was being prepared for more transcendental conceptions of Judgment and Salvation.

There is no lack of material, as is evident, for reconstructing in a rough fashion the general prophetic picture of the End, or rather, final epoch—a picture which, in its main outlines, we can trace also in the Psalms. Its original basis, the conviction that the scene of God's Kingdom will be a regenerated earth; that its centre will be the holy city Jerusalem; that from thence God, or His representative the Messianic King,[2] will rule in wisdom and righteousness and mercy over Israel and those Gentiles who have come to the light which shines from Zion—this conviction will necessarily involve the use of imagery derived from human experience.[3] No doubt the prophets themselves are often conscious that their

[1] *Cf.* Davidson in *H.D.B.*, iv. 121; Drummond, *Jewish Messiah*, p. 328.

[2] It is interesting to note the rarity of the Messianic idea in the literature of the Maccabæan period. Apparently the triumph of the Maccabees satisfied the popular hopes. It was the experience of hardship and calamity that followed, which kindled the Messianic Hope throughout the nation as a whole. *Cf.* Drummond, *op. cit.*, p. 269.

[3] "The moral and religious element is the essential part of

images are only inadequate approximations to the truth lying within their field of vision, for the transfigured earth and the new Jerusalem will be the home of spiritual forces, expressions of the Divine energy, such as men have never dreamed of. Still, the features of the picture will be essentially anthropomorphic; the sounding of the trumpet, which summons to the great assize; the Theophany itself, with its awe-inspiring accompaniments of fire and tempest and glowing clouds; the voice of thunder, which will shake the earth; the valley of Hinnom, where the bodies of the slain shall be consumed in heaps, or left a prey to the worms. No other setting could so vividly have represented to their contemporaries the terrific realities of judgment and retribution, and the consummation of blessedness for all who have been faithful to their covenant with Jehovah. May we not say that it is almost impossible to give practical value at any time to the conceptions of the final transcendent processes of God's moral order, without calling to our aid the ordinary human realisations of penalty and judgment?

The prophecies of the Book of Daniel may be regarded as standing by themselves in this connection.[1] They belong to that influential department of Jewish literature known as *Apocalyptic.* They are concerned almost exclusively with the events of the End. They deal in a mysterious, perhaps one might

the prophecy, the form in which it is to verify itself is secondary. The form was of the nature of an embodiment, a projection or construction, and the materials of which the fabric was reared were those lying to the hand of the prophet in each successive age" (Davidson, *op. cit.*, p. 126).

[1] Closely parallel are the Visions of *Zechariah* (see Smend, *Alttest. Religionsgeschichte*, p. 473).

say, in an esoteric manner, with those movements of history which lead up to the manifestation of the kingdom of the saints of the Most High. In an exceedingly compressed form, the fortunes of the chosen people, as these are moulded by the sway of successive foreign princes, are traced through a group of symbolic visions. In chap. xi., certain remarkable characteristics are ascribed to some of the most impious heathen kings, gross irreligion and daring sacrilege and overweening insolence, which appear to the seer's mind as the culmination of an almost superhuman wickedness. The colours of this picture seem to have made a profound impression on readers of the prophecy, for, as we shall discover, they reappear frequently in the apocalyptic tradition, and supply a setting for some of the most obscure of St Paul's eschatological forebodings.

Even from this meagre outline, which will be filled in, more or less, in subsequent chapters, we receive a glimpse of the eschatological background which lies behind the religious thought of St Paul. It is, indeed, a current fashion to minimise his relation to the ancient Scriptures of his people, as compared with his indebtedness to the teachings of post-canonical Judaistic literature, in its various branches. Thus, *e.g.*, Weizsäcker: "The same apostle, who freed the oldest Christianity from the limitations of the Jewish people and its religion, has, perhaps, chiefly contributed, on another side, to retain the Jewish spirit in it" (*Apostol. Zeitalter*, p. 105). We must understand here by the "Jewish spirit," that which prevailed in the Rabbinic circle in which St Paul received his early training. Now, as we shall have frequent occasion to show, his writings reveal every here and there affinities with his native environment. But the remarkable fact remains that these affinities are largely superficial, that they disclose themselves at the circumference rather than at the centre of his thought. It is the *spirit* of his religion which is essentially alien to contemporary Judaism and in profound harmony with the prophets and psalmists of the Old Testament. In this he is a true follower of his Master. Jesus also felt in His deepest consciousness the enduring significance of the Divine revelation as contained in the Old Testament. He recognised its permanent elements, and used them in His own presentation of spiritual truth. He found in the spirit of prophetism the genuine evidence of a direct fellowship with God, and hence a discernment of the eternal principles of the Divine operation. St Paul occupies a similar standpoint. We know, indeed, that the apostle employed Scripture proofs, repeatedly, according to the fashion of his time, regarding the original historical sense of passages as of minor importance in comparison with their bearing on the facts of the Christian dispensation (*e.g.*, Rom. iv. 24, xv. 2; 1 Cor. x. 11).[1] But this is a phenomenon of superficial importance as compared with his far-reaching appreciation of the inward vitality of the prophetic religion.[2] He is able to lay aside the fantastic imaginations and the pedantic hair-splitting which have obscured so much that is of high ethical worth in Rabbinic theology. As the true successor of the great prophets, who has discovered in the Christian revelation the summing up and attainment of their highest ideals, he is equipped by the very

[1] See Clemen, *S.K.*, 1902, p. 178 ff.

[2] *Cf.* Heinrici on 2 *Corinthians* (*Meyer*, [8] 1900), p. 451.

possession of their spirit for the world-embracing vocation of missionary to the nations. The truth is that his conversion seems to have sent him back with fresh vision to the Old Testament. However ready he shows himself to emphasise the preparatory, pædagogic purpose of the law enshrined in it, he assimilates by an inherent sympathy its most lofty spiritual doctrines, and esteems them with an intensified devotion, just because their deepest and perennial significance dawns upon him in the light of his fellowship with the Lord. Here and there he may make a purely dialectic use of passages for argument's sake, a use so foreign to our habits of thought that we are apt to do injustice to a man whose reverence for the Divine revelation was as profound as his spiritual life. To realise his genuine sympathy with the purest strain in Old Testament religion, we have only to compare him with subtle thinkers like Philo, with ardent enthusiasts like the Jewish apocalyptic writers, or with devout Christians like the Apostolic Fathers. This man, from the vantage-ground which he has found in Christ, recognises in prophet and psalmist real mediators of God's self-disclosure to mankind. While the stream of Divine revelation has been infinitely deepened and broadened, it has not left the rivulets of prophetic inspiration to stagnate in isolated pools.

It need hardly be said that the apostle has transformed the prophetic ideas of the Old Testament under the influence of the new Christian revelation. Thus the culmination of the Providential development is found in Jesus Christ, the crucified and risen Son of God, in whom all things are finally summed up (Eph. i. 10). Acceptance in the day of judgment is determined by men's attitude to the Gospel of Christ (Rom. iv. 25, v. 8-10, xiv. 9, 18; 1 Cor. iii. 11). Hence, of course, it follows that all national restrictions have vanished. For "there is neither Jew nor Greek, there is neither bond nor free, there is neither male or female." All are "one man in Christ Jesus" (Gal. iii. 28). But this higher stage in the knowledge of God to which men have been called in no way conflicts for the apostle's mind with the prophetic principle. It is the copestone of the great edifice of salvation. Therefore it is not too much, we believe, to assert that St Paul has rediscovered the Old Testament for himself as a Christian, and the Church has inherited the benefits of his discovery.

The Old Testament has furnished the apostle with a remarkable teleology. Strangely enough, he makes scanty use of that expression for the new Divine order which crystallised the deepest conceptions of the prophets, and was so frequently found upon the lips of Jesus—the Kingdom of God. Yet the terms in his Epistles which perhaps most nearly express its meaning, *σωτηρία* and *ζωή*, are much more closely linked to the Old Testament standpoint than might at first sight appear. In our next chapter we shall examine the conception of *ζωή* in detail, and its Old Testament basis will then become abundantly clear. We have already observed that *σωτηρία* and its cognates seem uniformly, with St Paul, to have an eschatological significance. The beginning of the saving process, indeed, may be so described, and any particular stage in its development. But in his use of the term the apostle, as we have sought to show, keeps ever in view the events of the last time, more especially the ὀργὴ θεοῦ, "the wrath of God," which must form part of the revelation (ἀποκάλυψις) of the exalted Lord. Salvation, in its full sense, is final deliverance from the Divine wrath and judgment. For St Paul, as for all the earliest Christians, the Day of the Lord is as cogent a reality as for the ancient prophets. The Incarnation has by no means made it superfluous. Rather has its meaning received new clearness. For men are now in a position to give definiteness to its conditions. Christ is to be the Mediator of the Divine judgment on sin. Sin culminates in the rejection of Him whom God has sent. Salvation is the ultimate deliverance, wrought through faith in Christ as the Redeemer, from the penal consequences of men's disobedience to God. This decisive σωτηρία, with all the blissful consequences which flow from it both now and hereafter, may be justly termed a Pauline equivalent for the Kingdom of God. It belongs to the community of believers. It is realised now, so far as that is possible under the conditions of earthly life, in the Christian brotherhood. Already it is their possession ideally. From the Parousia onwards, all restrictions shall have been removed. And the saints will enter on their eternal heritage, which is ζωὴ αἰώνιος.

Thus the Day of the Lord, which for the prophets was to be the inauguration of the new era, continues to hold its prominence in St Paul. And he has no hesitation, more especially in his earlier Epistles, in using the ancient imagery to describe its accompaniments. Noteworthy instances occur in the Epistles to the Thessalonians. There we find a veritable mosaic of quotations from, and reminiscences of, the Old Testament, the books chiefly drawn upon being

Isaiah and *Daniel*. God's Son is to come from heaven with all His holy ones. *Cf.* Zech. xiv. 5; Dan. vii. 13.[1] He is to descend with a shout, with the voice of the archangel and the trumpet of God. *Cf.* Isa. xxvii. 13; Exod. xix. 11, 13, 16, 17, 18.[2] The Day of the Lord will surprise them as a thief in the night. *Cf.* Joel ii. 1-11, especially ver. 9. The Lord Jesus is to be revealed from heaven in flaming fire. *Cf.* Isa. lxvi. 15; Ps. xviii. 8; Exod. xxiv. 17; Deut. iv. 24. He takes vengeance on them that know not God. *Cf.* Isa. xxxv. 4; Jer. x. 25. They are punished with destruction from the face of the Lord and from the glory of His power. *Cf.* Isa. ii. 10. He shall be glorified in His saints. *Cf.* Isa. lxvi. 5, xlix. 3; Ps. lxviii. *ad init.*[3]

[1] The O.T. parallels throughout our discussion must be examined in the LXX. For, as a general rule, St Paul used the Greek Bible.

[2] This parallel is peculiarly remarkable.

[3] Bornemann (on 2 Thess. i. 6-10) supposes that verses 7*b*-10*a* are a portion (perhaps altered here and there) of an early Christian psalm or hymn. The following is a remarkable group of parallels which he gives to show the O.T. basis of the passage:—

Isa. lxi. 2	—	2 Thess. i. 6, 7, 10.
Isa. lxvi. 4 f., 14 f.	—	2 Thess. i. 6, 8.
Lam. iii. 63	—	2 Thess. i. 6.
Obad. 15	—	2 Thess. i. 6.
Isa. lxiii. 4, 7	—	2 Thess. i. 6.
Isa. xix. 20	—	2 Thess. i. 6.
Isa. lix. 18	—	2 Thess. i. 6.
Jer. xxv. 12	—	2 Thess. i. 8.
Isa. xxix. 6	—	2 Thess. i. 8.
Isa. iv. 2 ff.	—	2 Thess. i. 10.
Ezek. xxxviii. 23	—	2 Thess. i. 10, 12.
Ezek. xxxiv. 8	—	2 Thess. i. 5, 6.
Ps. lxxviii. 6	—	2 Thess. i. 8.
Dan. vii. 9, 21 f.	—	2 Thess. i. 10, 11.

The portrayal of the "man of lawlessness" in 2 Thess. ii., whatever other elements it may contain, has certainly modelled many of its features on various passages in Daniel. Notable parallels to the passage will be found in Dan. xi. 30 to end, v. 20, 23, vii. 25, viii. 23-25. This last reference is suggestive. In the LXX. of Dan. viii. 23-25 (both versions) we have the picture of a king who shall arise "when their sins are fulfilled" (πληρουμένων τῶν ἁμαρτιῶν αὐτῶν). The filling up of the tale of their sins is the signal for a terrible crisis. Here we come upon one of the most marked points of contact between St Paul's expectation of the Parousia and the Old Testament. It is instructive for his whole point of view. At the time when the letters to the Thessalonians were written, the apostle appears to have been peculiarly impressed by the attitude of his own nation towards the Gospel. Not only did they refuse to accept the message of salvation for themselves, but in heathen cities like Thessalonica and elsewhere they stirred up the inhabitants against the Christian missionaries. Their methods were so shameful and their enmity so bitter, that Paul saw in their conduct a sort of concentration of the spirit of evil. In his view, they were wholly

Isa. xlix. 3	—	2 Thess. i. 10, 12.
Ezek. xxxix. 21	—	2 Thess. i. 10
Ezek. xxxv. 4	—	2 Thess. i. 6.
Jer. xv. 25	—	2 Thess. i. 8.
Isa. iv. 5	—	2 Thess. i. 9.
Isa. ii. 10	—	2 Thess. i. 9.
Ezek. xxviii. 22	—	2 Thess. i. 10, 12.

Possibly we have here some evidence for Weizsäcker's hypothesis that St Paul "arranged a kind of system of doctrine in the form of proofs from Scripture for use in giving instruction" (*Apost. Zeitalter*, p. 113; see also p. 119).

ripe for judgment: the wrath had come upon them to the full (ἔφθασεν . . . ἡ ὀργὴ εἰς τέλος). Everything seemed to await the direct intervention of God. Of course there were other elements in his experience which helped to quicken St Paul's expectation of the Parousia, as we shall discover in chap. iv. The position under review, however, is absolutely true to the prophetic standpoint. For to the minds of the prophets the rapid development of spiritual movements in any direction seemed to presage the Day of the Lord. At the same time, it is important to note that this Christian adaptation of the prophetic outlook is largely confined to the predominantly missionary Epistles. It is much less marked, for example, in the letters to Corinth, where the apostle has to deal with a quick-witted, argumentative community, who have intellectual difficulties on eschatological questions such as the Resurrection.[1] No doubt the Macedonians were a simpler people, and St Paul finds it fitting to set the events of the End before them by the help of impressive imagery. Probably in this direction rather than in that of a development of the apostle's views, we may look for an explanation of the diversity in his presentation of eschatological conceptions.

We have been considering the influence of the Old Testament upon St Paul in one or two of its aspects, from the side of its Eschatology of the nation. This may perhaps appear to us of secondary interest, as compared with the final condition of the individual. All recent discussions of the subject have taught us how we must approach the Old Testament treatment of immortality and its cognate conceptions. The

[1] We do not ignore such passages as 1 Cor. vii. 25-31.

best scholars are agreed that not until a late date in the history of religious thought in Israel did such questions appeal for discussion.[1] At the first glance, a fact like this seems to place the religion of which it is true on a lower level than the faiths of contemporary peoples, which reveal many highly-developed conceptions of the life after death. But such a conclusion is by no means warranted. Other elements in the religion must be taken into account. Thus, in Egypt, as Wiedemann points out, we have "the unique spectacle of one of the most elaborate forms of the doctrine of immortality side by side with the most elementary conception of higher beings ever formulated by any people" (*Ancient Egyptian Doct. of Immortality*, p. 2). That is the precise converse of the condition of belief in Israel. The prophetic conception of God is marvellously pure and lofty. He is pre-eminently the Living and the Holy One. He fills existence as they know it. The supreme question of religion is their actual attitude towards Him. The enjoyment of His favour, as that was evidenced by a happy and prosperous life, they regarded as their highest boon. Length of days and material blessedness were the rewards of righteousness and obedience. This earthly life was precious as the scene of fellowship with Jehovah. The dreary, shadowy existence in Sheol[2] meant the privation of

[1] Jeremias suggestively points out that, in the case of the peoples of the Euphrates valley, "occupation with the claims of this world absorbed all their religious interest. There is no room for that painful reflection and philosophising as to the Whence and Whither of the soul, which was so characteristic of the Egyptian people" (*Babylon.-Assyr. Vorstellungen*, p. 2).

[2] Probably the original popular notion was that of the family grave, as indicated, *e.g.*, by the recurrence of the phrase, "he

that and all other privileges. Only the living could praise God. The dead were shut out from access to Him in the land of silence. But as reflection on human life and destiny was deepened, perplexing problems forced themselves on earnest minds. On the one hand, the trials of righteous men, and the good fortune of many who were ungodly, undermined the simple and straightforward theory of religion which had been prevalent. Facts refused to square with it. Thus there arose the intellectual and moral demand for a future order of things, in which the apparent inequalities of the present should be adjusted, in which righteousness should be recompensed and evil visited with punishment. The reference of this spiritual balancing of accounts to a future life which was ultimately arrived at, is scarcely enunciated in the Old Testament, although in the Book of Job and several Psalms most significant hints and foreshadowings of it are apparent. In the epoch of the canonical writings it seems still to be assigned to a purified State existing under earthly conditions, in which the sway of God is supreme. But from another standpoint, a closer approximation was made to the New Testament conception of immortality. In various Psalms, notably the sixteenth, the forty-ninth, and the seventy-third, we find remarkable expressions of confidence in God.[1] The godly in Old Testament times had reached a

was gathered to his fathers." Gradually there arose the conception of a "unified realm of shadows," "the house of meeting for all living" (Job xxx. 23). See Bertholet, *Israelitische Vorstellungen v. Zustand nach d. Tode*, p. 18.

[1] We are scarcely prepared to believe, with Charles, that for the authors of Pss. xlix. and lxxiii. Sheol is the future abode of the wicked only, and heaven of the righteous (*Eschatology*, pp.

marvellously vivid sense of the Divine fellowship. The full emphasis of their piety was laid upon this experience. It determined their philosophy of life.[1] They possessed a unique sensitiveness to the Divine presence.[2] It was no metaphor in their religion. Now this intense realisation of the nearness of the spiritual world in the present would largely account for their slowness in attaining a full-fledged doctrine of immortality. But it forms also the basis of those yearning utterances in the Psalms which we have mentioned. As they became more self-conscious, more introspective, the horror of death grew upon them. The cessation of all activity, bodily, intellectual, spiritual; the nerveless and phantom-like existence of the under-world became a grim nightmare. And the deeper their religious consciousness, the more profoundly they were affected. To conceive of a state in which they should be isolated from God, in which communion with Him was impossible—that was the bitterest element in their notion of Sheol.[3] And so by the sheer force of their religious vitality they are

73, 74). They do indeed recognise clearly the distinction between the righteous and the ungodly, but the emphasis of their hope is not laid upon the escaping from punishment and the attaining to bliss. It is the thought of overcoming death, the common lot of men, and the conviction that their life of fellowship with God will not be interrupted, which buoys up their souls. The Psalms contain no material for such detailed conceptions as Charles would derive.

[1] *Cf.* the apt words of Dr Salmond: "It (*i.e.* the O.T.) deals not with what man *is*, but with what he is to *God*" (*Christian Doct. of Immortality*, p. 217).

[2] "The consciousness of God (in the O.T.) is God's giving Himself in the consciousness" (Davidson, *H.D.B.*, i. p. 741).

[3] In the Babylonian religion, "the blessedness of the pious is fellowship with the gods: abandonment by the gods is the

carried past the current, popular beliefs, and crave an unbroken union with God. Not only so, but their deepest experience and their confidence as "covenant members of the theocracy," assure them of such a relation. Their forecast of the future may be vague enough, but they refuse to contemplate an interruption of the Divine fellowship by death. Even if God cannot abide with them through death, He will by some merciful provision ransom them from it. This belief is, to all intents and purposes, a belief in immortality.[1] It is the inevitable result of their religious development. For "immortality is the corollary of religion. If there be religion, *i.e.* if God be, there is immortality, not of the soul, but of the whole personal being of man, Ps. xvi. 9" (Davidson, *Job*, p. 296). It is easy to see how this conviction prepared the way for the doctrine of the Resurrection on its more spiritual side. There were, indeed, various influences which led to the formation of this great conception. Some of these will come before us in our brief survey of the eschatological development of Judaism, and among them will be found several elements which do not possess a directly religious value. For there is possible a view of the Resurrection which leaves it little more than a piece of eschatological scenery. Such was not the conception which takes a central place in the teaching of St Paul. It touched his religious life in its deepest essence, communion of life with the

punishment of the wicked. . . . The certainty of being snatched from the saving hand of the gods in death is the bitterest drop in the cup of death" (Jeremias, *op. cit.* pp. 46, 48).

[1] It may be truly said that when the ideas of "communion with God" and "life" become synonymous, the religious belief in immortality is already there. See Schultz, *O.T. Theol.* (E. Tr.), ii. p. 82.

risen Christ. But that experience upon which all his hopes of the future were based, is really the crowning development of the remarkable conviction which finds expression in the Old Testament psalm: "I have set the Lord always before me: because He is at my right hand, I shall not be moved. Therefore my heart is glad, and my glory rejoiceth: my flesh also shall dwell in safety. For Thou wilt not leave my soul to Sheol; neither wilt Thou suffer thy godly (or beloved) one to see the pit" (Ps. xvi. 8-10).[1]

Perhaps enough has been said to indicate generally the lines on which both the direct and the indirect influence of Old Testament conceptions of the Last Things upon the mind and speculation of St Paul may be expected to reveal themselves. Separate details will frequently demand consideration in subsequent chapters. One caution, however, ought to be noted before we pass from this subject. There can be little doubt that St Paul, as we shall try to show later, was powerfully influenced by the apostolic tradition of the eschatological teaching of Jesus. This is revealed, for example, with remarkable clearness in those passages which we have singled out as intimately related to the prophetic teaching. The most striking instance is to be found in 2 Thessalonians ii. The parallels between that chapter and the discourse of Jesus on the Last Things, as reported in Matt. xxiv. (and parallels), are unmistakable. *Cf.* 2 Thess. ii. 1 with Matt. xxiv. 31, ii. 2 with xxiv. 6, ii. 3 with

[1] The sense of vagueness of which we are conscious in the utterances of the above-quoted Psalms, is due to the fact that the eternal fellowship with God to which they point is conceived not so much *post-temporally*, as rather *super-temporally*. See Kleinert, *S.K.*, 1895, p. 726.

xxiv. 12, 4, ii. 4 with xxiv. 15, ii. 9 with xxiv. 24. It is no exaggeration to say that Matt. xxiv. is the most instructive commentary on the chapter before us. It may be difficult to determine in what form this material lay before St Paul, but it is impossible to resist the conclusion that he was familiar with it.[1] No doubt the eschatological utterances of Jesus must have constituted a prominent element in the apostolic preaching and instruction. Perhaps no portion of the tradition of His ministry would appeal so powerfully to Christian circles, at a time when to believers the end of the age seemed imminent. Thus there is always the possible hypothesis that St Paul availed himself of the conceptions and the imagery of Old Testament Eschatology partly through the medium of the sayings of Jesus. But many of his applications of the earlier ideas are so distinctive, that we may safely attribute them to a patient and careful study of prophets and psalmists in the Greek version of the Old Testament. We lay stress on the *version* because, to an extent not yet sufficiently recognised, the thought of St Paul, and not merely his language, has been profoundly moulded by the LXX. Perhaps this is most apparent in a noteworthy subdivision of his eschatological speculation; we mean, the psychology which lies at its foundation. In the strictest sense, indeed, the apostle has no system of psychology.[2] And it is vain to attempt to construct one.[3]

[1] The curious position has been assumed (*e.g.* by Bousset), that Matt. xxiv. is to be explained by 2 Thess. ii. (see *The Antichrist Legend*, p. 23). This is surely one of the paradoxes of New Testament criticism.

[2] This holds good of the Biblical writers as a whole. As Dr Davidson expressed it, Biblical "Psychology" is a part of its ethics. It is not a physiology of the mind.

[3] An example may be found in Simon's *Psychologie d. Ap.*

But he was deeply interested in the mental and spiritual basis of religious experience. He was obliged to reflect on those functions of the inner life of man to which Divine influences attached themselves. He is in no sense scientific in his use of psychological terms. And if we presuppose or expect a rigorous terminology, we shall often miss his meaning. But he must employ an analysis of the religious consciousness, and his usage is closely related to the Old Testament, especially as it is interpreted by its Greek translators. In treating of St Paul's fundamental conceptions of the Last Things, we shall require to examine his use of such important terms as *ψυχή, πνεῦμα, νοῦς*, and others; and in order to appreciate the special aspects under which he views their content, it will be always needful to keep in touch with the Old Testament, bearing in mind that the apostle has used, for the most part, the Septuagint translation. It seems to us fairly clear that Hellenic and even Hellenistic influences play a small part in his psychological conceptions as compared with the tradition of the Old Testament, slightly modified by its adaptation to a Greek terminology.

We have already emphasised the fact, that at times the influence of the Old Testament upon St Paul's eschatological thought must probably be conceived as mediated by the teaching of Jesus. A similar hypothesis might be put forward, as we bring within our view another great epoch of religious thought with which the apostle stood in close contact, namely

Paulus, Göttingen, 1897. Simon approaches the Epistles from a definite, philosophical standpoint, and uses their material in accordance with his psychological scheme. The discussion sheds little new light on the thought of the apostle.

that of *Judaism.* It may be difficult to decide how far Judaism was a *direct* channel of Old Testament influence for St Paul. And the question is really of little importance. But it immediately touches our investigation to inquire to what extent the apostle was affected by the conceptions of the Last Things current among his contemporaries.[1] It is reasonable to expect that the atmosphere in which he was trained must have had a permanent meaning for his thinking.[2] The profoundest spiritual genius is, to some degree, a product of his surroundings. That fact in no sense collides with a genuine inspiration. For the Divine Spirit never works, so far as His operations are disclosed to us, independently of human thought. The highest spiritual truth must ever resemble a gem in a setting (*cf.* 2 Cor. iv. 7). The setting cannot possess the same worth as the precious jewel it encloses, yet without it the jewel would be lost, or damaged, or prevented from being worn. We know with some accuracy the nature of St Paul's environment. He was educated as a Pharisee. The Rabbi at whose feet he sat as a pupil was Gamaliel, the first

[1] The discussion of this subject in Thackeray's *Relation of St Paul to Contemporary Jewish Thought* (London, 1900), pp. 98-135, is rather a collection of notes than a coherent investigation. The truth is, that Judaistic influences cannot be treated in severance from the other elements in the Eschatology of the apostle.

[2] Dr Bruce appears to us to have overstated the truth when he says: "On no subject, perhaps, was Paul, in his way of thinking, more a man of his time than on that of Eschatology" (*Expos.*, iv. 10. p. 300). This applies almost exclusively to the framework. The spirit and central principles of his eschatological conceptions were totally divergent from those of Pharisaism. We are all men of our time as regards the drapery in which we clothe our ideas of the Last Things.

of the seven famous teachers who were distinguished by the title *Rabban* ("our Master"), and grandson of the celebrated Hillel. It would be unwise to lay too much stress on Gamaliel's personal idiosyncrasies, in estimating his influence on Paul. Tradition tells us that he was versed in Greek literature, an uncommon accomplishment for a Pharisee. This is borne out, perhaps, by the account of his tolerant attitude towards the Christians in the book of Acts, an account suspected by Baur on the ground of the persecuting zeal displayed by his pupil. A judgment of this kind reveals the dangers to which the critic is exposed in endeavouring to trace the influence of one mind upon another. It is much easier to tabulate probable points of contact under certain definite headings, than to follow out those subtle hints of shaping forces which are the truest indications of indebtedness of thought. It is possible that, under Gamaliel's tuition, St Paul may have moved in a larger air than some of his contemporaries. But at best, there was a Pharisaic tradition which would be normative for his earlier theology.

It has been pointed out on a preceding page (p. 49), that the apostle goes back to *Daniel* for many features in one, at least, of his eschatological pictures. But *Daniel* belongs to a class of writings which had gained a great vogue in the time of our Lord, and long before that. Jewish apocalyptic literature is a species of the genus prophecy. It is by no means accidental that its products did not appear until after the era of the great prophets. A profound and inspiring religious literature must necessarily be the result of an intense and far-reaching spiritual movement in a nation or community. It is a spontaneous creation.

It is the expression of a new kindling of spiritual intuition. It endures as a commanding type. But after the movement has done its work, after its vital energy has been diffused, there usually follows a period of greater or less stagnation. There are always earnest minds concerned about the spiritual prosperity of their time, and they attempt, by a process of reflection, to tread in the footsteps of their predecessors. They have a model to imitate. They can copy the phrases, and to some extent, the thoughts of the former days, but the inspiration is lacking. We are conscious of an artificiality in the whole standpoint of the apocalyptic writers. It is prophecy severed from history. The Old Testament prophets follow the track of movements, beginning to reveal themselves in the present, out into the future, interpreting the development by their insight into the eternal moral principles of the Divine operation, which they have gained by their experience of history and their fellowship with God. The apocalyptic writers turn the history of the past and present into prophecy, by mechanical methods. This they place in the mouth of some seer of the bygone ages, Enoch, or Moses, or Baruch. They recognise the doleful experiences of their own people. They are sadly conscious of their present prostration as a nation. Their political life is gone. They are only a downtrodden religious community. As individuals, also, they are exposed to suffering, in spite of their acknowledgment of the true God. Yet amidst all their depression, the amazing characteristic which has been a permanent possession of this indomitable people, comes to the rescue and asserts itself. Their *hopefulness* cannot be quenched. To the ancient seers of the

Apocalypses has been granted a glimpse into the age-long development of the secret purposes of God. The calamitous experiences of this present world, in which righteousness seems to be crushed and godlessness to triumph, are not the conclusion of the whole matter. In direct antithesis to this Æon there is the new Æon, "the world to come." In it both the righteous community and the righteous individual will be recompensed according to their deeds. No doubt there is a terrible obverse side to the coming retribution, for a woeful fate awaits the sinner, and sin is the transgression of the Divine law. But this apprehension is seldom found in the earlier Apocalyptists.[1] They console themselves with the hope of eternal life.

The apocalyptic writers, to use Prof. Charles's expression, really present "a Semitic philosophy of religion" (*Book of Enoch*, p. 23). Thus righteous individuals can find comfort in the knowledge that their trials are only part of a universal plan of God.[2]

[1] See Gunkel (in *Kautzsch*), pp. 338, 339. He connects with this thought the feelings of St Paul before his conversion.

[2] See Gunkel, *op. cit.*, p. 357. Bousset, *Offenbarung Johannis* (*Meyer*, [5]), p. 5, has the interesting suggestion that the Judaistic conception of the world "as a unified whole, developing according to definite laws, was derived by Judaism from the outlook presented to it through its historical experience by the arising of the inwardly-unified world-power and civilisation of Greece. At the moment when Judaism, which had again wakened up to national consciousness, met the dominant power of Greece, there arose with Daniel Jewish Apocalyptic." This idea has to be modified by the recollection that the Jewish conception of God in its ethical and spiritual transcendence was bound to lead up to a unified view of the world. This would be the main factor: the influence to which Bousset refers could be only secondary. And a further secondary motive in the

In the new epoch, which will be inaugurated by a stern crisis of judgment, the enemies of Israel and of God will be destroyed or subjugated. God will vindicate Himself and His people. Evil will be extirpated. The sovereignty will belong to the righteous. The End will be brought back into the likeness of the beginning, when "God saw everything that He had made, and behold it was very good" (Gen. i. 31). Obviously, in this view of the future, a view which was promulgated with enthusiasm, there is a mingling of political with religious elements. And we know how that combination remained influential in the later development of the Messianic Hope. It was a momentous step in the history of religion when Jesus stripped the faith He was shaping into universal validity of this hampering constituent. St Paul was the true successor of his Lord when, in nascent Christianity, he gave the deathblow to all thoughts of a national prerogative.

It is important to notice that, in apocalyptic literature, the pictures of the Last Things have become far more detailed. The judgment, the torments and destruction of the wicked, the bliss of the righteous—all these are portrayed in forcible colours, and with a bewildering variety of images which are often fantastic and grotesque. And now, for the first time, a conception of vital import is added to Jewish Eschatology. The *Resurrection* begins to occupy a fixed place among the events of the final period of transition. Probably the actual conception originated directly in the consciousness

advance to this position must have been the effect upon the mental outlook of the Jews of their dispersion among the nations.

that the future purified theocracy, the earnestly-desired Messianic Kingdom would be incomplete, were it not to include those godly members of the nation who had not survived to see it established. Such a feeling would be intensified by the events of the cruel persecutions under tyrants like Antiochus Epiphanes. Some of the noblest representatives of Judaism had perished as martyrs. It was impossible to believe that they could never have a share in the glory of their nation, for whose redemption they had suffered.[1] Must not God Himself, by the exercise of His almighty power, deliver them from Sheol, and restore them to a life of felicity among their brethren? Thus the idea of resurrection is prepared for by their confidence in the Divine retribution.[2] We can see the originally intimate connection between the hope of Resurrection and the Messianic Hope. It was at a later date, when the reign of Messiah was regarded as preliminary to the final Æon, that the two expectations became separated.[3]

It must not, however, be supposed that this far-reaching conception would be attained along any single line of reasoning or belief.[4] We have seen

[1] "Tacitus remarks that the Jews only attributed immortality to the souls of those who died in combats or punishments" (Renan, *L'Antechrist*, p. 467, quoting *Hist.* v. 5). Can this dictum of the historian have any connection with the view in the text?

[2] *Cf.* Cheyne on Isa. xxvi. 19. Plato also regards the ideas of retribution and immortality as involved in each other. See Zeller, *Plato*, p. 408.

[3] See Schürer, *H.J.P.*, ii. 2. pp. 175, 176.

[4] Gunkel (*Schöpfung und Chaos*, p. 291, note 2) apparently believes that the emergence of the Resurrection-doctrine in Judaism is due to Babylonian influences. Stave (*Ueber d. Einfluss d. Parsismus auf d. Judenthum*, p. 203) finds traces of

how some of the psalmists uttered a religious protest against the thought of separation from the living God. It may be difficult to discover whether they had a definite idea of resurrection: in any case, they groped eagerly after it. We have also to keep in mind the individualistic trend of religious thought which had revealed itself from the days of Jeremiah onwards, and was propagated by the indirect Persian influence. "Precisely the circumstance that the doctrine of resurrection occurs in close union with an apocalyptic view of the world, which has a noteworthy connection with Parsism, leads to this conclusion. In this general apocalyptic view, there are several features which more than prove . . . Persian influence. To these belong the universal-historical survey of history, its periods and their restriction to a definite space of time, which ultimately issues in the doctrine of a real world-renewal: the development of the power of evil spirits . . . and their defeat at the last judgment, and finally the doctrine of the beginning of future retribution in Sheol, transferred to Hell, from which resulted the separation of the ungodly from the pious immediately after death." It seems to us that there is little need to have recourse to these extraneous influences for the explanation of the Resurrection-idea. As parallel religious phenomena they are of high interest and value, for they reveal a persistent trend of human thought in the spiritual domain. It is more reasonable to look for the origins of such a conception in the spiritual experience of Judaism itself. It would be absurd to deny the contact between Judaism, on the one hand, and Babylonian and Persian influences on the other, and the cosmological strain which appears in the former may, at least, be partly due to Persian stimulus (see Bousset, *Religion d. Judenthums*, p. 478), but epoch-making conceptions like the one before us cannot be interchanged like counters. They rather presuppose a gradual growth from roots fixed deep in the soil of the religious consciousness. That such presuppositions existed in Judaism we hope to have shown in the text. See also Bertholet, *Vorstellungen v. d. Zustand n. d. Tode*, p. 27; Böklen, *Verwandtschaft d. jüd.-christ. mit d. parsisch. Eschatologie*, pp. 147-149.

influence of the Diaspora. While the righteous State or community still occupied the foreground, the individuals who composed it could never again be ignored. Hence, in the pseudepigraphal literature of Judaism anterior to and contemporary with St Paul, the fates of godly and ungodly *persons* in the future world have become a favourite subject of discussion. Participation in that eternal life which is attained through the Resurrection, and exclusion from it, are themes which now stand in the forefront of Jewish theology.

We need not attempt, within the space of a few pages, to give any adequate sketch of the eschatological conceptions of Judaism. This for obvious reasons. On the one hand, Eschatology may be said to form the main content of a whole branch, and that perhaps the most important branch, of later Jewish literature, the apocalyptic. On the other, there are so many modifications of the leading conceptions, and these are so frequently presented in a highly pictorial guise, that they could not be summed up under a few general headings. When treating of St Paul's conceptions in detail, we shall have occasion to discuss their parallels in Judaism. All that can be done at present is to state in a few paragraphs the main categories with which the apostle, from his early training, must have been acquainted.[1]

[1] The following useful table of Jewish literature is compiled from the masterly article by Prof. Charles on "Eschatology," in *Encyclopædia Biblica*:—

Writings of Assideans (2nd cent. B.C.).

Eth. Enoch, 1-36 . .	Sibyll. Oracles: *Proemium*, and iii. 97-818.
Daniel	Testaments of XII. Patriarchs (some of its apocalyptic sections).
Eth. Enoch, 83-90 . .	Judith (?).

In endeavouring to sketch even the fundamental positions of Judaistic Eschatology, one is perplexed by the confusing nature of the facts which have to be dealt with. It is impossible to assign a definite eschatological standpoint to many of the writings, as in certain very important instances, such as the Ethiopic Enoch and the Apocalypse of Baruch, there are sections which proceed from various hands and belong to different dates. To add to the complication, leading scholars are by no means agreed as to the dividing lines between these various sections. As an example, we may refer to the divergent theories described on pp. 9-20 of Prof. Charles's *Book of Enoch.* Not only so, but again and again the same writer shows an elasticity in his conceptions of the Last Things which seems to make classification impossible.[1] This is altogether natural in such a province of thought. We shall find that, to some extent, it holds good for St Paul himself. But it imposes the necessity of extreme caution in any attempt to construct from the extant literature the

Authorities for 104-1 *B.C.*

Eth. Enoch, 91-104 .	. Psalms of Solomon.
Eth. Enoch, 37-70 .	. Sibyll. Or. iii. 1-62.
1 Maccab. . . .	. 2 Maccab.

Authorities for 1*st Century A.D.*

Book of Jubilees .	. Apoc. of Baruch.
Assumption of Moses	. Book of Baruch.
Philo	. 4 Ezra.
Slavon. Enoch .	. Josephus.
Book of Wisdom .	. 4 Maccab.

[1] *Cf.*, for example, the wide variation in the significations of עוֹלָם הַבָּא, as described by Cheyne, *Origin of Psalter*, p. 414; Castelli, *J.Q.R.*, i. p. 320.

current eschatological doctrines of Judaism. Even so able an investigator as Prof. Charles has, in our judgment, not always avoided the danger of making affirmations which are too definite, in stating the positions occupied by individual apocalyptic writers. We must content ourselves here with somewhat broad generalisations.

The chief differences between the Eschatology of the Old Testament, if we may apply that name to a group of dim surmises and vague yearnings, and that of Judaism (and to these we mainly confine ourselves), seem to be due to the developments of the doctrine of a Divine retribution.[1] Thought still wavers as to the scope of this process. Some writers are inclined, at least, to keep in the forefront the future bliss of Israel as a nation, and the future woes of her heathen oppressors. But individualism steadily makes its way. And while in certain books it has reached full maturity, it has left its mark, more or less, upon all. Hints have already been given as to the causes which have brought the idea of future retribution into so marked a prominence. The phenomenon reveals a quickened

[1] "Already in the *Exhortations* of Enoch (chaps. xci.-civ.), the belief of retribution in the future has become the shibboleth of the pious. The ungodly receive a new distinguishing mark: they become the deniers of retribution after death, deniers of judgment, and consequently blasphemers and representatives of an Epicurean worldliness. In the opening chapters of Wisdom . . . the conception of judgment forms the essential distinction between the pious and the ungodly" (Bousset, *Religion d. Judenthums*, p. 174). It is interesting to note the extraordinary emphasis laid upon the idea of retribution in the Christianity of the second century A.D. See, *e.g.*, Von Engelhardt, *Das Christenthum Justins*, p. 199: "[For Justin] belief in God means belief in retribution."

sense of the moral order of the universe, backed up by an undying confidence in the Divine purpose for Israel. Separate thinkers, no doubt, would reach the conception in its clearness entirely along the line of reflection on the hard problems of personal life. The godly, whose lot here is one of suffering and sorrow, must some day reap the fruit of their devotion to righteousness. The sinners, who enjoy an unaccountable prosperity on earth, must ultimately pay the penalty for their disobedience. Parallel to this development of the conception would be the other, already manifest enough in the prophets, as we have seen, which was determined by the fortunes of Israel. So far as the present order of things could be judged, their situation was one of paralysing hopelessness. They had been trodden down by heathen foes. They had had to submit to a foreign tyranny. Where was Jehovah, the God of Zion? And then, at the moment when all seemed lost, God had interposed. The victories of the Maccabæan rising kindled new hopes. There was still to be a future for God's chosen people. Signs were dawning of a new era. The day was hastening on when they should be vindicated before all nations, when their oppressors should be overwhelmed with awful judgments. Thus the developed conviction of Divine retribution took a pre-eminent place in their religious thought. Perhaps we may say that the two great eschatological results of the doctrine were: (1) the transformation of the old idea of Sheol, (2) the Resurrection from Sheol. These came to be linked with the Advent of Messiah, the final Judgment, and the Future State both of righteous and of sinners.

In attempting to trace the history of those developments, we must bear in mind that the literature with which we are dealing stretches, roughly speaking, from about 200 B.C. to 100 A.D. During this period there must have arisen various alterations in feeling.[1] For after the glorious revival of the early Maccabæan age there came that era of decline which ended, after some discreditable episodes, in the submission of the Jews to the hated yoke of Rome. Naturally, therefore, in writings belonging to the latter part of the epoch with which we are concerned, we shall find the centre of interest transferred from the nation to the individual, for there are now national and anti-national parties within Judaism, and the bliss of the End is reserved for those who have remained true to the God of their fathers. As it happens, the writings we possess spring chiefly from the Pharisaic school. Their thoughts all circle around the Messianic Hope, however variously they may conceive of its realisation. The majority of the writers belong to the Quietist wing of the sect, and that standpoint, of course, regulates their eschatological conceptions.

We have seen that in the Old Testament, Sheol denotes the under-world, the receptacle of the dead, both righteous and wicked. Its inhabitants possess an existence which cannot be called "life." They are excluded from contact with God and man. No moral distinctions appear to prevail. A striking picture of their dreary plight is set before us in Isa. xiv., in a highly dramatic form. But a change of view begins to be manifest. The currents of thought, which have been briefly described above, make themselves felt. Thus when we come to examine the Book of Enoch,

[1] For the vagueness of the Messianic Hope during this epoch, see Drummond, *Jewish Messiah*, p. 199 ff.

in some respects the most influential of all Jewish Apocalypses, belonging in its earliest sections to the second century B.C., we are confronted by a remarkable development. Sheol has now become an Intermediate State. All men enter it at death, but it has a very different significance for various classes. According to chap. xxii. of this work, assigned by Charles to a date, at the latest, anterior to 170 B.C., it has four divisions. The first contains the souls of the righteous who suffered a violent, unmerited death The second also is allotted to the righteous, but to such as have escaped the hard fate of their brethren. The third is for sinners who escaped punishment in this life. "Here their souls are placed in great pain, till the great day of judgment and punishment and torture." The fourth is reserved for sinners who did suffer in this earthly life, and therefore incur a milder penalty afterwards. "They shall be with criminals like themselves, but their souls shall not be slain[1] on the day of judgment." We have here a more detailed analysis of Sheol as the Intermediate State than is usually to be found, but it reveals the position which has been reached by an authoritative thinker at the beginning of the second century B.C.[2] The

[1] This "slaying" does not imply annihilation. See Enoch, chap. cviii. 3.

[2] This is apparently the first occurrence of the idea of separate compartments in Sheol (*cf.* Clemen, *Niedergefahren zu d. Toten*, p. 148). For a fourfold lot in the state after death according to Plato, see Zeller, *Plato*, p. 394. Contrast the Rabbinic doctrine of the school of Schammai: "The Schammaites taught that there were three classes: the first two are those mentioned in Dan. xii. 2; the third, in whose case merits and guilt are balanced, incur purifying fire, in which those to be purified waver up and down until they rise out of it purified,

righteous[1] and one portion of the ungodly rise to be finally judged. The former (see chap. v. 7-9), after their resurrection, are, apparently, to live an untroubled life on this earth. The latter will be condemned to Gehenna, the proper hell, which is thus definitely separated from Sheol. The other group of sinners remains in Sheol for ever. We need not expect to find this view reappearing without alteration in other writings. Indeed, in the remaining sections of Enoch there are important divergences from it. Thus, in the section embracing chaps. xci.-civ., which Charles assigns to 134-94 B.C., Sheol appears to be synonymous with Hell. Probably this arises from the circumstance that in this section the writer (as so frequently in Judaism) thinks only of a resurrection of the righteous.[2] The wicked continue in the condition which they entered after death. That is a state of misery and condemnation. This writer, however, does not presuppose a temporary abode of the righteous in the place of woe. He possesses the conception, which appears repeatedly in

according to Zech. xiii. 9; 1 Sam. ii. 6. The scholars of Hillel, however, gather from the words "rich in mercy" (Exod. xxxiv. 6), that God allows the decision for this third class to incline towards mercy: it must have been with regard to them that David wrote Ps. 116" (Bacher, *Agada d. Tannaiten*, i. p. 18). Almost exactly parallel to this middle state is the Pehlevi conception of *hamîstakân*, see Söderblom, *La Vie Future d'après le Mazdéisme*, pp. 125-128.

[1] The idea of Hades as the provisional abode of the righteous after death is the ordinary Pharisaic one. See Schwally, *Leben n. d. Tode*, pp. 166-168.

[2] The expectation of a *universal* resurrection seems to be taught distinctly, for the first time, in the *Similitudes* of Enoch (*i.e.*, chaps. xxxvii.-lxx.); see especially chap. li. 1-3; and *cf.* xxxviii. 1, 6; xlv. 1-3; lxi. 5.

Apocalyptic, of certain special chambers, designated in 4 Ezra *promptuaria* (*e.g.*, iv. 35, 41, v. 37, vii. 32, 95), reserved for the righteous, where they are kept in peace until the final judgment. The same view is to be found in the Apocalypse of Baruch, chaps. xxi. 23, xxiv. 1, xxx. 2 (where see Charles's notes). As an instance of the flexibility of eschatological ideas of Sheol (and the state after death) during the period under review, we may refer to the Slavonic Enoch,[1] perhaps written in our Lord's lifetime, in which, to begin with, a portion of the *heavenly* region is reserved as the place of final torture for the wicked (chap. x.). In a later passage, however, the writer speaks (chap. xl. 12) of seeing "the mighty Hell laid open" in the under-world, the Old Testament Sheol. Thus the earlier and later notions remain side by side in this apocalypse without reconciliation, a phenomenon which is characteristic of eschatological speculation. To sum up on our special question, it may be said with accuracy that the main current of apocalyptic literature ends by recognising two contrasted abodes for the righteous and the wicked. The one is Heaven (occasionally Paradise). The other is Gehenna (sometimes iden-

[1] The book, which is held to be a product of Alexandrian Judaism (see Charles, *Eschatology*, pp. 251-253) departs at this point, in any case, from the ordinary position of Hellenistic Eschatology, which leaves no room for a doctrine of Sheol or an intermediate state, affirming that souls, *at death*, receive their final reward of blessedness or torment. But Bousset has given good ground for asserting that "a sharp distinction between Alexandrian and Palestinian eschatology does not exist" (*Religion d. Judenthums*, p. 260). In case the discussion in the text should create misconception, it ought to be noted that up to a late period in apocalyptic literature there are still traces to be found of the idea of a universal realm of the dead. See especially, Volz, *Jüdische Eschatol.*, p. 289.

tified with Sheol). Our conclusion may seem, indeed, at variance with statements already made as to the hope of a purified theocracy, in which, after the destruction of all their stubborn heathen foes, God or His representative, the Messiah, should rule from Zion over a restored Israel and those Gentiles who had submitted to Israel's dominion. That prospect shines forth clearly in the prophets. And there are many reflections of it in the earlier apocalyptic writings. But while, as truly national, it remains deeply rooted in the popular consciousness, another tendency of thought grows up beside it. This is the larger outlook, so noteworthy in Apocalyptic, which is occupied with the *coming Æon* of glory, as opposed to *the present*, with its depression and gloom. As the cleft between them becomes deeper, the hopes concerning the future grow ever more transcendent. No doubt we find them blended in strange and bewildering combinations in some of the writings of Judaism (see Volz, *op. cit.*, p. 2). But gradually the more spiritual ideas press to the forefront. They fit in with the wider view of the world and its destiny which is forced upon the Jews by their contact with other civilisations. Finally the ultimate goal of the *world*-history assumes a far larger importance in the apocalyptic writings than the crowning destinies of Israel. The righteous and the sinners as such come to occupy as prominent a place as Israel and the heathen. A great extension of categories is manifest. The redemption of Israel is enlarged into the future bliss of the godly. God's judgment upon the foes of the chosen nation becomes the universal judgment in which each individual receives the verdict of the Judge. Instead of a renewal of the Holy Land, a renovation of the world is proclaimed. Side by side with the doctrine of the permanence of the Messianic community stands that of the permanence of the individual, which finds its chief expression in the conception of the Resurrection. In this expectation of the new Æon, the coming blessedness assigned in the earlier period to Palestine and Jerusalem is associated with Heaven, the future dwelling-place of the saints of God. Of course, all the forces which will constitute the coming Æon are already in existence. The supra-mundane order of things and the heavenly world have existed from eternity. As yet that world is veiled, concealed. The main function of the Apocalypses is to penetrate its secrets, to unfold its mysteries. Hence the supra-mundane position of God, His transcendence, and that of all those conditions which await His servants, assert themselves with growing persistence in Apocalyptic. Sometimes it is difficult to determine how far the nationalistic hope preponderates, and how far the transcendental. In 4 Ezra, *e.g.*, the national and universal Eschatologies are found in close conjunction. But the interesting phenomenon may be noted that the doctrine of Chiliasm, the earthly reign of Messiah for a thousand years, is, in its origin, due to the attempt to harmonise the earlier and the later groups of ideas. It is, as Gunkel tersely expresses it, "a compromise between the ancient hope of the prophets which belongs to this world, and the modern, Jewish transcendental hope" (on 4 Ezra vii. 28, in *Kautzsch*). The intermediate, Messianic kingdom becomes the scene for the realisation of those earthly blessings so long held in prospect. The great Judgment and the Resurrection of the dead usher in the final epoch.[1] Hence, when the world is spoken of within the circle of ideas occupied with the coming Æon, it is the world as renewed, the "new heaven and new earth."

In close correspondence with the widening cleft between the two types of eschatological expectation described above, and the growing predominance of the more spiritual conception of the new Æon (עוֹלָם הַבָּא), is to be found the emergence into clearer view and more authoritative position of the momentous doctrine of the Resurrection.

We have seen how several psalmists passionately demand a continuance of fellowship with God in defiance of death. Probably their strongest expressions rather imply a miraculous deliverance from death than that which we mean by a resurrection. The idea may have assumed clearer shape under the pressure of the terrible experiences of persecution in the reign of Antiochus Epiphanes. In Isa. xxvi. 19 (belonging to a section of the book, chaps. xxiv.-xxvii., which most scholars hold to be post-exilic), there is a remarkable utterance, which forms a kind of link between the cravings of Job and the Psalms, and the developed theory of Judaism. Its expressions, indeed, are not isolated. The way has been prepared for them by imagery like that of Hos. vi. 2, and (more emphatically) Ezek. xxxvii. Here, it seems to be the nation, returned to its desolated land, that is speaking. "Thy dead" (as if addressing the land) "shall live: my dead body shall arise. Awake and sing, ye that dwell in dust: for thy dew is a dew of lights, and the earth shall bring forth (to life) the shades." This bold assertion is doubtless born of

[1] See, *e.g.*, Volz, *op. cit.*, pp. 62-67.

the conviction that God's purpose for the remnant of His people is incomplete, if those who perished in the downfall of the nation, and those whose graves had been left behind in the land of exile, have no share in the final restoration. It is of great significance to trace the leadings of the Divine Spirit in the human consciousness towards the attainment of this remarkable resurrection-hope. It is the claim of the people upon their God. And that continues to be the dominant motive in the formation of the conception. After a further period of depression under the Seleucidæ, the Maccabæan rising, as we have noted, again kindles glad expectations. And the demand that those who have died as martyrs for their faith should not be excluded from the felicity of their people, takes this unique shape.

It is very difficult to make definite statements as to the precise scope of the Resurrection in the view of the apocalyptic writers. Professor Charles, whose authority in this department is universally acknowledged, affirms, in a note on Enoch li. 1, that "no Jewish book except 4 Ezra teaches indubitably the doctrine of a general resurrection, and this may be due to Christian influence."[1] "The whole history of

[1] Bousset boldly declares: "We ought at least to say that the Jewish conception of resurrection has developed under the influence of Eranian Apocalyptic into the universal conception of a general resurrection and the world-judgment" (*Religion d. Judenthums*, p. 480). In our judgment, this statement can neither be affirmed nor denied. For lack of sufficient evidence, the question must be left open. But we are inclined to agree with Söderblom (*La Vie Future d'après le Mazdéisme*, pp. 316-318) in holding that such a hypothesis is not necessary. There are elements, that is to say, in Judaism itself, containing the germs of the development in question. The conception of a final

Jewish thought," he asserts, "points in an opposite direction." No doubt there is much truth in the latter statement, but, unless we are permitted to read a great deal between the lines, it is precarious to dogmatise upon the question. Dr Charles himself admits that a resurrection of *all Israel* is assumed, *e.g.*, in Dan. xii. 2; Enoch 37-70, 83-90, etc.; 2 Macc. vii., xii. 43-44; Apoc. Bar. l.-li. 6 (see his notes on Enoch li. 1). If that be so (although we are not quite convinced of it), it will require great caution to distinguish in several of the places quoted between a general and an Israelitish resurrection. But it may be frankly acknowledged that the more comprehensive view was, at least, very limited. Many passages plainly pre-suppose that only the God-fearing will enjoy the high privilege of resurrection. That is to be expected, when we recall the religious basis of the doctrine. And it is natural that members of the chosen community should exhaust the category of the righteous, as, for the writers of that period, in the narrowest sense, salvation was of the Jews. As examples of the restriction in question, we may quote Psalms of Solomon iii. 13-16: "The destruction of the sinner is for ever, and he shall not be remembered when He (*i.e.* God) visiteth the righteous; this portion of the sinner is for ever. But they that fear the Lord shall rise to everlasting life, and their life shall no more fail in the light of the Lord" (*cf.* xiv. 6, xv. 15); Apoc. Bar. xxx.: "And it

transcendent Divine retribution for the individual, combined with the earlier prophetic idea of the Messianic judgment, as it must often have been, would necessarily give rise to the picture of the world-judgment, in which the ultimate fates of men are decided. With a view to this event, there must be a universal resurrection.

shall come to pass after these things, when the time of the advent of the Messiah is fulfilled, and He shall return in glory (*i.e.* to heaven, so Charles, Ryssel), then all who have fallen asleep in the hope of Him shall rise again. And it shall come to pass at that time that the treasuries shall be opened in which is preserved the number of the souls of the righteous, and they shall come forth. . . . But the souls of the wicked, when they behold all those things, shall then waste away the more. For they shall know that their torment has come and their perdition has arrived." So Josephus, *Ant.*, xviii. 1 (3), in describing the views of the Pharisees, states that they hold that for evil souls "an eternal prison is appointed" (εἱργμὸν ἀΐδιον προτίθεσθαι), for the good, "an easy way of coming to life again" (ῥαστώνην τοῦ ἀναβιοῦν). This is probably, in general, the doctrine current in the Rabbinic literature. Various important passages, quoted by Weber (*Lehren d. Talmud*, pp. 372, 373), admit of no other interpretation. That there were traces of the wider view, however, is shown by a discussion between Eliezer b. Hyrkanos and Joshua b. Chananja. In an argument on the Resurrection, Eliezer proved the exclusion of the Sodomites from Gen. xiii. 3, while Joshua proved from Ps. i. 5, that "sinners" should rise to judgment, not indeed in the congregation of the pious, but in that of the impious (Bacher, *Agada d. Tannaiten*, i. p. 141; see, on the whole question, Volz, *op. cit.*, pp. 246, 247). It is possible that, as Schwally (*Leben nach d. Tode*, p. 151) and others suppose, the resurrection-hope originated rather as a popular belief, and then, gradually penetrated to the more learned classes. In any case, when the subject became a matter of reflection and study, thinkers would attempt to adjust the resurrection-doctrine to their general views of the world and human life. Accordingly when we come to a book like 4 Ezra, written probably within the last twenty years of the first century A.D., it is not unreasonable to expect a wider outlook. This work is peculiarly interesting and important for our inquiry, as originating probably in the same circle of thought as that in which St Paul himself had moved, and forming a kind of compendium of contemporary Judaistic Eschatology (see Gunkel in *Kautzsch*, p. 348; and Volz, *op. cit.*, p. 31). Like the apostle, 4 Ezra despises the fantastic, mythological ideas prevalent in Apocalyptic. He scarcely speculates at all on the fate of sinners, leaving that, as St Paul does, shrouded in darkness. He is content, at times, to allow what one might almost call divergent strains of eschatological theory to remain side by side, without apparent consciousness of their discrepancy. Speaking generally, it may be said that his horizon is far wider than that of the earlier apocalyptic writers. And the assertion is exemplified by his references to the Resurrection. According to his conception, it appears to be universal. His language is unmistakable. "The earth restores those who rest in it; the dust sets free those who sleep therein; the chambers yield back the souls which were entrusted to them. The Highest appears on the Judge's throne; then comes the end, and pity passes away; compassion is remote; long-suffering has disappeared; my judgment alone will remain, truth will stand, faith will triumph; reward follows after; retribution appears; good deeds awake; evil ones sleep no longer. There appears the hollow of pain, and opposite, the place of reviving. The oven of Gehenna becomes manifest, and opposite, the paradise of blessedness" (4 Ezra vii. 32-36).[1]

We have attempted very briefly to trace the main developments of eschatological doctrine in the thought of Judaism as the immediate background and environment of St Paul's mental life. Perhaps enough has been said to indicate the nature of the conceptions with which the apostle, from his earliest days, must have been more or less familiar. It ought not to be difficult, when we are dealing with his separate eschatological ideas, to discover approximately how far he accepted and how far he modified the traditional theories of his nation.

But we must now turn to that factor whose influence was supreme in shaping the eschatological as well as every other element in his religious thought, his personal Christian experience.[2] Here we are concerned with one of those mysterious problems which really elude matter-of-fact discussion. The conversion of St Paul has a place among the most remarkable events in all spiritual history. Numerous and ingenious attempts have been made to minimise its significance, or, at least, to account for it on purely natural grounds. Great stress, for example, has been laid upon the psychological preparation of Saul the Pharisee.[3] The process is conceived on some such

[1] *Cf.* his many expressions of dread at the thought of the world-judgment. That presupposes a *general* resurrection.

[2] Holtzmann puts the truth expressively when he says: "It (*i.e.*, St Paul's entire system of doctrine, *Lehrbegriff*) . . . simply means the exposition of the content of his conversion, the systematising of the Christophany" (*N.T. Theol.*, ii. p. 205).

[3] See, especially, Holsten's acute discussion, *Die Christusvision d. Paulus* in his *Zum Evangelium d. Paulus u. Petrus*, pp. 2-114.

lines as these. In the heat of Saul's persecuting zeal his mind has been disturbed. Probably before now he has been tormented, at times, by the consciousness of failure perfectly to keep the Divine law. And thus he is often uncertain as to his standing before God. He cannot help contrasting the calm confidence and heroism of the followers of the crucified Nazarene with his own experiences of inward turmoil. Their demeanour, their spirit, the triumphant loyalty which does not quail even before death—these things leave an overpowering impression on his ardent and sensitive nature. He envies them their firm assurance. It has something unique, something superhuman about it. His opposing faith begins to tremble. He has gained a partial knowledge of the history and claims of Jesus from the preaching of the apostles. As he reflects on these elements in the Christian Gospel, and compares them with the predictions of the Old Testament, he becomes inwardly less and less positive concerning his own legal status. At length the crisis comes, when his whole being has been wrought up to high nervous tension by the scheme he has undertaken—a scheme by which he strives to hide from himself the doubts which torture him. "Saul, Saul, why persecutest thou Me?" The voice is the echo of his surging thought and feeling. But it attaches itself to the image of that Figure which haunts him night and day. He can hold out no longer. The Crucified has conquered.

No doubt there is a measure of truth in such hypotheses. We cannot conceive a nature like that of St Paul remaining indifferent to the evidences of Christian certainty of which he was so frequently a witness. Not only so, but the very words reported in the narrative of his conversion, "It is hard for thee to kick against the goads," are full of significance. They show that deep misgivings concerning his religious position were asserting themselves in his inmost soul. Plainly (and this is borne out by passages, *e.g.*, like Rom. vii.) the painful conviction was pressing itself upon him, that by the deeds of the law no flesh is justified. And his whole nature craved a right standing before God. The very fact that he had to defend his position against a honeycombing doubt, would urge him forward more fiercely than ever as a champion of Judaism.

But there is no evidence to prove that he suspected the real truth to lie in the direction of the new sect of the Nazarenes. Their position was a blasphemy against God. Their so-called Messiah had been crucified as a common criminal. What insolence to see in him the culmination of God's revelation to His people! St Paul had been nurtured on the Messianic Hope of Israel. What a caricature was this of the glorious fulfilment for which devout Jews had yearned![1] They spoke, indeed, of a resurrection of Jesus, their

[1] Beyschlag supposes that St Paul's antipathy to the claims of Jesus did not rest on the fact of His shameful death (see Deut. xxi. 23: "He that is hanged is the curse of God," applied by St Paul to Christ in Gal. iii. 13), but was the result of their opposite conceptions of δικαιοσύνη παρὰ θεῷ (*S.K.*, 1864, pp. 245-247). It is very probable that this last consideration should be included. But it appears to us that the total inversion of the Jewish conception of Messiah and His work in the life and experiences of Jesus, culminating in the disgrace of the Cross, must have been the decisive factor in leading Saul the Pharisee to despise and thwart, with all his might, the Messianic faith of the first Christians. The passages quoted above corroborate this view.

Messiah,[1] but no one had seen Him save some of their own company. The young Pharisee was far from being at peace within himself. Yet he would never dream of expecting to find it among the deluded rabble whom he was hounding to their death.

Then his life was suddenly cleft in twain. It would be absurd to look for a perfectly clear or detailed account of an experience like this. The immediate effect of it, both on the mind and the whole sensory system, would be far too overwhelming to admit of any explicit analysis of the circumstances. But the accounts in Acts seem to show a remarkable agreement with the brief references in the Pauline Epistles. The definite points are these. In 1 Cor. xv. 8 he makes no distinction between his own "sight" of Jesus and that of the other apostles to whom He showed Himself after His resurrection: ἔσχατον δὲ πάντων . . . ὤφθη κἀμοί. It is worth while noting that the word used here for His "appearing" (ὤφθη) occurs in one of the strongest passages bearing on the Resurrection, Luke xxiv. 34: "The Lord has really risen and appeared to Simon." Similarly in 1 Cor. ix. 1: "Have not I *seen* (ἑόρακα) Jesus our Lord?" In striking accord with these passages, the accounts of the incident in Acts do not describe it as a "vision," although this idea was perfectly familiar to the historian. For he tells of a vision (ὅραμα) which appeared to Paul at Troas (xvi. 9); of another at Corinth (εἶπεν . . . ὁ κύριος ἐν νυκτὶ δι' ὁράματος τῷ Παύλῳ, xviii. 9). He speaks of the apostle as being

[1] This notion also had nothing to correspond to it in the beliefs of Judaism (see Teichmann, *Paulin. Vorstellungen v. Auferst. u. Gericht*, p. 34).

ἐν ἐκστάσει in the temple at Jerusalem, and seeing the Lord (xxii. 17, 18). Also, he describes the knowledge which Ananias of Damascus received concerning Paul as given ἐν ὁράματι. We quote these instances simply to show that for the writer of Acts there was a distinction between St Paul's first experience of the risen Jesus and some other experiences which came later. As we shall see in a moment, the reports on which he based his narrative agreed in relating a phenomenon perceived by his senses, a light which shone round about him.[1] Klöpper (*ad loc.*) finds a reference to the extraordinary event in 2 Cor. iv. 6, where the apostle speaks of "the illumination of the knowledge of the glory of God in the face of Christ" (φωτισμὸν τῆς γνώσεως τῆς δόξης τοῦ θεοῦ ἐν προσώπῳ Χριστοῦ). The concluding words appear to him to present the outer and objective side of the experience whose inward aspect is described by the preceding phrase, "who shone in our hearts" (ὃς ἔλαμψεν ἐν ταῖς καρδίαις ἡμῶν). While we would not lay the stress of any argument on this passage, Klöpper's interpretation ought not to be summarily dismissed.[2]

[1] Chap. ix. 3, περιήστραψεν φῶς; xxii. 6, περιαστράψαι φῶς; xxvi. 13, περιλάμψαν . . . φῶς.

[2] Heinrici refuses to allow such a reference, because he holds, (1) that the expression of details in the passage is regulated by the quotation of the creative word (ὁ θεὸς ὁ εἰπών· ἐκ σκότους φῶς λάμψει) in the opening clause, and (2) that the words "in our hearts" (ἐν ταῖς καρδίαις ἡμῶν) exclude a *personal* confession on the part of the apostle (see his notes *ad loc.*). The latter objection is by no means valid, for both in the preceding and following verses it is plain that St Paul has himself chiefly in view, although he invariably uses ἡμεῖς. *Cf.* the convincing verses at the beginning of chap. iii. As to the former, we should have an equal right to assert that the creative word about the light was introduced just because of its analogy with the experience which the apostle had in his mind.

Some weight has been attached to the important expressions in Gal. i. 15: "When it pleased Him . . . to reveal His Son in me" (ἐν ἐμοί), as bringing into prominence the inward nature of the experience. But Lightfoot (*ad loc.*) gives excellent reasons for taking this clause in close connection with the words immediately following, "that I might preach Him," etc. (ἵνα εὐαγγελίσωμαι αὐτόν), and understanding "He that called me by His grace" (ὁ . . . καλέσας διὰ τῆς χάριτος) as a reference to the actual event on the Damascus road.

Although there are some variations in the separate accounts of the occurrence as given in Acts, these do not touch the central phenomena in the experience. The following facts, at least, stand out in clear relief. (*a*) A great light from heaven suddenly shone round about the traveller, as he journeyed. (*b*) From the shock of this dazzling appearance, Saul falls prostrate on the ground. (*c*) He hears a voice, which he discovers to be that of Jesus, speaking to him in words which he can understand. The divergences in the narratives relate to his companions. It is easy to realise how vague and conflicting reports of *their* impressions of the event would speedily circulate. In the case of so unique and mysterious a phenomenon, we have no criteria whereby to estimate their situation. They saw (ἐθεάσαντο) the light, but no person (μηδένα).[1] In Acts ix. 7 they are described as ἀκούοντες . . . τῆς φωνῆς. In xxii. 9 we read, τὴν δὲ φωνὴν οὐκ

[1] Had the narrator of the story in Acts ix. been disposed to embellish his history or to draw on his imagination, as some critics have suggested, we can scarcely conceive of his leaving the details in this colourless condition. He had a magnificent opportunity here of supplementing the tradition.

κουσαν τοῦ λαλοῦντός μοι. It is possible that this variation, when examined closely, has real significance. They may have heard a vague sound (φωνῆς, genitive), and yet not the articulate, intelligible voice (φωνήν, accusative), which fell upon St Paul's ear with a definite meaning (see Brugmann, *Griechische Grammatik*, [3] pp. 385, 386).[1] In any case, their experience cannot affect St Paul's part in the event, unless we venture to assert that all percipient intelligences, when placed in the same situation, must necessarily be affected *in the same manner and degree* by some phenomenon which comes within the field of sensation. This would be a rash position to adopt, even with reference to those objects for which we can account by definable natural laws. But it is wholly precarious, when we are concerned with the mysterious borderland which lies between the physical and the spiritual. A wise and comprehensive psychology will hesitate to assert, in presence of the strange variety of evidence which is brought within its ken, what is possible or impossible in this dimly-lighted region. When we consider the extraordinary gradations of capacity in human intellects for apprehending different aspects of scientific or philosophical truth, when we bear in mind the varied stages of refinement in the sense-perception of separate individuals, it would be, in the highest degree, hazardous to rule out as incredible an abnormal intensity of sensitiveness to spiritual forces expressing themselves in forms the most fitted to achieve their aims. It is, indeed, useless to speculate on the objective phenomena which came within St Paul's horizon.[2] But we know with certainty the

[1] *Cf.* the incident narrated in John xii. 28-30.

[2] Prof. James speaks of "one form of sensory automatism,"

immediate inferences which he drew from them. He became absolutely convinced that Christ was risen from the dead and reigning in glory. These convictions laid so firm a grasp upon him as to transform his whole life and aspirations. That he himself regarded the crucial event as more than a spiritual experience, is clear from the plain, matter-of-fact language which has been quoted above: "Have not I *seen* the Lord." And he uses these terms with the express purpose of vindicating his apostleship against his detractors, who reduced it to a lower level than that of the other twelve apostles, partly on the ground that they had seen and known Jesus, while he had not. There is no trace throughout the epistles of any doubts thrown upon the occurrence, although no accusation could have been more conveniently brought against St Paul by his opponents than that his apostolic status was based upon a mere vision. The truth is, that the epoch-making crisis in the apostle's life can only be explained along the lines which he himself has indicated. In view of the manifold attempts which have been made to prove a gradual, psychological development, terminating in a

which he calls a *photism*, an "hallucinatory or pseudo-hallucinatory" phenomenon. To this class he assigns St Paul's "vision" and Constantine's Cross in the sky (*Varieties of Relig. Experience*, p. 252). He quotes several modern instances, but we must confess that we fail to see that they are, in any sense, valid parallels to the experience of St Paul. The subjects of these phenomena immediately recognise that they were altogether mental. Years after, St Paul with the utmost calmness uses Christ's appearance to him as a proof of Christ's "bodily" (*i.e.*, as we shall see = possessing a spiritual organism) resurrection, and hence also as a proof of the future "bodily" (in the sense already described) resurrection of believers. (See also Beyschlag, *S.K.*, 1864, p. 226.)

remarkable and entirely subjective experience, it is interesting to note the verdict of so fearless and unprejudiced a critic as H. J. Holtzmann. "It is certain," he says, "that the apostle himself knows nothing of a gradual process, which had led him nearer to Christianity, but only of a sudden halt to which he was brought in the midst of an active career. He recognises only an instantaneous transformation, but no bridge which had conducted him from one bank to the other (Phil. iii. 5-9). He looks upon himself, in 2 Cor. ii. 14, as a suddenly-subdued rebel, whom God leads in triumph about the world. . . . Wholly unassailable, personal testimonies, which corroborate the essential contents of our narrative (*i.e.* in Acts) with powerful demonstration" (*Hand-Commentar*, [3] Bd. i. Abtheil. ii., pp. 70, 71).[1]

But account must also be taken of the *development* of St Paul's Christian experience. This meeting with the risen Jesus does not remain an isolated event in his history. It forms the starting-point of a remarkable series of religious phenomena. Henceforward he knows himself to be in real contact with the exalted Lord. His inner life has been brought into relation with the Divine πνεῦμα, which is the life-principle in the ascended Christ. The incoming and indwelling of that πνεῦμα produces a new creation. His human existence receives a new basis. "Christ liveth in me" (Gal. ii. 20 ff.: perhaps the most crucial

[1] Holtzmann notes the number of separate accounts of St Paul's conversion, a number without any parallel in the book of Acts, which is to be explained from the fundamental significance of the event (*op. cit.*, p. 59). *Cf.* Gunkel (*Wirkungen d. heiligen Geistes bei Paulus*, [2] p. 75), on St Paul's conception of the Christian life as established by a break, by the inroad of the supernatural, a new thing, *i.e.*, "the Spirit of God."

passage for his conception of the new life). We dwell upon this entire experience, because it is of decisive importance for St Paul's eschatological conceptions. The Resurrection of Jesus Christ, indeed, may be described as the foundation of all that is most vital, all that is most central in the apostle's view of the Last Things. That tremendous fact is sufficient proof to Paul of the life beyond death. The risen Christ is the First-fruits of them that sleep (1 Cor. xv. 20). For those who have fallen asleep in Jesus, resurrection is a certainty (1 Thess. iv. 14). And it will take place on the lines of the resurrection of Jesus (1 Cor. vi. 14).

We believe that the apostle arrived at his conception of the resurrection-body, the spiritual organism, by reflection on this amazing event in his personal history. He was convinced that he had met Jesus, and by some marvellous method the risen Lord had impressed upon him His own objective reality. It was not a mere inward thrill of his soul, as under some hidden spiritual influence. It was the stamp of a personal revelation which was left upon him. It was the same *kind* of revelation, in his judgment, as that made to Simon Peter and John and the rest, after the Resurrection (1 Cor. xv. 4-8). Plainly, they were thoroughly conscious of a "bodily" presence, and yet it was quite distinct from His former state, for now He was raised above the ordinary conditions of a material organism.[1] He could manifest Himself

[1] See some suggestive thoughts in Westcott, *Revelation of the Risen Lord*, p. 68; and *cf.* Forrest, *Christ of History*, p. 153: "The temporary union in Him (*i.e.* the Risen Christ) of two diverse modes of being will not seem strange to us, if we realise that only by this means could God assure us that the redemption

when the doors were shut. He could vanish from their sight in a moment. St Paul believed his experience to be in line with theirs. Does it not seem probable, therefore, that he formulated his doctrine of a spiritual "body" as a direct inference from his wonderful contact with the risen Christ? This conception would necessarily be corroborated by the subsequent course of his religious experience. Through faith in the living Lord, he was conscious of intimate fellowship with Him. This fellowship was mediated by the *πνεῦμα.* Occasionally he identifies the *πνεῦμα* with the living Christ (2 Cor. iii. 17, 18; Rom. viii. 2). Sometimes he speaks of *τὸ πνεῦμα τῆς υἱοθεσίας* (Rom. viii. 15), or *τοῦ υἱοῦ αὐτοῦ* (Gal. iv. 6). Sometimes he ascribes to the Spirit an independent existence, the Life of God operating upon the life of man in a personalised activity (*e.g.*, Rom. viii. 9, 14, 16; 1 Cor. ii. 10, xii. 3; Eph. iv. 30 *et al.*). In any case, the *πνεῦμα* is the death-conquering principle in Jesus Christ. It was in virtue of the *πνεῦμα τῆς ἁγιωσύνης* that He rose from the grave (Rom. i. 4). It is this *πνεῦμα*, which is His life, that acts directly upon the souls of those who cling to Him in lively faith (Rom. viii. 2). They may therefore be said to possess the *πνεῦμα* (Rom. viii. 9). And their possession is also the pledge of their victory over death (Rom. viii. 23; 2 Cor. v. 4, 5). The flesh perishes, the spirit survives (Rom. viii. 10). But it does not lose individuality; that is to say, it bears on the personality into the glorified life. That personality retains its identity with its

of Christ was no less the rectification of the material than of the spiritual universe. Yet it is precisely such an assurance that is needed to give religious faith a final basis and guarantee, by showing that it cannot be explained as a psychical hallucination."

past. The spirit has an "organism" (σῶμα) corresponding to itself (1 Cor. xv. 44 f.). The organism of humiliation (ταπεινώσεως) is changed into the organism of glory (δόξης), which is the form (σύμμορφον) of Christ's exalted life (Phil. iii. 21).

We are also inclined to suppose that the circumstances of St Paul's experience of the risen Christ on the Damascus road helped to contribute certain pictorial elements, if we may so call them, to his conception of the future glorified life. His conception of *δόξα,* by which, as we saw in our last paragraph, he describes the spiritual organism of Christ (σῶμα τῆς δόξης, Phil. iii. 21) is a highly suggestive one. We must return to it in a future chapter, but it is necessary at this stage to point out its connection with the apostle's impression of the exalted Lord. No doubt the basis of the idea is to be found in express form in the Old Testament. In ancient Israel, God's real presence, His actual self-revelation conceived as living energy, was constantly associated with His glory (כָּבוֹד). Cf., *e.g.*, Exod. xl. 34, "The glory of the Lord filled the Tabernacle"; Ezek. i. 28, "This was the appearance of the likeness of the glory of the Lord." These, and numerous other instances which might be quoted, present the more material side of the conception, God's presence, as it were, revealing itself to the senses. From this aspect of the conception was derived the notion of the Shekinah, so frequently found in the Targums, *e.g.*, Targum on Isa. lx. 2: "In thee the Shekinah of the Lord shall dwell, and His glory shall be revealed upon thee." The Shekinah is the localised presence of God, *cf.* Enoch xiv. 20: "And the great Glory sat thereon, and His raiment shone more brightly than the sun." Hence light radiates from the place of His earthly abode. But the Old Testament has also a more figurative conception of God's glory; see, *e.g.*, Psa. xix. 1, "The heavens declare the glory of God," *i.e.*, are a witness to His omnipotent energy; Psa. civ. 31; "The glory of the Lord shall endure for ever," *i.e.*, His power and authority, as manifested in the universe; Hab. ii. 14, "The earth shall be filled with the knowledge of the glory of the Lord"; Psa. lxiii. 2, "To see Thy power and Thy glory." And there are many instances which seem capable of being assigned to either aspect, such as Isa. xl. 5, "The glory of the Lord shall be revealed, and all flesh shall see it together"; Ezek. xxxix. 21; "I will set my glory among the heathen"; Isa. lviii. 8, "Then shall thy light break forth as the morning, and thine health shall spring forth speedily; and thy righteousness shall go before thee; the glory of the Lord shall be thy rereward." In close connection with the conception of God's glory, it must be borne in mind that *light* is the symbol of salvation in the Old Testament. Hence, in many post-canonical writings, the life of the blessed is pictured as radiance, the result of their fellowship with the God whose most characteristic self-manifestation is conceived as light. See, *e.g.*, Ps. Sol. iii. 16, "Their (*i.e.*, the risen God-fearers) life shall no more fade in the light of the Lord"; Enoch xxxviii. 4, "The light of the Lord of Spirits is seen on the face of the holy and righteous and elect"; civ. 2, "Soon ye will shine as the stars of heaven; ye will shine and ye will be seen."[1] In the New Testament there are traces of the same

[1] For numerous additional examples, see Grill, *Untersuchungen über die Entstehung d. vierten Evangeliums* (Tübingen, 1902), i. p. 265.

conception, kept, however, within careful limits. St Paul speaks, *e.g.*, of the "inheritance of the saints in light." It is quite possible to exaggerate this and other statements of the apostle in a grossly materialistic direction, as, *e.g.*, Kabisch has done (*passim*) in his *Eschatologie d. Paulus*.[1] But it would almost appear as if his experience on the journey to Damascus confirmed or gave a new meaning to the familiar imagery of the Old Testament for the mind of St Paul. There, at least, he received the impression of a radiant light shining about him. And it is probable that when afterwards he attempted to picture the unseen future of those who should be with Christ, he was led, under the influence of the supra-earthly manifestation which had burst upon him, to conceive a condition of glowing brightness, the effulgence of the God of glory Himself. It would be hazardous to press this conception of *δόξα* (as we shall afterwards see), for its Old Testament basis reminds us that its content is apt to fluctuate between the actual and the figurative; but it is highly probable that it formed a real element in the thought of the apostle.

The recognition of a foundation for his ideas of the Last Things in his personal Christian experience, is supremely important in estimating the limits of his Eschatology. We have already treated of its fragmentary character. We have already observed that there are certain sides of the subject which he has barely touched. Probably when we remember the facts of his own history, which were of such paramount importance in fixing the direction of all his religious

[1] For an excellent caution against literalising the metaphor of *light* as applied to the Divine nature and Spirit, see Drummond, *Philo*, i. pp. 217, 218.

thinking, it will be easier to understand why he has merely alluded to, or even passed by in silence, some aspects of the question, fraught with far-reaching significance. Thus, in the light of the circumstances which we have been considering, we can discover why his utterances on Eschatology are chiefly positive. This is not the usual trend of modern speculation. Such topics as Eternal Punishment, the fate of the Lost, the Intermediate State, etc., have called forth the most animated discussion. St Paul does little to satisfy his reader's curiosity on such problems. His letters are addressed to Christian communities. The main interest for him and for them is the promise of eternal life in Christ. And the certainty with which he clings to this glorious prospect is founded on the conviction, reached at the crisis of his history, that Christ *has* risen, and become the First-fruits of them that sleep. Hence even such apparently central questions as that of a general resurrection receive little elucidation on his pages. He looks out upon the problems of the Last Things, not from a speculative, very seldom even from a theological, standpoint, almost invariably from that of Christian faith and experience. And after all, is not this by far the most momentous aspect of the field to keep in view? The supreme fact which makes Eschatology a subject of living interest, at least to Christians, is the pledge of immortality assured through the risen Christ. Men cannot, indeed, refrain from asking questions concerning the fate of those who have passed away without apparently laying hold of the mercy of God extended to them in the Redeemer. The processes of moral retribution press heavily upon human minds. And it is possible to give the rein to innumerable speculations regarding the future destinies of the world and its relations to the kingdom of God. Many of those speculations never appealed to St Paul. Subjects like Conditional Immortality or Eternal Punishment certainly did not present themselves to *his* mind in the guise or in the terms which form the battle-ground of modern discussions. Yet if we endeavour to place ourselves at his point of view, and to become familiar with the precise significance of his language, we may at least gain valuable hints as to the truths involved in such discussions. We emphasise the "point of view" and the "precise significance of his language," because St Paul is often cited in modern books as an authority for views which he would not have understood, as a witness to theories foreign to his entire method of thought. Keeping in mind, therefore, that his eschatological ideas are, in the main, of a positive character, as arising out of his personal contact with the risen Christ, we shall be obliged in the subsequent chapters to give more ample space to the Eschatology of the Christian life and the Kingdom of God.

But, before leaving the present phase of our inquiry, there is a further subdivision of the Formative Influences in St Paul's conceptions of the Last Things which we must very briefly notice: the Christian tradition of the eschatological teaching of Jesus. To discuss this difficult subject with any degree of fulness, would require a separate volume. It must suffice for our purpose to endeavour to trace in a few sentences the fundamental parallels between the thought of the Master and that of His apostle. Both of them make large use of the terms and ideas current in their time. Both lay the basis of their Eschatology in the Old

Testament revelation. Both of them employ as their ormal starting-point the hopes which possessed the earts of their fellow-countrymen. The background nd environment of the eschatological teaching of esus, as of Paul, have been outlined in the former art of this chapter. It remains simply to recognise hose transformations of Jewish Eschatology wrought y Jesus, which Paul assumes as axioms in representng the Last Things both to himself and to his readers.

It is quite self-evident that, after his conversion, St Paul must have gone back to the teaching of esus as authoritative for the Christian Church. While the glorified Christ who had appeared to him vould always remain the predominantly normative actor for his religious thought,[1] we can easily coneive with what eagerness the apostle, in the light f his new and wonderful experiences, would inquire nto the actual views of God and the world which he Master had set forth in His earthly career. That hrough converse with the Twelve and others he ecame acquainted with these, is plain from the background of his thinking throughout the Epistles. The ntimate relation of his doctrine to that of Jesus is ometimes ignored because it does not always appear ipon the surface. But a deeper penetration reveals remarkable kinship of spiritual ideas. Comparaively often he directly refers to words of Jesus.[2] And these references are, no doubt, merely a sample

[1] For the subordination of interest in the detailed sayings of esus and the events of His earthly life to that in the crucified nd risen Messiah, in the early Apostolic Age, see the emarkable essay of Von Soden, *Das Interesse d. apostol. Zeitalters an der evangel. Geschichte* in *Theolog. Abhandlungen C. v. Weizsäcker gewidmet*, pp. 113-169 (Freiburg i. B., 1892).

[2] See Titius, pp. 11, 12.

of his practice in his oral instruction. Numerous important parallels to the sayings of Jesus may be noted in his ethical teaching.[1] But more important than these, which may often be accidental, is the common basis of their central religious conceptions. We can only call attention to those which seem most decisive for Eschatology. We shall have occasion to show in a subsequent chapter how, in what may be called the more "pictorial" conceptions of the Last Things, Jesus, as well as His apostles, used the current imagery of His time, an imagery which had descended from the prophets, and was extended, often in grotesque directions, by the apocalyptic writers, to set forth the great crises of the future, the Parousia and the Judgment. He spoke with absolute conviction of His own coming, His personal intervention in the consummation of all things. He proclaimed His place as Judge in the final decision of human destinies. To express these momentous facts, He employed the only kind of terms which would convey the lessons He sought to enforce upon His hearers. As will be clearly seen at a later stage, St Paul was very directly influenced by the tradition of Jesus' teaching concerning the Parousia and Judgment. For the same pictures appear in the Epistles, and the same elements in the situation are emphasised. For the Parousia, we may quote the following parallels:[2] Mark xiv. 62 = Rom. xiii. 11 ff.; Matt. xxiv. 19 ff. = 1 Thess. iii. 4; 1 Cor. vii. 26, 28 (preparatory woes); Matt. xxiv. 43 = 1 Thess. v. 2; Matt. xxiv. 31 = 1 Thess. iv. 15 ff.; Matt. xxiv. 42 = 1 Thess. v. 6 f. On the Judgment, the following are note-

[1] See Titius, pp. 13-15; *cf.* Von Soden, *op. cit.*, pp. 127-129.
[2] See Titius, pp. 15, 16

worthy: Matt. xxv. 31, 32=2 Cor. v. 10; Matt. xix. 28=1 Cor. vi. 2; Mark xii. 36=1 Cor. xv. 25.

But more decisive for St Paul's relation to the teaching of Jesus are the deeper elements of his eschatological thought. Two of these we would emphasise: his conceptions of the *basis* of the Future Life and the *nature* of the Future Life.

Again and again Jesus uses the term "Life" (ζωή) to sum up the whole range of the blessings of salvation which the believer is to inherit. In the Fourth Gospel the attribute "eternal" (αἰώνιος) is usually added. The objection may be raised that the prevalence of the epithet in that Gospel is due to the fact that our Lord's conceptions have passed through the mind of the writer, who delights to view the Christian verities *sub specie æternitatis*, but for whom "eternal" means primarily that which belongs to the coming Æon, the higher order of things, and thus is virtually equivalent to "supra-earthly."[1] Whether this objection have force or not, it is plain that in the Synoptic Gospels, where the epithet αἰώνιος occurs very seldom, ζωή by itself really includes all that is involved in the idea of "eternal." This appears even from the ideas with which it is contrasted. These are ἀπώλεια (Matt. vii. 13, 14), τὸ πῦρ τὸ αἰώνιον (Matt. xviii. 8), τὴν γέενναν (Matt. xviii. 9; Mark ix. 43, 46). In Matt. xix. 16, 17, he answers the phrase ζωὴν αἰώνιον, spoken by the young ruler, with the simple ζωήν. This usage had already existed in Jewish literature, see *e.g.*, Ps. Sol. xiv. 6, ix. 9; 2 Macc. vii. 14.[2] It was not, therefore, the conception of "Life" (virtually equivalent to participation in the Kingdom of God) that was

[1] See Haupt, *Eschatol. Aussagen Jesu*, p. 84 f.

[2] See Dalman, *Worte Jesu*, p. 129.

new on the lips of Jesus. The difference consisted in the conditions which He laid down for possessing it; and the spiritual view of the Kingdom in which it was to be possessed, which He substituted for that of Judaism. The knowledge of God as the Father, and the fellowship which was the outcome of that knowledge, constituted the idea of Life for Jesus. In this real relationship, a sharing in the very life of God, the whole future was embraced. It was indeed the pledge of immortality. The truth is tersely stated in His discussion with the Sadducees: "God is not the God of the dead, but of the living" (Mark xii. 27). To be brought into genuine contact with God, to know God in His actual character, was in itself the assurance of perfected life in communion with God for ever (*cf.* John xvii. 3). This is precisely the position which is occupied by St Paul. The God who has revealed Himself to him in Christ is worthy of all confidence. He has "sent forth the spirit of His Son into our hearts, crying, Abba, Father. Therefore thou art no longer a slave, but a son; and if a son, then an heir (*i.e.* of the eternal inheritance) through God" (Gal. iv. 6, 7). It is on that fatherly love which has been proved towards him by the death of Christ (Rom. v. 8) that St Paul takes his stand. "I am convinced that neither death, nor life, nor angels, nor principalities, nor powers, nor things present, nor things to come, nor height, nor depth, nor any other creature, shall be able to separate us from the love of God, which is in Christ Jesus our Lord" (Rom. viii. 38, 39). As already a son of God in Christ Jesus, he possesses the earnest of the Spirit. This is the pledge of completed redemption in the future. And his confidence is marvellously corroborated by his actual experience of the risen Christ. He was raised from the dead by the glory of the Father (Rom. vi. 4). "Now, if the Spirit of Him who raised Jesus from the dead dwell in you, He that raised from the dead Christ Jesus shall quicken also your mortal bodies through His Spirit dwelling within you" (Rom. viii. 11).

St Paul is also in harmony with his Master on the all-important question of the *nature* of the Future Life. Here again we must refer to our Lord's discussion with the Sadducees. In a single sentence He describes the condition of the risen. "When they rise from the dead they neither marry nor are given in marriage, but are as the angels of God in heaven" (Mark xii. 25). In Luke it is given in the following form: "The sons of this age marry and are given in marriage, but those accounted worthy to attain that (coming) age and the resurrection from the dead neither marry nor are given in marriage: nor can they any more die, for they are like the angels (ἰσάγγελοι), and are sons of God, being sons of the resurrection" (xx. 35, 36). That is to say, they possess a heavenly or spiritual organism, and are conformed to the likeness of God. Jesus merely hints in these words at the non-earthly nature of the risen life. There is no trace of the idea, so prevalent in Judaism, that, in the first instance at least, the dead should be raised in the form in which they had been buried.[1] The whole process is conceived to be of

[1] *Cf.* Apoc. Bar. l. 2: "For the earth shall then assuredly restore the dead, which it now receives, in order to preserve them, making no change in their form, but as it has received, so shall it restore them, and as I delivered them unto it, so also shall it raise them." It must be noted, however, that the *final* form of the righteous, after their resurrection, is often represented as angelic. See, *e.g.*, Enoch li. 4; Apoc. Bar. li. 5, 10.

a supra-earthly character.[1] The apostle follows the same lines. Titius has pointed out parallels to or reminiscences of Jesus' interview with the Sadducees in 1 Cor. xv. He compares 1 Cor. xv. 34 with Mark xii. 24, and 1 Cor. xv. 33 with Mark xii. 24, 27. He regards xv. 35 ff. as an illustration of the "power of God" (Mark xii. 24). And in the contrast between χοϊκός and ἐπουράνιος (xv. 40, 47-49) he finds a reminiscence of ὡς ἄγγελοι ἐν τοῖς οὐρανοῖς (Mark xii. 25).[2] It is easy to recognise the intimate connection between the conception of Jesus and that of Paul. The "image of the heavenly" (εἰκόνα τοῦ ἐπουρανίου) which risen believers are to wear in virtue of their σώματα πνευματικά is the precise equivalent of the ἰσάγγελοι, which is found in Luke xx. 36. Both of these ideas find a fitting expression in the σῶμα τῆς δόξης αὐτοῦ of Phil. iii. 20, which is to be the transfigured form of the earthly organism. In Jesus and in Paul, as contrasted with Judaism, the emphasis is laid on heaven, not as a new and glorious dwelling-place, but as a new type of life, the perfected life of God. In this idea there has been accomplished a transformation of the current Eschatology.

We have attempted no more than a bare outline of the close kinship between Jesus and Paul as that can be traced in the two basal conceptions of their eschatological teaching. Frequent occasions will occur in subsequent chapters of pointing out the influence of the Master on the apostle.

[1] See Haupt, *op. cit.*, pp. 89-92; Feine, *Jesus Christus u. Paulus*, pp. 181, 182.

[2] Pp. 15, 16.

CHAPTER III

ST PAUL'S CONCEPTIONS OF LIFE AND DEATH

It is obvious that if we are to form a true conception of St Paul's forecast of the Last Things, we must endeavour to discover with as much accuracy as possible the precise force of certain fundamental terms which constitute the elements, so to speak, of his eschatological construction. Pre-eminent among these are the basal ideas of Life and Death.

Nothing has been the cause of greater confusion and error in estimating the apostle's point of view than the tacit assumption that his use of terms is identical with ours. Indeed, the more familiar the terms, the more unhesitating the assumption. As a consequence, lines of argument have been frequently drawn from statements of St Paul, which he would not ave under-stood, far less sympathised with. We believe that this erroneous hypothesis is especially misleading in the instance before us. Life and Death are notions belonging to the common stock. It scarcely occurs to us to inquire whether their connotation is the same for us as it was for a Jewish apostle in the first century of our era. But the inquiry is of supreme importance, as we shall find, for our whole discussion. As an example of the misconceptions which may arise from neglecting to penetrate to the foundation of an idea, we may quote a few sentences from Matthew Arnold's *St Paul and Protestantism.* "Paul's conception of life and death," he says, "inevitably came to govern his conception of resurrection. What indeed . . . is for Paul life, and what is death? Not the ordinary physical life and death;—death, for him, is living after the flesh, obedience to sin; life is mortifying by the spirit the deeds of the flesh, obedience to righteousness. Resurrection, in its essential sense, is therefore, for Paul, the rising, within the sphere of our visible earthly existence, from death in this sense to life in this sense" (p. 143). There could scarcely be found a more glaring misrepresentation of the apostle's thought than that contained in these sentences, as we hope immediately to show. And the words are the more misleading, inasmuch as they emphasise to the exclusion of all others, an element which, of course, does belong to St Paul's ideas of life and death. The error really springs from an ignoring of the Old Testament background, out of which the apostle's conceptions emerge. This source of confusion too frequently reveals itself, even in the discussions of trained theologians.[1] The inferences, therefore, which may or may not be deduced from many important affirmations of St Paul regarding Life and Death must depend on the exact content which these terms held for him.

Let us deal with the negative concept in the first place. Careful readers of the Old Testament must

[1] See, *e.g.*, Kabisch's discussion of θάνατος in St Paul (*Eschatol. d. Paulus*, p. 101). So, to a slighter extent, Prof. Beet's treatment of "life" and "death" (*Expos.* iv. 1. pp. 203-207) suffers from a neglect of the roots of these conceptions in the Old Testament and Judaism. It is more important to keep these sources in view than to refer to the Homeric ideas.

have observed the horror which death inspires in the Hebrew mind. One or two instances may be quoted. In Ps. lxxxviii. 2-5 we have this appeal: "Let my prayer come before Thee: incline Thine ear unto my cry; for my soul is full of troubles, and my life draweth nigh unto Sheol. I am counted with them that go down into the pit: I am as a man that hath no strength: cast off among the dead, like the slain that lie in the grave, whom Thou rememberest no more: and they are cut off from Thy hand." A similar note is heard in Ps. vi. 3-5: "My soul also is sore vexed: and Thou, O Lord, how long? Return, O Lord, deliver my soul: save me for Thy loving-kindness' sake. For in death there is no remembrance of Thee: in Sheol who shall give Thee thanks?" In giving thanks for his recovery, Hezekiah expresses his fear at the approach of death: "I said, In the noon-tide of my days I shall go into the gates of Sheol; I am deprived of the residue of my years. I said, I shall not see the Lord, even the Lord in the land of the living: I shall behold man no more when I am among them that have ceased to be. My habitation is removed, and is carried away from me as a shepherd's tent: I have rolled up like a weaver my life; He will cut me off from the loom. . . . Like a swallow or a crane, so did I chatter; I did mourn as a dove: mine eyes fail with looking upwards. . . . But Thou hast in love to my soul delivered it from the pit of corruption . . . For Sheol cannot praise Thee, death cannot celebrate Thee: they that go down into the pit cannot hope for Thy truth" (Isa. xxxviii. 10, 12, 14, 17, 18). The description of Sheol in Job x. 20-22 sheds light on their shuddering apprehensions: "Let me alone . . . before I go whence I shall not return, even to the land of darkness, and of the shadow of death: a land of thick darkness, as darkness itself; a land of the shadow of death, without any order, and where the light is as darkness." According to the Old Testament conception, life is the opportunity for all joy, for all good. Death, indeed, is inevitable. And its calamity is mitigated when it presents itself as the close of a long earthly career, rich in well-being. The man who dies full of years and honour is like a shock of corn reaped when it is wholly ripe (Job v. 26). The life of such an individual is carried on in his descendants (Ps. ciii. 17).[1] But death under any other conditions is an utterly doleful fate. It robs men of all prospect. It shatters human power and capacities. It is a paralysis of the entire personality.[2] For throughout the earlier stages of Hebrew religion, there is no thought of one part of the *person* surviving death. The spirit, indeed, the *ruah*, which has been imparted by God, cannot die. It returns to Him who gave it (Ps. cxlvi. 4; Eccl. xii. 7). But the *nephesh*, the natural principle of life, which is closely dependent on the *ruah*, and is the bearer of the personality, shares in the fate of the physical organism. It is not a mere separation of soul and body. For the conception of a disembodied soul is foreign to Old

[1] These conditions diminished the horror of death also for the Greeks. *Cf.* Kaibel, *Epigramm. Gr.* 68, ὄλβιον εὐγήρων ἄνο[σον] . . . τύμβος ὅδ' εὐθάν [ατον] . . . ἔχει ; also *C.I.A.* 2, 2541, εὐδαίμων δ' ἔθανον παίδων παῖδας καταλείπω[ν] (Herkenrath, *Studien zu d. griech. Grabschriften*, Feldkirch, 1896, p. 27).

[2] Death, in the Old Testament, "is the phenomenon *which we observe*" (A. B. Davidson, *H.D.B.*, i. p. 739). The recognition of this tersely stated truth would often have saved pages of useless discussion.

Testament thought. It belongs to Hellenism, as *e.g.*, Plato, *Cratylus*, 403 b.: ὅτι τε γάρ, ἐπειδὰν ἅπαξ τις ἡμῶν ἀποθάνῃ ἀεὶ ἐκεῖ ἐστι, φοβοῦνται, καὶ ὅτι ἡ ψυχὴ γυμνὴ τοῦ σώματος παρ' ἐκεῖνον ἀπέρχεται, καὶ τοῦτο πεφόβηνται: "For they fear that, when once any of us dies, he is always there, and of this also they are afraid that the soul, disembodied, departs to him" (*i.e.* Pluto). For the Hebrew, death is the reducing of the person, in the sum-total of his energies, to a nerveless and phantom-like existence in Sheol, the place of assemblage for the dead. There, no moral distinctions prevail. There is a dreary equality among the shades (*rephāîm*). Up to this point, we may find parallels in other ancient civilisations. Thus the Greeks reveal the dark shadow which death casts across the gladness of their life by the epithets which describe it on their sepulchral inscriptions, epithets such as "bitter," "ruinous," "relentless," etc. Euphemisms were far rarer in this connection than in modern times. The under-world stretches hopelessly before the wistful gaze of men. It is called φθιμένων ἀέναος θάλαμος, "the eternal chamber of those who have withered" (so an inscription in Kaibel, *Epigr. Gr.* cxliii. 2, quoted by Herkenrath, *op. cit.*, p. 22. See also pp. 19, 21, 24). The bucolic poet Theocritus has the mournful line, ἐλπίδες ἐν ζωοῖσιν, ἀνέλπιστοι δὲ θανόντες: "Among the living hope endures, but hopeless are the dead" (*Idyll.* iv. 42). It was the same in the Roman world. Catullus laments: *Nobis quum semel occidit brevis lux, nox est perpetua una dormienda:* "When once the short-lived light has vanished, we all must sleep through an unbroken night" (v. 5 f.). And Seneca, speaking of the courage of Socrates, tells how he remained in prison, *ut duarum rerum gravissimarum hominibus metum demeret, mortis et carceris:* "that he might set men free from the fear of two most grievous fates, imprisonment and death."

But there can be little doubt that the horror of death was heightened for Hebrew minds by the predominantly religious cast of their thought. The value of the present life is immensely enhanced by the fact that it is only with the living that *God* can enter into relation. He is conceived pre-eminently as the *living* God, and only the living can respond to His claims. The true purpose of life, indeed, is fellowship with God. It has often occasioned surprise, that so devout a people as the Hebrews should, for generations, have rested content with the conception of an earthly relationship to Jehovah. Probably the explanation is due to the circumstance that that relationship was one of peculiar intimacy, of unique power and reality. They felt the Divine presence with a wonderful thrill of immediate consciousness. Human life from beginning to end could be alive with God. Hence a long and prosperous existence is the recognised mark of God's approval, the most convincing evidence of true piety. "Honour thy father and thy mother, that thy days may be long upon the land which the Lord thy God giveth thee" (Exod. xx. 12). "If thou were pure and upright, surely now would He awake for thee and make the habitation of thy righteousness prosperous" (Job viii. 6). "For evil-doers shall be cut off, but those that wait upon the Lord, they shall inherit the earth. For yet a little while and the wicked shall not be: yea, thou shalt consider his place, and it shall not be. But the meek shall inherit the earth, and shall delight themselves in the abundance of peace" (Ps. xxxvii. 10, 11). For the earlier stages of their religious reflection, death is that which robs of all blessedness.[1] They that go down to Sheol cannot praise God. All bonds of intercourse with the Most High are snapped. Sometimes the dead are described as if existing in the under-world almost beneath the sway of another tyrannical power. There is a kind of personification of Death, resembling that of the Greek Hades, when it is said in Ps. xlix. 14: "Like sheep they are laid in Sheol; death shepherds them."[2]

But further elements disclose themselves in the conception. It may be difficult to fix the time at which the connection between sin and death came to

[1] On the special horror of death felt by the Jews, see Smend, *Alttest. Religionsgeschichte*, pp. 504, 505. An interesting aspect of the same fundamental idea appears in *Philo*, who, as Drummond points out, regards the *body* as antagonistic to the soul, "not because it is material . . . but because it is phenomenal, transient, mortal" (*Philo*, ii. p. 297).

[2] In ancient literature it is hard to distinguish between a person and a personification. Animistic ideas lie deep in the naïve, popular consciousness. Bousset, grouping together such passages as Isa. xxv. 7 f.; 4 Ezra viii. 53; Apoc. Bar. xxi. 23; Test. Levi 18; 1 Cor. xv. 26, 55, all of which treat of the destruction of death at the end, would relate the figures of θάνατος, Hades (*cf.* Rev. xx. 13), and the angel of Hades closely to that of the devil, finding in them personal opponents of God (*Religion d. Judenthums*, p. 241, note 3). So also Kabisch on 1 Cor. xv. 20 (*Esch. d. P.*, p. 162) and Titius, p. 220 (on sin and death in Paul). We need hardly refer to the frequency of such personifications in Greek literature. A striking instance is Pindar, *Olymp.* ix. 35-38. "In the Vosges . . . Death's personality is accepted as an act of creation. 'Votre vie aura un fin,' God said to Adam, 'et la mort fut créée'" (*Edin. Review*, 1902, p. 381).

be emphasised in the popular consciousness.[1] In any case it was a natural inference to draw. Sin separates from God. In their view, this is also true of death. Unrelieved death was felt to be a judgment, a doom. Sin and death were inextricably interwoven. "The soul that sinneth, it shall die" (Ezek. xviii. 4; *cf.* the Genesis-narrative, chap. ii. 17: "In the day thou eatest thereof thou shalt surely die"). In the prophetic period the religious horizon is extended.

[1] Probably this doctrine was based on a literal interpretation of Gen. iii. So Denney on Rom. v. 12. See especially Wisd. ii. 23 f: *ὅτι ὁ θεὸς ἔκτισεν τὸν ἄνθρωπον ἐπὶ ἀφθαρσίᾳ, καὶ εἰκόνα τῆς ἰδίας ἰδιότητος ἐποίησεν . . . φθόνῳ δὲ διαβόλου θάνατος εἰσῆλθεν.* St Paul was in all likelihood acquainted with this book. *Cf.* 1 Clem. ad Cor. iii., *ζῆλον ἄδικον . . . ἀνειληφότας, δι' οὗ καὶ θάνατος εἰσῆλθεν εἰς τὸν κόσμον*; and Evang. Nicod., chap. xxiii., p. 736, *ὦ ἀρχιδιάβολε, ἡ τοῦ θανάτου ἀρχή, ἡ ῥίζα τῆς ἁμαρτίας.* Mr F. R. Tennant has sought to show in his recent work, *The Sources of the Doctrines of the Fall and Original Sin* (Cambridge, 1903), that the earliest indication of the idea that death is a consequence of our first parents' sin, occurs in Sirach xxv. 24. From that time onwards it appears frequently in Judaistic literature—*e.g.*, Enoch lxix. 11; Slavon. Enoch xxx. 16; Apoc. Bar. liv. 15; 4 Ezra iii. 7. It was the usual teaching of the Rabbis. In commenting upon 4 Ezra vii. 116 f., which he compares with Rom. v. 12 f., Mr Tennant remarks: "In neither place is it explained how Adam's sin made his posterity sinful. Perhaps in neither case had the writer developed or received any definite theory on the point" (p. 229). His own view is that St Paul has "clothed the current notion of Adam as the cause of human death, and the root of human sin, in the language of his mystical realism" (p. 266). Certainly St Paul has given us nothing in the nature of a theory on the subject, but is not his conception of race-solidarity something deeper than a Judaistic speculation? Strangely enough, to most primitive peoples, death seems an abnormal event, and immortality the normal course. (See C. P. Tiele, *Inleiding tot de Godsdienstwetenschap*, ii. p. 197 f.; qu. by Söderblom, *op. cit.*, p. 52.)

The vision of the future glory of the Kingdom of God dawns upon the broken nation. Thus the darkness of death is deepened. Not only is it an event which deprives of the present opportunity of fellowhip with Jehovah, but it also shatters all prospect of oming blessedness. Further, the frailty and transiency of which it is the crowning proof, the sharp pangs which accompany its approach, the unsightliness and decay which follow its presence, the bitter pain of soul t inflicts on those who are left behind—all these, its associations, impress them as an outrage upon a reation made in the image of God. Plainly, thereore, we may say that for the Hebrew mind the physical fact has a spiritual significance. And so viewed, it is only typical of that remarkable strain of thought, discernible throughout their reflection on the universe, which assumes that the physical s always the medium, the vehicle of the moral, such being its purpose and meaning in the Providential order. Thus death is only intelligible to them in he light of the weakness and sinfulness of humanity. And surely at this point their conception bears witness to the great truth of the ultimate unity of he physical and spiritual worlds, a unity which we egularly break up in our theoretical arguments, and as regularly presuppose in our working, personal experience.

We know that a striking change passed over the Jewish view of the condition of things ushered in by death. This was stimulated by the powerful influence of the doctrine of a Divine retribution, a doctrine which took shape, as we have seen, amidst the strange revolutions of the fortunes of the Jewish nation. There had been various isolated yearnings for uninterrupted fellowship with God. Several remarkable psalms give ample proof of that. We can scarcely suppose that the idea of a resurrection, as we understand it, passed before the psalmists' minds. Rather was it the passionate cry that, in some miraculous manner, God would deliver them from the gloomy lot of Sheol. But in the Maccabæan period these cravings and hopes took a more concrete form. Victory had roused afresh the sense of national unity. God's people were still a factor to be reckoned with. The glorious heritage of the past could still be honoured and defended. The triumphal mood was not, indeed, of long duration. Too soon the people again became conscious of their bondage. But an inextinguishable hope had been kindled. The present was the Æon of distress and anguish, in which God's arm seemed to be shortened. But it was only the precursor of the great Æon to come, when the holy seed should be vindicated, when the Divine purpose for Israel should be laid bare in the eyes of all the nations. Who, then, were to share in that era of felicity? Necessarily, the remnant of the people, the survivors of the chosen stock. Yet, as we have noted, this did not satisfy the sentiment of the nation. Were the heroes of their history, the men who had shed their blood for the faith, to have no part in the joyful restoration? The sense of justice revolted from the thought. The omnipotent God could rectify the inequality. His power could invade Sheol. He could bring the righteous dead to life again. This bold conviction laid the foundation for the great resurrection-hope. Now they could follow the workings of the Divine retribution. Resurrection would be the recompense at least of the eminently righteous. Nevertheless, the expectations of many devout hearts must have been mingled with fear. Would they live to see the redemption of Israel? If not, had they any right to expect a place amongst those favoured ones whom God should ransom from the grave? The more tender their consciences, the more hesitating would be their hope. Superficial minds might picture a resurrection which was little more than a mechanical scene amid the events of the end. The deeper and more earnest thinkers, conscious of failure and transgression, would still view death with gloomy forebodings, for the hope which shone beyond was flickering and dim.

Perhaps enough has been said to account for their dread of death, as that appears in the Old Testament and in the Hebrew mind. It is time now to ask, What relation does the Pauline conception of death hold towards that which we have been considering? Unless we have strong evidence to the contrary, we must believe that the apostle uses the term in its current significance. But we have distinct corroboration of the fact. As it happens, St Paul makes very definite statements concerning death. "As by one man sin entered the world, and death by sin, and so death hath come upon all men, in that all have sinned" (Rom. v. 12). "The wages of sin is death" (Rom. vi. 23). "O wretched man that I am, who shall deliver me from the body of this death?" (Rom. vii. 24). He speaks of "the law of sin and death" (Rom. viii. 2). He describes "the sting of death" as sin (1 Cor. xv. 56). Death is the last enemy to be destroyed in God's warfare with evil (1 Cor. xv. 26). The final issue of God's redeeming purpose is that death is swallowed up in victory (1 Cor. xv. 55).

These examples, and there are many more, may help us to realise the prominent elements in the apostle's view of death. Of course there are passages where he uses it in an apparently colourless sense, but it is only by following such clues as these just given that we can penetrate to his real inner thought.

Evidently, for St Paul, as for the men of the Old Testament, death signifies something far deeper than the natural close of life. Too commonly a false analysis has been made of his conception. His idea of death has been qualified by various limiting adjectives. Thus the apostle is supposed in some passages to speak of "physical" or "natural" death; in others of "ethical," in others still of "spiritual." In some places he is assumed to have "temporal" death before his mind, in others "eternal." We believe it is no exaggeration to assert that such distinctions would have been meaningless for St Paul. In this respect he is thoroughly true to the essential nature of Hebrew thought. Theirs was a synthetic view both of life and of death.[1] And no fact has to be borne more carefully in mind than this when we attempt to estimate the conceptions of St Paul. For him death is one indivisible experience. It is the correlative of sin. Like all the Biblical writers, he never distinguishes between "moral" (or "spiritual") and "physical." It is to miss the permanent ethical element in the apostle's thinking, when the assertion is made that the physical experience of death in itself was the supreme evil to the mind of St Paul. Thus Kabisch, to whom the merit belongs of emphasising the bearing of this aspect of that experience on the

[1] See this admirably brought out by Dr Davidson in *Expos.* v. 1, p. 330.

ιpostle's feelings, is led into exaggeration and con-
ιequent misconception by ignoring the other aspects vhich have to be reckoned with. "Sin," he says, 'came (according to St Paul) into the world. But his, in itself, is not the evil, were it not that by it leath also came into the world. For we actually ind the apostle dwelling upon the thought, that vithout law, sin is not imputed. Therefore the nisery does not lie in sin itself, but in that which s decreed on account of it" (*i.e.* death, *Esch. d. Paulus*, p. 86).[1] This appears to us a complete listortion of the apostle's teaching. However obscure nay be the reference to the imputation of sin in Rom. v. 13 (a statement belonging to a passage vhich, as Dr Denney well expresses it,[2] "in spite of he enormous place it has filled in the history of

[1] *Cf.* Kabisch, pp. 88, 89: "There are religious views which eceive no support from this deep, overpowering impulse to live, vhich puts other ideas in the background. To them pure death, he mere cessation of existence, is not the most dreadful thing vhich can be conceived. . . . (For Paul) death, passing away, is he sum of all that is fearful. . . . By the æsthetic, equally with the thical side of his consciousness, it (*i.e.* death) is abhorred." Such ssertions are untrue to the whole basis of Pauline theology. They cannot be supported by any relevant evidence. The same nisconception, arising from an illegitimate partition of the postle's thought, is found in an otherwise most suggestive dis-
ussion of Steffen's: "How greatly at times, in certain moods f his religious life, the physical-hyperphysical outweighs the thical, may be recognised for Paul in the fact that his power-
essness under the law culminates in the crushing utterance of voe, 'Who shall deliver me from the body of this death.' He ighed, as none other has done, beneath the curse of the transiency f all that is earthly," (*Z.N.T.W.*, 1901, H. 2, p. 124). It is the ransiency, *as charged with the issues of sin*, that weighs him lown.

[2] *Expos.* vi. 4, p. 304.

dogma, is hardly more than an *obiter dictum* in the Epistle to the Romans"), St Paul asserts in the preceding sentence that death passed upon all men, *because all sinned* (ἐφ' ᾧ πάντες ἥμαρτον). In whatever speculative fashion the apostle may have conceived the connection between the sin of Adam and that of his descendants, we know from his whole religious outlook that when he makes the statement, "all sinned," he can never have in view an unmeaning, mechanical fiction. Apart from any theorising on inherited guilt, we have his position clearly stated in Rom. iii. 23: "all sinned (πάντες γὰρ ἥμαρτον) and fall short of (ὑστεροῦνται) the glory of God." All are blameworthy. Death, therefore, in St Paul's view, is not something which works, as it were, mechanically. It is, as it speaks to the sensitive conscience, the shadow of the wrath of God. It is for that reason the apostle shrinks from it in terror. "Who shall deliver me from the body of this death" (Rom. vii. 24). He exults to think of a time when its sway shall be abolished. "O death, where is thy sting? O death,[1] where is thy victory? The sting of death is sin; and the strength of sin is the law: but thanks be to God, which giveth us the victory through our Lord Jesus Christ" (1 Cor. xv. 55-57). The latter passage is decisive for the view we advocate. Not the mere physical experience, not the mere consciousness of mortality, nor, on the other hand, a spiritual doom ushered in by death, but viewed as belonging entirely to the soul, and out of relation to the physical experience:—not with alternatives such as these have we to deal in estimating St Paul's standpoint, but with an event which includes and implies them all.

[1] So ℵ* BCD as against ℵc A.

This quailing in the presence of death is very marked throughout the New Testament, and a careful appreciation of it is of real importance for the comprehension of early Christian thought. We may recall the striking instance in Heb. ii. 14, where Christ is said "through death" to destroy "him that hath the power of death—that is, the devil"—and to set free "those who through fear of death were, throughout the whole of their life, subject to bondage."[1] Plainly, this recoil from death is precisely

[1] An interesting passage may be quoted from Boswell's *Life of Johnson*:—"I expressed a horror at the thought of death. *Mrs Knowles*: "Nay, thou shouldst not have a horror for what is the gate of life." *Johnson* (standing upon the hearth, rolling about, with a serious, solemn, and somewhat gloomy air): "No rational man can die without uneasy apprehension." *Mrs Knowles*: "The Scriptures tell us, 'the righteous shall have *hope* in his death.'" *Johnson*: "Yes, madam; that is, he shall not have despair. But, consider, his hope of salvation must be founded on the terms on which it is promised that the mediation of our Saviour shall be applied to us—namely, obedience; and when obedience has failed, then, as suppletory to it, repentance. But what man can say that his obedience has been such as he would approve of in another, or even in himself upon close examination, or that his repentance has not been such as to require being repented of? . . ." *Boswell*: "Then, sir, we must be contented to acknowledge that death is a terrible thing." *Johnson*: "Yes, sir. I have made no approaches to a state which can look on it as not terrible" (IV. 297, 298, Birrell's ed.). *Cf.* the dictum of La Rochefoucauld: "Everything that is most calculated to persuade that death is not an evil has been written . . . Yet I doubt whether any sensible person ever believed it, and the trouble taken in order to persuade others as the writers themselves of it shows plainly that it is no easy enterprise. Every man who can see death as it is, feels it a terrible thing." Prof. Shaler treats the fear of death from a very different standpoint. "It is well to remember," he says, "that the instinctive fear of death is not, as our forefathers deemed it, a dread of

in line with that which we have noted in the Old Testament. Death is regarded as separation from God. The tender conscience shudders at the prospect as merited separation. So death, conceived as the final word on human destiny, becomes the synonym for hopeless doom. Probably, therefore, St Paul could not picture a more appalling penalty for sin than death, and all that death, in its complete paralysis of the personal being, must involve. With his tremendous experience of the inner conflict between self and the holy law of God, and of all the misery which that conflict stirred within him, he perhaps felt little need of emphasising extraneous penalties in addition to the awful crisis of death. A death which was death pure and simple, with the sharp sting of sin in it, with nothing to mitigate the soul's isolation from the living God, with no hope or prospect in it, an existence robbed of all that makes existence worth having, would loom before his eyes as an overpowering judgment. As we shall see presently, this view of death sets in an extraordinarily vivid contrast the revelation of eternal life made in Jesus Christ. Indeed, to recognise its significance to the full, we require to have before our minds the apostle's view of the "life everlasting."[1]

coming to a place of judgment, though that idea has added to the pang. Its source is to be looked for in our animal ancestry, where this fear, blind and unconscious of its object, was absolutely demanded for the fit preservation of the individual" (*The Individual*, p. 200). But does this explanation lead us any deeper into the meaning of the experience for a rational, ethical being?

[1] It is not our aim in this investigation, even if we were competent for the task, to examine St Paul's conceptions of such experiences as death or life in the light of current scientific theory. Unquestionably, biological science would rule out as

But before we leave St Paul's conception of θάνατος as a bare and gloomy fact of human existence, a fact which, in the words of Professor Kähler, "as we

rrelevant the intimate connection between sin and death which s so important for the apostle. And yet science can only go a very short distance in pronouncing upon the meaning of death. 'It must be admitted," says Weissmann (and we quote from him as a representative biologist), "that we can see no reason why the power of cell-multiplication should not be unlimited, and why the organism should not therefore be endowed with everlasting life. In the same manner, from the physiological point of view, we might admit that we can see no reason why the functions of an organism should ever cease. It is only from the point of view of *utility* that we can understand the necessity of death . . . I consider that death is not a primary necessity, but that it has been secondarily acquired as an adaptation . . . Death is to be looked on as an occurrence advantageous to the species as a concession to the outward conditions of life, not as an absolute necessity, essentially inherent in life itself . . . (Death) is an adaptation which first appeared when, in consequence of a certain complexity of structure, an unending life became disadvantageous to the species" (*Essays upon Heredity*, ed. 2 (E. Tr.), i. pp. 23, 25, 111). Of course, this theory regards man merely as an animal. But, viewing him as a self-conscious ethical being, must not the union of his rational life with the bodily organism be conceived differently from the relation of the vital functions of the "lower" animals to their bodies? And keeping in mind the break, which science has never surmounted, between rational and merely animal life, may we not conceive, even from the scientific standpoint, a situation in which, for self-conscious *persons*, "utility," coinciding with a domination of the spiritual over the material, might have demanded the transition of the individual into a higher stage of life, without the occurrence of the adaptation called death? In the event of man's acting in perfect harmony with his highest good, might not the whole organism have followed other lines of development which would have still further differentiated it from that of inferior species, and more directly and immediately assimilated it to the nature and existence of God?

sinners experience it, has remained the preacher of responsibility," it is necessary to examine briefly the closely related term ἀπώλεια, "destruction," as it is employed in the Pauline Epistles. This is of importance, because many arguments have been based upon it, in the attempt to establish the theory of annihilation, which forms so essential an element in the hypothesis of Conditional Immortality. We must confine ourselves to St Paul, but his use of the term and its cognates is sufficiently clear and instructive. The noun ἀπώλεια occurs but rarely in the apostle's writings. There are about a dozen instances of the verb, ἀπολλύναι. In 2 Thess. ii. 3, he describes the "man of lawlessness" by the epithet, "son of ἀπώλεια." In Rom. ix. 22, he speaks of "vessels of wrath fitted out for ἀπώλεια." The *camaraderie* of Christians in courageous adherence to their faith is to be to their adversaries a proof of their ἀπώλεια, but of the Christian's σωτηρία (Phil. i. 28). And to the same Church he writes of a group of nominal members of the Christian community, who are "enemies of the Cross of Christ, whose end is ἀπώλεια" (Phil. iii. 18, 19). The verb occurs most frequently as a designation of those who reject the Gospel of Christ: they are *οἱ ἀπολλύμενοι* as opposed to *οἱ σωζόμενοι* (so 1 Cor. i. 18; 2 Cor. ii. 15, iv. 3; 2 Thess. ii. 10). In Rom. ii. 12, it is said of those who sinned without having the law (ἀνόμως), that without having the law, ἀπολοῦνται. The fate of those Israelites in the wilderness who were bitten by the serpents (Num. xxi. 6) or died of the plague (*ib.* xiv. 37) because of their murmurings, is described by the same term (ὑπὸ τῶν ὄφεων ἀπώλλυντο . . . ἀπώλοντο ὑπὸ τοῦ ὀλοθρευτοῦ, 1 Cor. x. 9, 10). If Christ be not risen, hen those who fell asleep in Christ ἀπώλοντο (1 Cor. xv. 18). The apostle, in recording his own trials as ι worker for Christ, speaks of himself and his fellow-abourers as "cast down, but not ἀπολλύμενοι" 2 Cor. iv. 4, 9). In two interesting passages where ie is dealing with Christian liberty and its responsi-›ilities, he warns his brethren to walk warily: μὴ τῷ Ͻρώματί σου ἐκεῖνον ἀπόλλυε, ὑπὲρ οὗ Χριστὸς ἀπέθανεν Rom. xiv. 15), "Destroy not with thy meat him for vhom Christ died"; ἀπόλλυται γὰρ ὁ ἀσθενῶν ἐν τῇ ῇ γνώσει, ὁ ἀδελφὸς δι' ὃν Χριστὸς ἀπέθανεν (1 Cor. viii. 1), "For he who is weak is destroyed by thy know-edge, the brother on whose account Christ died." The only other occurrence of the verb is in 1 Cor. i. 9, where he quotes part of Isa. xxix. 14 from the XX.: ἀπολῶ τὴν σοφίαν τῶν σοφῶν, καὶ τὴν σύνεσιν ῶν συνετῶν ἀθετήσω, "I will destroy the wisdom of he wise and make void the understanding of the ›rudent." This quotation is interesting as occur-ing immediately after his use of the phrase οἱ ιπολλύμενοι, indicating that it is in harmony with he usage of the Septuagint. It is evident that in ll of the above passages which bear on the future lestiny of men, ἀπώλεια is used as the antithesis of ωτηρία, and ἀπόλλυσθαι of σώζεσθαι. The question of *xistence* is not before the apostle's mind at all. Blessedness and its converse are the ideas which oncern him. In one or two of the instances quoted, he verb is exactly equivalent to ἀποθνήσκειν (so 1 Cor. :. 9, 10; also 1 Cor. xv. 18, where ἀπώλοντο = "died" in he ordinary sense of the word, "died without the pos-ibility of a blessed resurrection"). The verse from the XX. is, of course, figurative, thus showing the wide ense in which the apostle knows the verb can be used.

And in this respect, the two remaining passages are extremely suggestive. He is warning against the damage which may be done by a reckless and selfish use of Christian liberty. Hence we may translate, "Do not ruin by what you eat, that brother for whom Christ died": "For he that is weak is damaged (or ruined) by your knowledge, the brother on whose account Christ died." Quite obviously, there is no hint of "destruction," or "extinction" here. He speaks, as we speak, of one man "ruining" another without in any way meaning to specify in what this ruin will formally issue.[1]

We have already pointed out how largely St Paul's terminology, as well as the complexion of his thought, was affected by the usage of the LXX. Now *ἀπώλεια* and its cognates are frequently found in the Septuagint. In the numerous examples which we have examined, its significance varies from what we should call a "calamity" to "destruction" in the sense of death, and the doom which that involves. Thus, Ezek. xxix. 12 (of Egypt), *δώσω τὴν γῆν αὐτῆς ἀπώλειαν*, where it means "desolation," or "devasta-

[1] Many instances of this sense of ἀπόλλυμι can be given from later Greek. The following are taken from an interesting paper by Prof. Massie in *Expos.* ii. 2, pp. 64-70. *Polyb.* xxxii. 19: "They did not wish the people in Italy κατ' οὐδένα τρόπον ἀπόλλυσθαι (to become in any way demoralised)" διὰ τὴν πολυχρόνιον εἰρήνην. In *Dion Chrysost.* xxxi. 348 c, the phrase τοῖς ἐσχάτως ἀπολωλόσι is used as a description of immoral character, "those who are utterly abandoned." Plutarch (*De Cupid. Divit.* chap. vii.), pointing out the bad training which misers give their children, says: "The children they think to educate ἀπολλύουσι καὶ προσδιαστρέφουσι (they ruin and pervert)." In his *Vita M. Antonii*, 66, he describes Antony at Actium as fleeing after the woman (Cleopatra) τὴν ἀπολωλεκυῖαν ἤδη καὶ προσαπολοῦσαν αὐτόν ("who had already ruined him, and would ruin him yet more.")

:ation" (Heb. שְׁמָמָה); Jud. vii. 25, καταστρωθῆναι . . ἐν δίψῃ καὶ ἀπωλείᾳ μεγάλῃ, co-ordinated with 'thirst"="sore calamity"; Prov. vi. 15, ἐξαπίνης ἔρχεται ἡ ἀπώλεια αὐτοῦ, where ἀπώλεια = Heb. אֵיד, listress, calamity (lit. = that under which one bends, B.D.B.); Isa. liv. 16, ἔκτισά σε οὐκ εἰς ἀπώλειαν φθεῖραι = destruction (in the sense of "kill" = Heb. שַׁחֵת). Perhaps our word "ruin" would most adequately cover the various applications of ἀπώλεια. Of special importance and value for our discussion is the use of ἀπώλεια and kindred words in the *Wisdom of Solomon*, a book which shows some singularly interesting points of contact with Pauline thought.[1]

The godless, we read, are to be wholly destroyed by God: εἰς ὕβριν ἐν νεκροῖς δι' αἰῶνος. ὅτι ῥήξει αὐτοὺς ἀφώνους πρηνεῖς . . . καὶ ἕως ἐσχάτου χερσωθήσονται (Wisd. iv. 19). This last expression, ἕως ἐσχάτου χερσωθήσονται, is one of the strongest conceivable for destruction. The verb has a more intense force than

[1] Grafe (in *Abhandlungen C. v. Weizsäcker gewidmet*, pp. 253-286) attempts to show that St Paul derived from *Wisdom* "a large number of words, ideas, and illustrations" to express "conceptions and convictions gained from other sources"; while "in a few not unessential points he shows himself materially influenced by *Wisdom*, in his doctrine of predestination, in his eschatology, and in his criticism of heathenism and its idol-worship" (p. 286). We are unable to accept his arguments for the latter position (see Additional Note, p. 344 f.). But there is much to be said in favour of his statement "that Paul, even if *Wisdom* were not his source, repeatedly shows a contact in expression with significant conceptions and groups of conceptions belonging to Hellenism, conceptions which, on the one hand, exercised the most powerful influence on the higher part of the heathen world, and on the other, by reason of the depth and earnestness of their content, could most readily form an alliance with Christianity" (*loc. cit.*).

ἀπόλλυμι. Yet the writer continues, καὶ ἔσονται ἐν ὀδύνῃ, "and they shall be in anguish." Thus their destruction is by no means conceived as annihilation, although it is described in the most drastic and vivid terms. They still possess a conscious *existence*, which, however, is sheer *ruin*, so far as the idea of life is concerned. The same notion is met with in apocalyptic literature. Thus, *e.g.*, Enoch cviii. 3 has the following description of the ungodly: "Their names shall be blotted out of the book of life and out of the books of the holy ones, and their seed shall be destroyed for ever, and their spirits shall be slain, and they shall cry and make lamentation in a place that is a waste wilderness, and they shall burn with fire where there is no earth." *Cf.* Enoch xcix. 11, xxii. 13. This is true to the Hebrew standpoint. The ungodly are destroyed. That is, they lose all true life, all that would count as life to a Jew. But they do not lose conscious existence.[1] Here, for example, they are still in anguish. The same interpretation will be found to hold strictly for St Paul. In his Epistles, ἀπώλεια and ἀπόλλυσθαι are the exact antithesis of σωτηρία and σώζεσθαι. Both sides of the contrast are concerned with the *true life* of the individual. It may be noted that repeatedly in the LXX., ἀπώλεια is the translation of אֲבַדּוֹן, the place of ruin in Sheol for the lost or ruined dead. All that makes life worth living is destroyed

[1] *Cf.* the Babylonian conception: "The body decays in the grave (Shalamtu = name given to the corpse, 'that which is done with'), but the soul lives in the gloom of Hades, and in that abode of horror leads an immaterial shadow-like existence" (Jeremias, *Babylonian Conception of Heaven and Hell*, p. 31).

'or them. The existence they still possess cannot be :alled life at all. That has been lost, shattered. 3ut even able writers ignore this distinction between 'life" and "existence." Thus Ménégoz: "It is not ›nly Paul's anthropology, but also the Pauline dea of redemption that is opposed to the under-:tanding of death as anything else than the ıbolition of existence"; and again, "The whole heological system of Paul falls to pieces if death be ınderstood to mean anything else than the suppres-ion of existence" (*Le Péché et la Rédemption d'après St Paul*, pp. 78, 84).[1] Similarly, Mr Edward White, :ommenting on the words εἰς ὄλεθρον καὶ ἀπώλειαν ı Tim. vi. 9), affirms that "the Greek language does ıot afford two stronger expressions than these for lenoting the idea of literal death and extinction of ›eing" (*Life in Christ*, p. 383). A closer acquaint-.nce with Hebrew and Jewish modes of thought vould have shown those writers who have established heir view of annihilation on such New Testament erms as ἀπώλεια, ἀπόλλυσθαι, ὄλεθρος, κ.τ.λ., the mpossibility of such a deduction. What moderns ıre apt to forget is, that for the Old Testament vriters and for St Paul, the question of the *existence* ›f the person had no interest whatsoever. They

[1] Dr Petavel, a leading exponent of this theory, defines ınnihilation in his sense of the term as "the gradual diminu-on of the faculties possessed by the individual *ego*, and the nal extinction of that master faculty by which we take ossession of the other faculties" (*Problem of Immortality*, p. o2). We are not here concerned with arguments for or against ınnihilation as a theory, but we have no hesitation in asserting ıat a definition like the above would have appeared altogether -relevant to St Paul. He deals with a different set of ategories.

were not concerned at all with considerations of immortality in the abstract. It was *life* which occupied their thoughts: the life of the community or the individual: that is, *existence in touch with God.* When that contact was lost, the outlook for the person was the most hopeless they could imagine. For death could then signify for him (in St Paul's view) nothing else than the experience in which the meaning of sin for God should be most overpoweringly felt. This is unmitigated disaster, ἀπώλεια, ruin.[1]

From the positions that have been stated, it is not difficult to approach St Paul's conception of Life, which is, perhaps, the most important of which we have to treat in view of the discussions before us. Let us begin, as before, with the Old Testament background of the conception.

Ζωή and *ζῆν,* the terms employed by the apostle, are almost invariably in the Septuagint translations of the Hebrew חַיִּים and חָיָה. These Hebrew words are, of course, frequently equivalent to "life," "live,"

[1] *Cf.* A. B. Davidson (*Expos.* v. 1, p. 333): "They (*i.e.* Old Testament saints and prophets) did not reason that the soul was immortal from its nature—this was not the kind of immortality in which they were interested—though for all that appears the idea that any human person should become extinct or be annihilated never occurred to them." Similarly, Prof. Robertson Smith: "We have no reason to suppose that there ever was a time when the Hebrews held the annihilation of the soul in death. But the continued existence of the Rephaim . . . is never thought of as life: nay, it is the very contrary of life, opposed to it as darkness is to light" (*Expos.* i. 4, p. 356). See also for St Paul's view, an admirable paragraph by F. Köstlin, *Jahrb. f. deutsche Theol.*, 1877, p. 275. For instances of ἀπώλεια and cognates in Judaistic literature, see Volz, *op. cit.*, pp. 282, 283.

in our common usage, as applied to the ordinary physical existence of mankind. Briggs, Brown, and Driver, in their Hebrew Lexicon, remark of חָיָה that it often has "the pregnant sense of fulness of life in the divine favour." Instances are, *e.g.*, Deut. viii. 3, "Man doth not live by bread only, but by everything that proceedeth out of the mouth of the Lord doth man live"; Isa. xxxviii. 16, "O Lord, by these things (God's promises?) men live, and wholly therein is the life of my spirit"; Ezek. xxxiii. 19, "When the wicked man turneth from his wickedness, and doeth that which is lawful and right, he shall live thereby"; Hab. ii. 4, "A righteous man by his faithfulness shall live" ("such a character has in it the quality of permanence," Davidson, *ad loc.*); Ps. lxxx. 18, "Quicken Thou us, and we will call upon Thy name"; Eccl. vii. 12, "The excellency of knowledge is that wisdom preserveth the life of him that hath it"; Deut. xxx. 15, "See, I have set before thee this day, life (חַיִּים) and good, and death and evil"; Prov. viii. 35, "Whoso findeth me, findeth life"; Ps. cxxxiii. 3, "There the Lord commanded the blessing, even life for evermore" (חַיִּים עַד־הָעוֹלָם).

The lexical note quoted above does no more than justice to the Old Testament conception of Life. It emphasises the large content that is included in it, a content amply attested by the examples which have been given. This wide significance of the idea of life is in full accord with the essential attitude of the Old Testament to natural phenomena. Their importance, for it, consists in their capacity of revealing the moral forces which work in and behind them. The Old Testament writers have no abstract interest in the meaning of life. Such statements as those of modern biological science that "perfect correspondence (to environment) would be perfect life" (so Herbert Spencer, *Principles of Biology*, i. p. 88), lie outside the region of their reflection. And yet, by a slight alteration we might affirm that, for them, perfect life consists in "perfect correspondence" with God.[1] It is just because He is the all-absorbing environment for their thought, that Life, like every other fundamental conception, assumes in the Old Testament a predominantly religious cast. We may gather, therefore, from the instances cited above, that there is a blending of the physical and the religious. Take Deut. viii. 3: "Man doth not live by bread only, but by everything that proceedeth out of the mouth of the Lord doth man live." We should be apt, in such a statement, to distinguish between the physical and the spiritual. The Old Testament writers are conscious of a unity in which the physical is always included, but taken up, as it were, into a higher synthesis. Of typical significance is the affirmation of Ps. xxxvi. 9: "With Thee is the fountain of life." Life, in its fulness, springs from God. This truth is emphasised by the Creation-narrative of Gen. ii. 7, in which it is said of God (we quote the Septuagint on account of its importance for St Paul's thought): *ἐνεφύσησεν εἰς τὸ πρόσωπον αὐτοῦ πνοὴν ζωῆς, καὶ ἐγένετο ὁ ἄνθρωπος εἰς ψυχὴν ζῶσαν*, "He breathed into his face the breath

[1] *Cf.* Mr Mivart's interesting admission from the scientific point of view: "It is impossible to adequately define life without taking into our definition the idea of '*an end*' in the orderly changes which it presents, and it seems needless to include within it a reference to the environment" (*Contemp. Review*, xxxv. p. 707).

of life, and man became a living soul." Life, that is to say, is the result of the impartation of the *ruah* of God. *Ruah* (πνεῦμα in the LXX. and St Paul) is the energy of God, going forth and acting, the energy of God in its definite operations. God, to the Hebrew, is pre-eminently the Living One. The chief factor in his conception of God is that of activity, an activity whose power cannot be limited. See, *e.g.*, Jer. x. 10-12, "The Lord is the true God; He is the living God, and an everlasting King: at His wrath the earth trembleth, and the nations are not able to abide His indignation. . . . He hath made the earth by His power, He hath established the world by His wisdom, and by His understanding hath He stretched out the heavens"; Dan. iv. 34, 35, "I blessed the Most High, and I praised and honoured Him that liveth for ever: for His dominion is an everlasting dominion, and His kingdom from generation to generation: and all the inhabitants of the earth are reputed as nothing: and He doeth according to His will in the army of heaven, and among the inhabitants of earth: and none can stay His hand, or say unto Him, What doest thou?"[1] Kleinert points out that that side of the life of God which is related to "enjoyment" is scarcely found in the Old Testament: it only appears in relation to His *activities;* see, *e.g.*, Ps. civ. 31: "The glory of the Lord shall endure for ever: *the Lord shall rejoice in his works*"; also, Zeph. iii. 17; Isa. lxii. 4; Josh. iii. 10,

[1] Grill (*Untersuchungen*, etc., i. p. 237) calls attention to the interesting fact that the New Testament writers, when they speak expressly of God as the "living," conceive the being of God as *Power*, in thorough accordance with the Old Testament usage and conception (*cf.* Matt. xxvi. 63; Acts xiv. 15; Matt. xvi. 16, 18, 19; 1 Thess. i. 9; Heb. ix. 14; 2 Cor. iii. 3).

(*S.K.*, 1895, p. 701). He notes further that all God's living energy is borne along by the constant knowledge and willing of itself: that is to say, it is *personal* (*op. cit.*, p. 706). This conception of God as the Living is most intimately related with the Hebrew idea of Him, not precisely (in the earlier stages of thought) *as* Spirit, but always as *having* Spirit.[1] Thus His most characteristic operation is the breathing out of His spiritual energy (*ruah*, N.T. πνεῦμα). The result in the creation of man is that he becomes εἰς ψυχὴν ζῶσαν, "a living soul." That is to say, man is constituted a "person." He possesses a principle of life (*nephesh*, in the New Testament, ψυχή), a rational principle with an intelligent side, or faculty, which St Paul designates by νοῦς. The Divine side of his personality may be termed the *ruah*, the human the *nephesh*, yet it would be hazardous to draw too sharp a distinction between them. It is important to note that in the Creation-narrative this "living soul" is ascribed only to man.[2] "It is this capacity for moral and spiritual action," says Kleinert, "in short, the distinctively human, which entirely determines the specific appreciation of life and the value of life, in the Old Testament" (*loc. cit.*, p. 679). At death, accord-

[1] See Siebeck, *Zeitschr. f. Völker-Psychol.* xii. p. 392.

[2] "According to *Bammidbar rabba*, chap. xvi., the first man, as the image of God, received eternal life: his transgression made him mortal" (Weber, *Lehren d. Talmud*, p. 208). *Cf.* the relation of Wisd. ii. 23 f. to Gen. i. 26, ii. 7, iii.; and see Grimm's instructive note on Wisd. ii. 23. Philo draws a sharp contrast between the δύναμις ζωτική, or physical principle of life, and the δύναμις λογική, or rational principle. The former belongs to all living organisms (ζῶα); the latter, found in the νοῦς, belongs exclusively to man, and differentiates him from the mere ζῶον (see *Quod. det. pot. insid. sol.*, 82, 83, C. W.).

ing to the Old Testament, the Divine *ruah* is withdrawn, and there can be no *life* without that: hence, with the paralysis of the whole person, the *nephesh* is shattered, ruined. We can already discern the preparation for a more spiritual psychology (although it is scarcely permissible to use so formal a term) such as we discover in the writings of St Paul.

But, to return to the Old Testament, Life is the supreme blessing. "See, I have set before thee this day *life* and *good*, and *death* and *evil*" (Deut. xxx. 15). "Whoso findeth me (*i.e.* wisdom), findeth life" (Prov. viii. 35). "Wisdom preserveth the life of him who hath it" (Eccl. vii. 12). This last passage (and it is only one of many which might be adduced) clearly shows that the physical permanence of life is to be included in what may appear the purely "spiritual" statements of those which precede it. Some of the verses quoted on a former page, more especially a group which is well represented by Ps. lxxx. 18, "Quicken (literally, 'make us to live') us, and we will call upon Thy name," may appear, at the first glance, to have an entirely spiritual connotation. Yet when we bear in mind the Hebrew conception of life as the inbreathing of the Divine *ruah*, it would be probably an exaggeration to assert that there was no trace of a physical element involved.[1]

When we pass on to the Apocryphal and Pseudepigraphal literature, we still move among Old Testament ideas, but these have been strikingly

[1] "Life (in the Old Testament) is what we so call when we see it, the subsistence of the complete personality in the unity of its parts, body and soul" (A. B. Davidson in *H.D.B.*, i. p. 739). *Cf.* Kleinert, *S.K.*, 1895, pp. 700-725, for the various religious aspects of Life in the Old Testament

modified. We may mention one or two significant passages in 2 Maccabees, where πνεῦμα and ζωή are directly co-ordinated: *e.g.*, vii. 22, τὸ πνεῦμα καὶ τὴν ζωὴν ὑμῖν ἐχαρισάμην—"I granted to you your spirit and your life"; xiv. 46, ἐπικαλεσάμενος τὸν δεσπόζοντα τῆς ζωῆς καὶ τοῦ πνεύματος . . . τόνδε τὸν τρόπον μετήλλαξεν—"Calling upon Him who is Lord of life and spirit . . . in this manner he departed." These find a close parallel in Ezek. xxxvii. 5: Ἰδοὺ ἐγὼ φέρω εἰς ὑμᾶς πνεῦμα ζωῆς . . . καὶ δώσω πνεῦμα μου εἰς ὑμᾶς καὶ ζήσεσθε· καὶ γνώσεσθε ὅτι ἐγώ εἰμι κύριος—"Behold, I bring to you the spirit of life . . . and I will put my Spirit into you, and ye shall live, and ye shall know that I am the Lord." Quite clearly, ζωή depends immediately on πνεῦμα.

In the pseudepigraphal writings, we find, as we should expect, the Old Testament idea of Life (with the physical side largely in evidence) as a recompense of righteousness. See, for example, Sibyl. Orac. iv. 45: "The righteous shall remain on the fruitful earth, as God gives them spirit and life and grace." This is a higher form, however, of the conception than that which appears, *e.g.*, in Enoch v. 9: "They (*i.e.* the righteous) shall not be punished all the days of their life, nor shall they die of plagues or visitations of wrath, but they shall complete the full number of the days of their life, and their lives shall grow old in peace, and the years of their joy shall be many, in eternal happiness and peace, all the days of their life." We are here reminded forcibly of the beautiful picture in Zech. viii. 4: "Thus saith the Lord of Hosts, There shall yet old men and old women dwell in the streets of Jerusalem, and every man with his staff in his hand for very age." There is nothing transcendental in these delineations. But now there comes into far greater prominence what we may designate the *eschatological* conception of Life. A few examples will make this clear. Slavon. Enoch l. 2, "Ye shall inherit the endless life[1] which is to come; Ps. Sol. iii. 16, "They that fear the Lord shall rise to life everlasting, and their life in the light of the Lord shall no more fail"; *ib.* ix. 9, "He that doeth righteousness heapeth up life for himself with the Lord"; Sibyl. Orac., *prooem*, 84, 85, "Those who reverence the true and everlasting God inherit life (*i.e.*, inhabit evermore the green garden of Paradise); Apoc. Bar. xlii. 7, "Corruption shall take those that belong to it, and life those that belong to it." Here we have precisely the idea which the New Testament calls "eternal life," and the later Jewish literature "the life of the future Æon" (see Dalman, *Worte Jesu*, pp. 129-131, where a brief summary is given of the process by which this conception has been reached). This forms, in our Lord's discourses, the antithesis to ἀπώλεια (see, *e.g.*, Matt. vii. 13, 14). It is largely

[1] Bousset notes how the expression חַיֵּי עוֹלָם dominates apocalyptic literature. He gives numerous examples (*Religion d. Judenthums*, p. 263). *Cf.* Volz, *Jüdische Eschatol.*, p. 306 (on the simple idea "live"): "The most universal but most pregnant word for participation in salvation is 'to live' . . . *Vivere*= be blessed (saved), in 4 Ezra vii. 21, 129, viii. 6; Ps. Sol. xiv. 3, xv. 13 (opp. ἀπόλλυσθαι) . . . the blessed (saved) are the *viventes*, Apoc. Bar. xlix. 2, li. 11 (*viventes vivimus*, 4 Ezra vii. 67); they attain to life . . . *vivicari*=be blessed (saved), 4 Ezra vii. 137 f." "In *sifra* 85d on Lev. xviii. 5, we see a characteristic transference from the present to the future; it is said there: 'He who keeps the law receives thereby life in the coming Olam: if thou sayest, In this Olam, is not his end death? Therefore it is to be explained, He shall live thereby in the coming Olam'" (*op. cit.*, p. 326).

equivalent, in His use of it, to the expression which predominated in His teaching, "the Kingdom of God."[1]

It is important to observe that the Old Testament idea of Life does not stand in isolation from this later conception. We can see already how the difference between them is bridged over in such passages as the following:—Ps. Sol. xiii. 9, "The life of the righteous endureth for ever"; Wisd. of Sol. iii. 2-4, "In the eyes of the foolish, they (*i.e.* the righteous) seemed to have died, and their departure was reckoned a misery. . . . but they are in peace. For even if they were punished according to the view of men, their hope was full of immortality" (so i. 15, "righteousness is immortal"); [2] Apoc. Bar. xiv. 13, "These (*i.e.* the righteous) without fear leave the world, and trusting with joy, they hope to receive the world which Thou has promised them."[3] Here, the

[1] See Haupt, *Eschatol. Aussagen Jesu*, pp. 85, 86. Von Schrenck puts the facts aptly: "That condition in which the rule of God is to be fully realised, and the children of God in fellowship with one another and in untroubled bliss are to see God and rejoice in His rule—that will be ζωή" (*Die johanneische Anschauung von "Leben,"* p. 37). He notes how Jesus took the Danielic and contemporary expectation of an eternal life and deepened it in accordance with His religious-ethical view of the coming βασιλεία of God. Volz traces the eschatological conception of "Life" through the following stages: (1) =Continuance, as presupposition of participation in salvation; (2)=Participation in salvation; (3)=Sum of blessings in the period of salvation; (4)=Eternal blessedness (see *Jüdische Eschatol.*, pp. 326, 327).

[2] *Cf.* the remarkable parallel in Philo (*Quod det. pot.* xlix., C.W.): ὁ μὲν δὴ σοφὸς τεθνηκέναι δοκῶν τὸν φθαρτὸν βίον ζῇ τὸν ἄφθαρτον. The same idea is highly elaborated in Enoch cii. 4-civ.

[3] A suggestive parallel from Greek religion is to be found in *Soph. Frag.* 753 (N): ὡς τρὶς ὄλβιοι κεῖνοι βροτῶν, οἳ ταῦτα δερχθέντες τέλη (*i.e.* those initiated into the mysteries at Eleusis)

thought of the continuity of the life of the righteous in the present with that which awaits them after death, is brought into full prominence.

It is difficult to determine precisely what theory these writers held as to the *basis* of the endurance of life in the righteous. Possibly hints towards the comprehension of such a theory may be found in passages like Slavon. Enoch xxx. 8: "I ordered My wisdom to make man of seven substances . . . his spirit from My spirit and from the wind." There is an immortal element in man, which, if rightly cherished, will be the pledge of immortality. This thought finds unique expression in Wisd. Sol. ii. 23, 24 (a passage already referred to, which cannot, however, be taken as a typical example of the literature or period in question): "God created man for incorruption (ἀφθαρσία), and made him a copy of His own peculiar essence (ἰδιότης), but by envy of the devil death entered the world, and they that are of his portion make trial thereof." It is quite possible that these writers (like Eccl. xii. 7) conceived the πνεῦμα as returning to "God who gave it,"[1] in the case of those who had defied God's will and yielded to the sway of

μόλωσ' ἐς Ἅιδου· τοῖσδε γὰρ μόνοις ἐκεῖ ζῆν ἔστι, τοῖς δ' ἄλλοισι πάντ' ἐκεῖ κακά. See Rohde, *Psyche*, [2] Bd. i. p. 294. Rohde points out that the continued life of the soul after its separation from the body was not so much *taught* at Eleusis as presupposed, for "this belief lay at the foundation of the universally-diffused soul-worship. What the initiated at Eleusis gained was a more vivid idea of the meaning of this existence of departed souls, which was left empty in the conceptions which lay at the basis of soul-worship" (*loc. cit.*).

[1] *Cf.* and contrast *Inscr. of Antiochus of Commagene* (69-34 B.C.): σῶμα . . . πρὸς οὐρανίους Διὸς Ὠρομάσδου θρόνους θεοφιλῆ ψυχὴν προπέμψαν, εἰς τὸν ἄπειρον αἰῶνα κοιμήσεται (Cumont, *Textes . . . relatifs aux Mystères de Mithra*, ii. 89).

evil. But it would be unsafe, where opinions are so vague and fluctuating, to attempt even the outline of any hypothetical theory.

From the foregoing brief investigation, we are able to realise the ideas which were in the air, more especially among the Pharisaic circles in which St Paul received his early training. It should prove of genuine interest to attempt to discover the new and the old in his formulation of his great primary conceptions. What content, then, did the idea of ζωή have for the apostle? The idea, even in its deeper suggestions, was, probably, in no sense foreign to his earliest thinking. Indeed, certain hints afforded by the Epistles would lead us to believe that the question of a true, victorious, indissoluble life was a pressing one for St Paul even in his pre-Christian days. There can be no doubt that the craving for life in the fullest sense of the term, is a factor of immense weight in the religious consciousness. A recent philosophical writer has said: "Not God, but life, more life, a larger, richer, more satisfying life, is, in the last analysis, the end of religion. The love of life at any and every level of development, is the religious impulse." (Prof. Leuba, *Monist*, xi. p. 572: quoted by James, *Varieties of Religious Experience*, p. 507). In the form in which it is here expressed, this dictum is an exaggeration, but certainly an exaggeration in the true direction.[1]

[1] *Cf.* Tennyson's well-known lines:—

"Thou wilt not leave us in the dust.
Thou madest man, he knows not why—
He thinks he was not made to die,
And Thou hast made him: Thou art just"
(*In Memoriam*, Prelude);

and James (*Human Immortality*, p. 11), "The whole subject of immortal life has its prime roots in personal feeling."

"The universe," writes Prof. James, "with every living entity which her resources create, creates at the same time a call for that entity, and an appetite for its continuance" (*Human Immortality*, p. 78). We have seen that death was an experience at which St Paul shuddered.[1] The correct interpretation of 2 Cor. v. 1 ff. (as we shall discover) adds emphasis to what has already been urged on this point. No thought has such power to kindle his soul into exultation as that of the final and complete vanquishing of the last enemy, which is death. But this is not all. Life, genuine life, in its widest connotation, appears to him as the original purpose of God for humanity. He speaks of the commandment of God as intended for life (Rom. vii. 10: ἡ ἐντολὴ ἡ εἰς ζωήν). He makes a very remarkable statement in Gal. iii. 21: εἰ γὰρ ἐδόθη νόμος ὁ δυνάμενος ζωοποιῆσαι, ὄντως ἐκ νόμου ἂν ἦν ἡ δικαιοσύνη: "If a law had been given which was able to make alive, then, *essentially*, righteousness would have sprung from the law." These words let us see deep into the texture of the apostle's religious thought. The supreme discovery which he has made is that of his own flagrant misconception of the way of salvation. He believed that he could attain complete satisfaction and peace with God by keeping the commandments. But this turned out a hopeless effort, and he then discovered that faith in Jesus Christ could do for him that in which the law was powerless. It authenticated itself to him as the means by which he could realise his true end. In the passage before us he identifies the highest conceivable purpose of God with ζωοποιεῖν,

[1] For the Judaistic fear of death, see Weber, *Lehren d. Talmud*, pp. 325, 326.

"making alive." But it is no incidental reference. The more closely we examine his religious outlook, the more distinctly shall we find that it is dominated by the conception of Life. Nothing reveals the fact more clearly than its relation to the apostle's conception of Justification, and its cognate, Salvation. Thus in Romans v., which sums up his discussion of justification by depicting its blessedness, the final contrast in which the humanity which starts from Adam is placed over against the humanity which originates in Christ, resolves itself ultimately into the supreme contrast between life (ζωή) and death (θάνατος). Life is, in fact, the issue and goal of justification (see the remarkable phrase in verse 18, εἰς δικαίωσιν ζωῆς, "justifying which confers or leads to life"). The normative function of this idea for his entire thought is no less marked in the succeeding section of Romans, which deals with the state of grace. Here again, the inference they are to draw from their new relation to Christ, that relation which he has described as "buried with Him by baptism into death," "united together with the likeness of His death," is that they are now "alive (ζῶντας) unto God through Jesus Christ our Lord" (vi. 11), or, in another place, as "made free from sin and become servants of God," they have their "fruit unto holiness, and the end (τὸ τέλος) everlasting life" (vi. 22). It is scarcely necessary, in view of some preceding sections in this discussion, to point out the prominence of the conception of Life in the group of ideas which centre round salvation. A typical example is 1 Cor. i. 18: "The preaching of the Cross is to them that perish (τοῖς ἀπολλυμένοις) foolishness; but unto us which are being saved (τοῖς σωζομένοις) it is the power of

God." The issues of those two decisive processes which must sift mankind are obviously the very same as have been emphasised above: ἀπώλεια and σωτηρία. Ἀπώλεια and θάνατος are, of course, synonymous for the apostle. Σωτηρία is merely the negative conception for that gift of God which is contrasted with θάνατος in Rom. vi. 23, namely, eternal life (ζωὴ αἰώνιος) "in Jesus Christ our Lord" (*cf.* the words of Rom. v. 10, which strikingly corroborate our position, "If, when we were enemies, we were reconciled to God by the death of His Son, much more, having been reconciled, we shall be saved in His life," σωθησόμεθα ἐν τῇ ζωῇ αὐτοῦ).[1] Life, that is to say, is for St Paul the *summum bonum.* Life eternal (ζωὴ αἰώνιος) is the supreme reward for a course of perseverance, through faith, in righteousness: it is the gift of God which is richly bestowed in Christ Jesus.[2]

[1] Titius, pp. 53-55, is very suggestive on this whole subject. See also p. 186: "The essential meaning of the kingdom of God is for Paul as for Jesus, life (in 1 Cor. xv. 50 βασιλεία alternates with ἀφθαρσία) and glory (*cf.* 1 Thess. ii. 12). The conception of blessing leads us to the same connection. In itself of universal meaning, and embracing all the Divine benefits, it is already in the Old Testament referred to the Messianic benefit of Life (*cf.* Deut. ii. 26-28 with xxx. 15, 19; Jer. xxi. 8), and as in Matt. xxv. 34, 41, so also in Gal. iii., Abraham's blessing is fully identified with eternal life. This shows the manner in which the conception of life is introduced into the context (iii. 11, 12) which treats of blessing and cursing." "It was *life*, which all these rules (*i.e.* the ritual of the Avesta) were destined to propagate and to foster: strong and wholesome life as they understood it, the life of the body which must not suffer diminution by sin or by want or by bad treatment . . . the life of the soul which is nourished by holy instruction and the adoration of God; the life of the race . . . the life of nature" (Söderblom, *op. cit.*, p. 115).

[2] It is scarcely relevant for Grill to remark (*Untersuchungen*,

Let us briefly endeavour to reach the basis of St Paul's thought on the subject. We have seen that the great blessing of the future order of things, in which God's sway should be paramount, was already in the literature of Judaism frequently summed up as life, or eternal life.[1] This included

i. p. 323): "How little determinism (election, working of Spirit, etc.) asserts itself in the Pauline consciousness at the expense of subjective conditions, or of the purely ethical manner of attaining final salvation, is evidenced by the fact that in the whole of the Pauline section of the New Testament world of ideas, the attribute 'eternal' is never applied to the present Christian life." Surely this is not a point which calls for emphasis, seeing that the ζωή which St Paul attributes to believers now virtually partakes of all the qualities embraced under the term αἰώνιος. As Haupt suggestively points out in dealing with the teaching of Jesus, the epithet αἰώνιος shows a tendency throughout the New Testament to pass from its quantitative sense of "endlessness" into the qualitative idea of "supra-earthly," having the quality of that Æon in which the dominion of God is complete (see *Eschatol. Aussagen Jesu*, p. 84). Undoubtedly the beginning of this transition is visible in St Paul, as Grill himself practically admits a few sentences before (*loc. cit.*). Indeed, his definition of "Life," as used in the Fourth Gospel, might hold of the apostle's conception: "Life . . . is the continuous, organically-unified activity of a capacity of forces, imparted by God through Christ to receptive (believing) men, according to its nature renewing itself continually and perfecting itself from its Divine source, which not only (and this in the first instance) in a wholly spiritual fashion on the side of consciousness, ethically, and in a moral-intellectual manner, is effectual as a principle of development, but also forms the real condition for physical glorification, the spiritual-bodily perfecting of the human personality, and from the beginning evokes the feeling of attaining blessedness" (*op. cit.*, p. 306). This definition, although inordinately cumbrous, is both deep and comprehensive.

[1] An interesting summary of the history of this conception in Judaism is given by Dalman, which we here abridge. Dan.

all that we mean by "physical" life, but it evidently regarded this as directly sustained by the power and fellowship of God. Our difficulty was to discover how this sustenance of life was mediated, and on what lines the original "natural" life of the body was raised, so to speak, to a higher power, charged with the potentiality of eternity. When we turn to the writings of St Paul, we are left in no such perplexity. It will always, indeed, be impossible to reach a complete analysis of delicate spiritual experiences; but the apostle has set forth clearly enough the general features of his own appropriation of the Divine gift of life, its conditions, and its channel. Whatever St Paul may have carried with him from his training in a devout Jewish home and subsequently in the schools of the Pharisees, the unique spiritual crisis of his own life formed the regulating factor in his conceptions of the Divine workings in human experience. It may be difficult for us to construct any coherent picture of the objective phenomenon which was pre-

xii. 2 first speaks of the "everlasting life" (חיי עולם) of the pious; then in the first pre-Christian century, Ps. Sol. iii. 16 (*cf.* xiii. 9); Enoch xxxvii. 4, xl. 9 (*cf.* lviii. 3); lxii. 14 (see Slavon. Enoch lxv. 10); 2 Macc. vii. 9, 36; 4 Macc. xv. 3. Also in the Onkelos-Targum, which does not speak of the "future Æon," the conception has found a place as חיי עלמא (Lev. xviii. 5), meant in this sense. Thus the collocation ייחי בחיי עלמא, "He shall live in the eternal life," makes clear in the passages cited, and in the Targum on Ezek. xx. 11, Hosea xiv. 10, that חיי עלמא is in these regarded as equivalent to עלמא דאתי. The rest of the older Jewish literature has the expression "eternal life" almost exclusively when it stands in contrast to "perishable life." Numerous examples (*Worte Jesu*, pp. 127-128.)

sented to the Pharisee as he journeyed to Damascus: objective we say expressly, for there are no arguments which can weigh against the calm conviction exhibited by St Paul as to this event. For except on the ground of unshaken conviction, no man, who, in describing other visions and revelations, employs so entirely different a tone, could have uttered the bare statement, "Have not I seen Jesus our Lord?" (1 Cor. ix. 1). But after all, the more important part of this extraordinary crisis, practically, was the spiritual transformation of which the apostle was conscious. This, or rather the result of this, he describes in language which fits in with remarkable aptness to that section of his thought which we are discussing. "I have been crucified with Christ, and it is no longer I that live, but Christ liveth in me, and the life which I now live in the flesh, I live by faith, faith in the Son of God, who loved me and gave Himself for me" (Gal. ii. 20). Here we have placed before us with unmistakable clearness what he conceives to be the genesis of the new life in him. The first clause holds the key. The Christ whom St Paul met on his memorable journey was the Christ who had been crucified. We know what that tremendous fact meant for the apostle. He found in the Crucified the propitiation for his sins. He found in His atoning death the supreme revelation of the love of God, the love of God as forgiving love, welcoming the sinner, setting him in a new relation to God, and also in a new relation to sin. His own response to that marvellous love was faith, complete trust in the Christ who had died for him, and by that faith he made Christ's death his own. Sin became to him what it was to Christ.

He was through faith introduced into a new environment, the environment of the victorious Lord. Henceforward, he breathes the atmosphere of that new realm, the realm of grace. He lives its life.

As all careful readers of the Epistles must have observed, the apostle regards the whole grand experience of salvation from two points of view, the one of which is really the obverse of the other. In a number of important passages the prominent conception is that of dying to sin with Christ, and living in Him to God. A striking example is Rom. vi. 5 ff.: "If we have been engrafted into the likeness of His death, we shall be also into the likeness of His resurrection, knowing this that our old man was crucified along with Him, that the body of sin might be annulled with a view to our no longer serving sin. . . . Now, if we die along with Christ, we believe that we shall also live along with Him, knowing that Christ, having risen from the dead, no more dies; death no longer rules over Him. For in that He died to sin, He died once for all; but the life He lives, He lives to God. So also do you conclude yourselves to be dead (νεκρούς) as regards sin, but living as regards God in Christ Jesus. Let not sin therefore reign in your mortal body, so as to obey its lusts, nor offer your members to sin as tools of unrighteousness." Here is the new life looked at from the human side, from the side of man's response to the divine mercy made manifest in Christ crucified for him. By faith in the virtue of that atoning death, the believer identifies himself with it. He shows his willingness to throw off the yoke of sin and to enter the service of righteousness. The best proof of his willingness, the best evidence of the meaning of his faith, is the actual refusal to yield his members as tools of unrighteousness (Rom. vi. 13). Accordingly, such an expression as that quoted at the outset, "I have been crucified with Christ," has a large and rich content. The fleshly nature has entered on a process of annulment and abolition, because in Christ it is cut off from its old environment, sin. Faith has brought the personality, as a whole, into contact with that new principle of life which belongs to the living Christ who was raised on account of our justifying (*διὰ τὴν δικαίωσιν ἡμῶν*), and the new life is really the full expression and self-evidencing of justification. But this wonderful process can be viewed also from its complementary side, namely, the operation of God in Christ, the activity of the Holy Spirit. We cannot, indeed, think of the two sides as apart from each other. For, as Prof. Denney admirably expresses it, "The faith which abandons itself to Christ is at the same time a receiving of the Spirit of Christ, or of what to experience is the same thing, Christ in the Spirit; *there are not two things here, but one* (the italics are ours), though it can be represented in the two relations which the words Faith and Spirit suggest" (*Expos.* vi. 4, p. 426). This intimate connection is strikingly shown, *e.g.*, in Gal. v. 5: "For we by the Spirit (*πνεύματι*), as the result of faith (*ἐκ πίστεως*), eagerly await the hope of righteousness" (*ἐλπίδα δικαιοσύνης*, lit., the hope which righteousness guarantees). But it is natural to find that the apostle, in speaking of the new life of the believer as something which has passed beyond its initial stage, the dawning of faith in Christ crucified, which unfolds the high possibility of breaking with sin once for all on the basis of God's forgiving love, should think most frequently of the power which sustains the new relationship, and is none else than He who has reconciled the sinner to God. Christ, that is to say, is his new life-principle. This fact he realises in a particular form. "The law of the Spirit of life in Christ Jesus made me (*v.l.*, thee) free from the law of sin and death" (Rom. viii. 2). "If Christ be in you, the body is dead on account of sin, but the Spirit is life on account of righteousness" (viii. 10). "Christ in" him, is equivalent to the "Spirit of life," or the Spirit which is life. He lives by the Spirit (*cf.* Gal. v. 25: *εἰ ζῶμεν πνεύματι, πνεύματι καὶ στοιχῶμεν*, "If we live by the Spirit, let us take each step by the Spirit," *στοιχεῖν* referring to the *details* of conduct). Here we touch a fundamental aspect of St Paul's religious experience. The primary importance of his meeting with Christ lay in the fact that, in response to his faith in the crucified and risen Redeemer, his soul was brought into a marvellous new contact with a power outside himself, which he could only attribute to the living Lord. This he could describe as the Spirit of God, or of Christ, dwelling in him. Henceforward he is led by the Spirit of God (Rom. viii. 14: *ὅσοι γὰρ πνεύματι θεοῦ ἄγονται, οὗτοι υἱοί εἰσιν θεοῦ*). "The Spirit itself (*αὐτὸ τὸ πνεῦμα*) bears witness with (*συμμαρτυρεῖ*) our spirit that we are children of God" (Rom. viii. 16). Here he concentrates his thought on the Divine part in the new life of salvation. Unquestionably, the existence of faith is presupposed all through, faith in the Son of God who loved him and gave Himself for him. Only by such means can his nature be linked to the Divine, the supernatural, the activity which springs from the living God. It was of no concern to him to inquire as to the relation in time, or sequence, of faith to the possession of the Spirit. Both were included in the same glorious unity of spiritual illumination. Both must ultimately be traced to God. "For by grace have ye been saved through faith, and that not of yourselves, to God belongs the gift" (θεοῦ τὸ δῶρον, Eph. ii. 8). The Spirit, therefore, is the Divine factor, working in the believing soul and sustaining the life of faith.

It will be of interest to ask, How is this gift of the Spirit, which is the principle of the new life, related to the apostle's psychology? As we have already observed, St Paul has, strictly speaking, no psychology. The phenomena of the inner life interest him solely on their religious side. He accepts in general the Old Testament view of the constitution of man, perhaps regulating his thought especially by the Creation-narrative in Gen. ii. According to the Old Testament, as we have seen, man consists of flesh (*bāsār*), soul (*nephesh*), and spirit (*ruah*). We need, it is true, to exercise caution in analysing the difference between *nephesh* and *ruah*. *Ruah* is not higher than *nephesh*, neither is it, strictly speaking, distinct from it. Rather is it *nephesh* possessing or manifesting power. All influences from God are influences from His *ruah*. And the immortal part of man, as *ruah*, receives these influences.[1] We noted, at an earlier point in our discussion, that at death the *nephesh*, as the bearer of the personality, descends into Sheol, while the *ruah*, which was the quickening influence in the person, returns to God from whom it came. Conceptions such as these lie at the basis of St

[1] These latter sentences are condensed from MS. notes of Dr A. B. Davidson's lectures.

Paul's view of the constitution of man. Only, as we might expect, certain important modifications have to be observed. The conception of "flesh" (*bāsār*, *σάρξ*), which predominates in the Old Testament as an inclusive description or definition of the bodily nature,[1] has, of course, an influential place in Paulinism. Side by side with it in the writings of the apostle, there appears the cognate term *σῶμα*, not often found in the Septuagint as a translation of *bāsār*, which may perhaps best be rendered in English as "organism." The term, that is to say, is colourless as compared with *σάρξ*. The latter, in St Paul's usage, almost always implies the bodily nature in its present condition, the bodily nature as we know it in experience.[2] It has already been pointed out that the apostle is not interested in the physical side of man as such. Its ethical import is that which concerns him. In this aspect of it, he is too well aware that it is corrupted by sin. We see nothing in his writings to justify the hypothesis so frequently charged upon him, that he took a dualistic view of human nature, holding the inherent evil of matter. The constitution of matter is a problem which would never appeal to him.[3] Man as a living person is made up of body

[1] For the use of σάρξ as designating the *body*, even in Greek philosophical literature of the first two centuries A.D., see Zeller, *Theolog. Jahrbücher*, 1852, pp. 293-297.

[2] See Cremer, in *Herzog* [3] vi. p. 104.

[3] *Cf.* Denney: "The Flesh belongs not to his psychology—he has no such thing—but to his moral and religious experience: it is that in him which does not submit itself to the law of God, and cannot, but lives in the perpetual revolt of sin. It is common to ask how Paul conceived man's nature to have become what it is, or whether he conceived it to have been what it is from the beginning. These are questions to which

(flesh) and soul (spirit). Man as a person is sinful: from that the apostle concludes that those elements in him which compose his personal being, are, as a matter of experience, tainted by sin. At this point we touch a difficult problem in St Paul's religious terminology. As we know it, *σάρξ*, the flesh, is corrupt. So is the *ψυχή*, the soul, which is the inward principle of the *σάρξ*, like the *nephesh*, the bearer of the personality, the natural life-centre of the individual. Neither of these can be conceived without the other. Σάρξ is meaningless apart from ψυχή. And ψυχή is never posited except as *informing* σάρξ.[1] But the ψυχή has what one may call a higher side. This the apostle generally designates νοῦς, the power of moral discernment, perhaps virtually equivalent to our term "conscience."[2] A closely allied expression is ὁ ἔσω ἄνθρωπος. Both of these terms (or in the case of the latter, an exact parallel) are to be found in Greek philosophy. In its philosophical usage, νοῦς denotes, according to Siebeck (*Geschichte d. Psychologie*, i. 2. p. 52), "the

no answer is supplied: they are questions, indeed, which it would have been as impossible for Paul to answer as it is for us. . . . We know what the Flesh means as soon as we have a *conscience* at all, and memory reaches no further, if indeed as far" (*Expos.* vi. 3, pp. 291, 293).

[1] See, *e.g.*, Lüdemann, *Anthropologie d. Ap. Paulus*, p. 4; also p. 33.

[2] The late, semi-philosophical term συνείδησις occurs repeatedly in the Pauline Epistles, but almost exclusively where he is discussing questions of Christian liberty. He never employs it when describing the processes of the new life which reveal themselves in the depths of Christian experience. The word is probably one of the few links which directly associate him with the intellectual activity of contemporary Hellenism.

thinking spirit, that part of the soul peculiar to man, which animals do not possess, linked to no bodily organ, in its deepest essence un-become (*ungeworden*) and incorruptible." Plato (*Republic*, ix. 589 A.) speaks of *τοῦ ἀνθρώπου ὁ ἐντὸς ἄνθρωπος*, which seems an exact equivalent of the Pauline phrase. It would be, of course, unsafe to infer that these conceptions occur in their Hellenic sense in St Paul. As regards the last-named, there is no need to look for its basis in Platonic thought. "The man within" is an idea which might quite naturally be found in popular currency. In St Paul's usage it seems practically identical with *νοῦς*, in the sense of that part of man's nature to which Divine influences and appeals will usually attach themselves. It is that aspect of the innermost life of man which lies open to God.[1] In the New Testament, *νοῦς* is almost confined to the Pauline Epistles. If St Paul did not adopt the term from contemporary Greek thought,[2] as is quite probable, he certainly modified it according to his own view of man's inner constitution.

Now, if the apostle had restricted himself to the use of the terms we have been considering, to express the factors in human consciousness, apart from the Divine operation, it would be a perfectly simple matter to delimit his conceptions. Thus we should be able to assert without reservation that, wherever he uses *πνεῦμα* to denote an element in the inner life of man, he has in view either the direct gift of the

[1] *νοῦς* occurs very rarely in the LXX. When it does, it usually translates the Hebrew לֵב or לֵבָב, heart.

[2] The Aristotelian *νοῦς*, *e.g.*, really finds its New Testament parallel in *πνεῦμα*. See Siebeck, *Zeitschr. f Völker-Psychol.* xii. pp. 397, 398.

Divine πνεῦμα imparted to the individual, or the human soul in its new condition as transformed by the Spirit of God. As a matter of fact, this may be stated as his normal standpoint. The conception of πνεῦμα has become gradually spiritualised, if we may so say, in Jewish thought. From the earlier Greek conception of it as a kind of air or breath, which came to be regarded as the bearer of vitality and a link between σῶμα and ψυχή, it had reached, among the Stoics, the position of the creative principle (the πῦρ τεχνικόν) through which the organic development of all things takes place. It was at the same time "the all-penetrating, quickening power and soul of the world, the breath of life in all, and as such the deity itself." Hence, from being conceived as the most highly refined "body," it came to be regarded as λόγος, reason. This aspect of πνεῦμα was developed by the Jew Philo, and naturally it came to be affected by the intensely ethical and spiritual character of the Old Testament conception of God.[1] St Paul carries the process to its highest point. For him the πνεῦμα, according to his normal view, is the Spirit of God, mediated through the exalted Christ. In one passage he expressly identifies the Spirit with Christ: "Now the Lord is the Spirit" (2 Cor. iii. 17; with this may be compared ver. 18, καθάπερ ἀπὸ κυρίου πνεύματος, "as from the Lord who is (the) Spirit"). The indwelling of the πνεῦμα is the basis and pledge of eternal life in the believer. We shall return to this point: but a difficulty must first be noted. There

[1] See, on the whole development, Siebeck's admirable essay in *Zeitschr. f. Völker-Psychol.* xii., especially pp. 373-395. *Cf.* his *Geschichte d. Psychol.* i. 2 pp. 148-155.

are about a dozen passages in which St Paul uses πνεῦμα in a looser sense. It is needless to enumerate all of these here. The following examples will suffice: 1 Cor. ii. 11, "For who of men knoweth the things of man save the spirit of man (τὸ πνεῦμα τοῦ ἀνθρώπου) which is in him" (*cf.* Rom. viii. 16, "The Spirit itself beareth witness with our spirit that we are children of God") a passage in which a distinctly human πνεῦμα is contrasted with the Divine; 1 Cor. v. 3, "Being absent in the body but present in the spirit" (τῷ πνεύματι, *cf.* vii. 34, xvi. 18; 2 Cor. ii. 13), where he uses πνεῦμα in a popular or colloquial sense; 1 Thess. v. 23, "May your spirit and soul and body, in their entirety, be preserved blamelessly" (ὁλόκληρον ὑμῶν τὸ πνεῦμα καὶ ἡ ψυχὴ καὶ τὸ σῶμα ἀμέμπτως . . . τηρηθείη), where we should suppose (with Dr A. B. Davidson) that this is a rhetorical combination, not to be interpreted prosaically, or as representing any psychological theory of the apostle's. We need not be in any way astonished at these exceptions to his stricter usage. Nor is there occasion, with Holsten (*Paulin. Theologie*, pp. 10-11), to look for special reasons why St Paul should employ πνεῦμα of the human spirit. No thinker is strictly accurate in his terminology. There are freer moods in which he avails himself of current terms, entirely unconscious of the fact that pedantry will demand uniformity in his language. There is some force, also, in the observation of Titius (p. 240, note 1), that St Paul, "with the exception of 1 Cor. ii. 11, nowhere speaks of the spirit of man, not even in 1 Cor. v. 3, 5, vii. 34, etc., but of the spirit of the Christian, and nowhere is this *Christian* determination of the spirit without importance in the context," although we doubt whether this distinction was to any large extent before the apostle's mind in the relevant passages.

But to return to his strict conception of the πνεῦμα. This implies undoubtedly the entrance of a new factor, the Divine energy into the inner life. He gives various descriptions of the experience. These are all involved ideally in the first genuine contact of the soul with God in Christ through faith. When the soul recognises the love of God in Christ as the Saviour, and appropriates that forgiving love by faith, it is brought into touch with God as living, and dealing with it. This is, in St Paul's view, an experience of the Divine πνεῦμα. Yet we find him urging it, at times, on those who have already been baptised. It is absurd to say (with some expositors) that the apostle associated the reception of the Spirit with baptism. Had this been the case, baptism would not occupy the comparatively insignificant place which it does in his teaching. Baptism is indeed a vivid picture or illustration of the saving process. On the one hand, it sets forth the unseen experiences which are attained through faith. As the baptised person is plunged out of sight in the water, and then rises out of the cleansing element a member of the Christian community, so does the believer, who by faith appropriates the benefits of Christ's atoning death and resurrection, pass out of contact with the sinful life of the flesh, annulled on the Cross, and rise in fellowship with the risen Lord to newness of life in the Spirit. But, obviously, the picture also symbolises the relation of the believer to the Spirit. For all that has happened to him in the experience of salvation, his death to sin (immersion beneath the water), and his entrance upon a new life (emergence from the water), is really accomplished for him in response to his faith, accomplished by the Divine operation; is the work, as St Paul would put it, of the Holy Spirit. Necessarily, in that sense, the experience of baptism emphasises the reality and significance of the gift of the Spirit, and thus quickens the believer's consciousness of its possession.

What happens in the reception of the Spirit may be described as an *ἀνακαίνωσις τοῦ νοός*, "a renewing of the *νοῦς*" (Rom. xii. 2). From the remarkable collocation in Eph. iv. 23, *ἀνανεοῦσθαι . . . τῷ πνεύματι τοῦ νοὸς ὑμῶν*, "to be renewed in the spirit of your mind," we may infer that St Paul regards the Divine *πνεῦμα* as taking possession of the *νοῦς*. This implies that there is now a new moral centre of the personal life. Yet we must not conceive the Divine Spirit as passing over, as it were, into the subjective, regenerated life of the believer. For the apostle always regards the Divine energy as continuing to act on the life of the believer as a distinct objective power.[1] This is evident from Rom. viii. 16. The person becomes *πνευματικός*, "spiritual," instead of *ψυχικός*, "natural" (virtually equivalent to "conditioned by human nature as such"). The *ψυχή*, or soul, which is the substratum, so to speak, of the *νοῦς*, is overshadowed, or rather supplanted in the government of the personality, by the *πνεῦμα*, which becomes the basis of the new life. Thus the new life may be said to be at the same time supernatural and psychologically mediated. It is very doubtful whether any trace remains of the more ancient quasi-physical side of the conception. Unquestionably *πνεῦμα* can mean "breath" and

[1] See Weiss, *N. T. Theol.* (E. Tr.) i. p. 477.

"wind," and some theologians imagine that St Paul does presuppose, in a sense, an inbreathing (material in the most refined degree) of the Divine life. Pfleiderer, for example, speaks of the *πνεῦμα*, according to St Paul's view, as "in itself a transcendent physical essence, a supersensuous kind of matter, which is the opposite of the earthly, sensuous materiality of the *σάρξ*" (*Paulinism*, i. p. 201). Kabisch holds that in St Paul "the *πνεῦμα* has a kind of physical, or, to put it better, *metaphysical*, substantial quality" (*Esch. d. Paulus*, p. 113). We can find no evidence in the Epistles for this position. It seems to attribute to the apostle an analysis of the new Divine life altogether foreign to his method of thought. But, bearing in mind his *synthetic* conception of life, to which we have already referred, we are justified in affirming that this experience affects what *we* should designate the physical life of the believer. This, at least in its essential element, shares in the quickening (*ζωοποιεῖν*), which is a main function of the *πνεῦμα*. Probably it would be truer to the apostle's conception to say that the *whole person* is quickened by the life-giving Spirit. Nothing less can be the meaning of the strong words of Rom. viii. 11: *εἰ δὲ τὸ πνεῦμα τοῦ ἐγείραντος τὸν Ἰησοῦν ἐκ νεκρῶν οἰκεῖ ἐν ὑμῖν, ὁ ἐγείρας ἐκ νεκρῶν Χριστὸν Ἰησοῦν ζωοποιήσει καὶ τὰ θνητὰ σώματα ὑμῶν διὰ τοῦ ἐνοικοῦντος αὐτοῦ πνεύματος ἐν ὑμῖν*: "If the Spirit of Him who raised Jesus from the dead dwell in you, He that raised from the dead Christ Jesus shall quicken even your mortal bodies through His Spirit dwelling in you."[1] This quickening has nothing spasmodic or

[1] *Cf.* Titius: "When he speaks of the Spirit which makes alive (2 Cor. iii. 6; 1. Cor. xv. 45), of the life of Jesus Christ, or of the Spirit in believers (Gal. ii. 20, v. 25; 2 Cor. iv. 10-12, v. 15; Rom.

abnormal about it. It is a gradual, orderly process, thus described in 2 Cor. iv. 16: ἀλλ' εἰ καὶ ὁ ἔξω ἡμῶν ἄνθρωπος διαφθείρεται, ἀλλ' ὁ ἔσω ἡμῶν ἀνακαινοῦται ἡμέρᾳ καὶ ἡμέρᾳ: "But although our outward man decays, our inner man is renewed from day to day." We shall have to discuss later on the relation of this process to the genesis of the σῶμα πνευματικόν, the "spiritual body," which is to be the organism of the glorified believer. Enough, however, has been said to indicate the steps which St Paul presupposes in the inauguration of new life in the individual, and his conception of its psychological mediation.

We are now, therefore, in a position to summarise his precise conception of Life. In many passages, of course, he uses ζωή in the more or less colloquial sense of existence in the world: *e.g.*, Rom. viii. 38 f., "I am persuaded that neither death nor life . . . shall be able to separate us from the love of God"; Phil. i. 20, "According to my hope that . . . Christ shall be magnified in my body, whether by life or by death"; 1 Cor. xv. 19, "It in this life we have only hoped in Christ." On these it is unnecessary to comment. At the other extremity, ζωή has for him the definite sense of a future reward

vi. 4, 11, 13, viii. 2, 6, 10), we must not interpret the 'life' metaphorically, as in 1 Thess. iii. 8, but in addition to the spiritual, ethical reference, the supernatural must necessarily be maintained. He deals with the real, higher life, . . . which . . . forms a transition-stage to that (*i.e.* eternal life)" (p. 263). The truth is, as Pfleiderer well expresses it, that "the two ideas of the ζωή, the 'eschatological' [a far better description than 'transcendent-physical' which he also employs, *e.g.* i. p. 204], and the 'ethical' interpenetrate one another" (*Paulinism*, i. p. 206). It has to be remembered that St Paul would never consider each by itself apart.

or boon which God will bestow. This may be designated as its "eschatological" usage. In this sense, ζωή is generally qualified by the adjective *αἰώνιος*. The phrase invariably denotes life looked at in prospect, in its complete realisation. Ἀιώνιος is an eschatological adjective. But even here, where the future outlook is so prominent, ζωή seems usually to be regarded as the end, or the crowning-point, or the reward, or the harvest, of a preliminary course of experience and discipline which leads up to it. Thus, in Rom. ii. 7, ζωή is the recompense of perseverance in righteous conduct and of the quest for glory and immortality; in Rom. v. 21, it is the goal and aim of the reign of grace through Jesus Christ; in Rom. vi. 22, it expresses the end (τέλος) or climax of the life of freedom from sin and bondage to God, and hence it is further defined as the gift of God (in contrast with the wages of sin) in Christ Jesus. Finally, in Gal. vi. 8, the apostle designates as ζωή the harvest reaped ἐκ τοῦ πνεύματος by him who sows εἰς τὸ πνεῦμα. Plainly, there is an organic connection between ζωή and that human experience of which it is the culmination. It is in no sense an acquirement added on at death or judgment or the inauguration of the coming Æon. Ἀιώνιος shows what is its quality. It partakes of the nature of God Himself, and of the new glorified life which He introduces. It is eternal. There are one or two passages which contain, apparently, this shade of meaning, although *αἰώνιος* is lacking: *e.g.*, Rom. v. 17, "Those receiving the superabundance of grace, and of the gift of righteousness, shall reign in life through one, Jesus Christ"; also Phil. iv. 3, "Whose names are in the book of life" (ἐν βίβλῳ ζωῆς). But St Paul always regards life as a *present* possession of the believer. As such, it is the direct result of the indwelling of the Holy Spirit, and may even be termed the actual presence of the Spirit in the human personality. We have seen how the apostle conceives this endowment, as related to the natural inner constitution of the individual. Most typical instances are: Rom. viii. 2, "The law of the Spirit of life in Christ Jesus made me free from the law of sin and death"; viii. 6, "The mind of the spirit is life and peace"; viii. 10, "If Christ be in you, the body is dead (νεκρόν) because of sin, but the Spirit is life because of righteousness." This last example leads us to one or two passages in which the ζωή of the believer is represented as the very ζωή of the exalted Christ: so 2 Cor. iv. 10-11, "Always carrying about in the body the dying of Jesus, in order that the life also of Jesus may be manifested in our body; for always we, the living, are delivered unto death for Jesus' sake, that the life also of Jesus may be manifested in our mortal body"; Col. iii. 4, "When Christ shall be manifested, our life (ἡ ζωὴ ἡμῶν), then you also will be manifested with Him in glory." With these verses may be compared the remarkable expression of Ephes. iv. 18: "Alienated (ἀπηλλοτριωμένοι) from the life of God." This life, as we have noted, belongs to earthly experience: *e.g.* 2 Cor. iv. 12, "Life works (ἐνεργεῖται) in you." It is by no means something abnormal. It was God's original design for man, for ἡ ἐντολή, the commandment of God, was one designed for life (ἡ εἰς ζωήν, Rom. vii. 10). "If a law had been given, able to make alive (ζωοποιῆσαι), righteousness would essentially have sprung from the law," Gal. iii. 21). The possession of "life" is really the ideal of humanity.

It forms the content of the Gospel of Christ which is a savour from life unto life (2 Cor. ii. 16). It is a transformation of the former condition, which was also, in a sense, ζωή. Through the power of the Spirit, the believer receives καινότης ζωῆς (Rom. vi. 4). The transformed life, which necessarily includes the "physical," swallows up death (which also, for St Paul, includes the "physical" aspect), and passes on into the eternal world (2 Cor. v. 4; 1 Cor. xv. 54).

All the evidence which we have examined corroborates our earlier statement that St Paul's view of Life is synthetic. He would not have affirmed of the believer that originally he possessed a natural life, but, when he surrendered himself to Christ, received a spiritual. The new life is a renewal of the old from its very foundations. It is not a renewal of one part but of the whole. It embraces the physical (to use our distinctions) as well as the ethical or religious. For St Paul, the sum of the believer's experiences is a unity. Life includes the totality of his energies. It cannot be divided up into provinces, of which one may be contrasted with another. Its only contrast lies in Death. Death for the apostle means the ruin of the whole personality. Life means its triumphant continuance in the power of the Spirit beyond the barriers of earth and time, in conformity with the nature of the glorified Christ, who is the Image of the invisible God.

CHAPTER IV

ST PAUL'S CONCEPTIONS OF THE PAROUSIA AND THE JUDGMENT

AT the stage we have reached in our inquiry, a difficulty occurs as to the question of *method.*

St Paul's statements regarding the Parousia are most intimately interwoven with his treatment of the Resurrection. Both belong to that inbreaking of the era of salvation, in which time is no longer reckoned. Yet his conception of the Resurrection is so crucial for the apostle's Eschatology, that it inevitably demands a separate discussion for itself. It is not easy to decide between the respective claims of the two groups of ideas as to priority of handling. Perhaps, however, a truer perspective will be gained in our presentation of St Paul's forecast of the future, if we deal first with the Parousia, and its chief content, the Judgment, and then pass on to the Resurrection, a subject which takes us into the very heart of his religious thought and experience. Unquestionably, in the former province, as we shall discover, he has followed much more closely what may be called the prophetic tradition. In the latter, he has remoulded current notions by means of that creative power which sprang from his wonderful contact with the risen Lord.

The careful reader of the Pauline Epistles must be forcibly impressed by their constant references, in one form or another, to that event which the Christian Church is accustomed to designate the Second Coming of Christ. This emphasis on the Parousia is, indeed, by no means peculiar to St Paul. All the New Testament writers seem to assign to it a like prominence. In proof, we have only to cite such passages as James v. 8: "Be ye also patient; stablish your hearts; for the coming of the Lord draweth nigh"; 1 Pet. iv. 7: "The end of all things is at hand; be ye therefore sober, and watch unto prayer"; Heb. x. 25: "Exhorting one another, and so much the more, as ye see the day approaching."[1] These are typical of a large class of passages. And the fact stands out in bolder relief, owing to the

[1] It is characteristic of all intense eschatological expectation to look for a speedy development of events. *Cf.* Rev. i. 1, "To show unto His servants things which must shortly come to pass." The earlier Jewish Apocalypses reveal the same trait: *cf.* Apoc. Bar. xxiii. 7, "My salvation has truly drawn nigh, and it is no longer distant as formerly"; also Enoch li. 2, "He (*i.e.* the Messiah) will choose out the righteous and holy among them, for the day of their redemption is near." Davidson refers to the same phenomenon in the O.T., "the peculiarity of prophecy, which compresses great momenta into a brief space, which brings up great movements close upon the back of one another, and takes them all in at one glance of the eye." He compares our Lord's prophecy of the End in which "the two great events which He has in view—the destruction of Jerusalem and the end of the world—seem immediately combined," and offers the hypothesis that "there may have been a powerful exercise of the intuitional faculty which presented the events together, taking little note of time, or contracting the time into what seemed a period of a very few years" (*O.T. Prophecy*, p. 353).

comparative receding of the conception in the later periods of the history of the Church.

It may be well to inquire at the outset into the special reasons which should be assigned for the phenomenon in question, although, in attempting such an inquiry, we must confine ourselves to the apostle Paul.

In many passages, more especially in the earlier Epistles, he seems to expect the Parousia in his own, or, at least, in his readers' lifetime. Writing to the Thessalonians, he rejoices at the success of his ministry among them, and reminds them how they turned "to God from idols, to serve the living and true God, and to await His Son from heaven, whom He raised from the dead, Jesus who delivers us from the coming wrath" (1 Thess. i. 9, 10).[1] He prays that their hearts may be "blameless in holiness before our God and Father, at the Parousia of our Lord Jesus" (1 Thess. iii. 13). He reassures those who were distressed because some of their friends "had fallen asleep," by the affirmation that "we, the living, who survive to the Parousia of the Lord shall not anticipate (φθάσωμεν) those who fall asleep. For the Lord Himself shall descend from heaven with a commanding word (κελεύσματι), with the voice of the archangel and the trumpet of God: and the dead in Christ shall rise first, then we, the living, who survive, shall be snatched up with them in the clouds to meet the Lord, into the air, and then shall we be ever with the Lord" (1 Thess. iv. 15-17). He seeks

[1] It is of importance to notice that St Paul's interest attaches to the Parousia solely along redemptive lines. For him, certainly, its vital import lies in the assurance that it is to be a deliverance from judgment and all that *that* involves.

to relieve their perplexity as to the precise time of the Parousia, by declaring that they are not in darkness so that "the day" (*i.e.* of the Lord) should come upon them (καταλάβῃ) as a thief. They are "sons of the light and of the daytime," therefore it accords with their character to watch and live soberly (1 Thess. v. 4-6). He prays that their "spirit and soul and body in their entirety (ὁλόκληρον) may be preserved blameless at the Parousia of our Lord Jesus Christ" (1 Thess. v. 23). In his *second* letter to Thessalonica, his expectation appears to be no less vivid. To his persecuted converts he predicts a stern judgment of God upon their cruel enemies, and for themselves "rest along with us at the revelation (ἀποκαλύψει) of the Lord Jesus from heaven with the angels of His might in flaming fire . . . when He shall have come to be glorified (ἐνδοξασθῆναι) among His saints" (2 Thess. i. 6-10). The Parousia of the Lord Jesus Christ and their "gathering together" (ἐπισυναγωγή) to Him, had become events of such acute and vivid anticipation at Thessalonica—apparently, in part, at least, from an exaggerated impression based on his teaching—that he is obliged to correct their expectation of its immediacy (2 Thess. ii. 2). His expectant mood continues more or less throughout the letters to the Corinthians and the Romans. Thus, he gives thanks for the rich gifts bestowed on the Corinthian Christians as they eagerly await (ἀπεκδεχομένους) "the revelation (ἀποκάλυψιν) of our Lord Jesus Christ," and expresses his confidence that they will prove without reproach "in the day of our Lord Jesus Christ" (1 Cor. i. 7, 8). He entreats them not to be misled by adversaries into hasty criticism of his work "before the time . . . until the Lord shall have come" (1 Cor. iv. 5). In view of what he believes to be the shortness of the interval (*ὁ καιρὸς συνεσταλμένος ἐστίν*), he advises them to make no new family ties, "for the fashion of this world passes away" (1 Cor. vii. 29, 31). And in the climax of the great Resurrection-passage he can look forward to a day when those of them who have not fallen asleep—and he appears, from the form of the sentence, to include himself—shall be transformed "in a moment, in the twinkling of an eye, at the last trumpet" (1 Cor. xv. 51, 52). In the second Epistle the emphasis on the probable imminence of the Parousia is by no means so marked. Indeed, we may even go the length of saying that the apostle seems to have a presentiment that he will not survive until that great crisis. This is suggested by such passages as 2 Cor. iv. 14, 16; v. 1 ff., 6-10. Some exegetes have accounted for the less vivid statement of his expectation by the serious perils through which he had lately passed at Ephesus (see 2 Cor. i. 8-10, vi. 4-10), perils which unquestionably have left their mark upon this Epistle. Perhaps no such definite reason need be given.[1] A man of the apostle's richness and variety of spiritual experience cannot be tied down by the logic of any merely external sequence of events. At certain moments in his career the vista of the Kingdom of God would lengthen out for him, at others it would seem to contract. Nothing, indeed,

[1] Heinrici observes with force, that so far from these great dangers in Asia leading him to give up all hope of experiencing the Parousia, his remarkable deliverance from them must have strengthened it (see his notes on 2 Cor. v. 4 f.).

is more fitted to convince us of the futility of postulating schemes of gradual development in St Paul's Eschatology (as, *e.g.*, Sabatier, Teichmann, Holtzmann, and others have done) than his utterances on the nearness of the Parousia.[1] For while his expectation has receded in 2 *Corinthians*, it revives in the Epistle to the *Romans*. In the eighth chapter he gives expression to eager yearnings for the redemption (ἀπολύτρωσις) of the body (viii. 23). We know from other passages that this redemption was to be accomplished at the Parousia. In chap. v. he exults "in the hope (ἐλπίδι) of the glory of God." In the later letters, as we shall see, ἐλπίς often represents his conception of the future of salvation. Towards the close of the Epistle his statements are more definite. "And this, knowing (or, taking note of) the season (καιρόν, fitting opportunity), that it is already high time for you to rise from sleep: for now our salvation (σωτηρία, always used by the apostle of the final, com-

[1] Of course we should admit the possibility of very considerable variation as to details in the apostle's conceptions at different times, for the simple reason that neither in Judaism nor in primitive-Christian circles does there seem to have been any rigid eschatological system (see this point well argued in Bornemann's *Thessalonians*, p. 186). Where we fail to trace any marked development, is in his presentation of the great central conceptions of Eschatology. Holtzmann is obliged to have recourse to the theory, based on 2 Cor. v. 1-7, that St Paul, having given up his old idea of resurrection, hopes, immediately after death, to be carried to Christ in heaven. "But this," he is forced to admit, "was certainly conceived only as an exceptional case, affecting merely himself and a few companions in spirit and fortune, as otherwise a total transformation of his entire eschatology must be assumed," etc., etc. (*N.T. Theol.* ii. p. 193). This hypothesis of the "exceptional case" appears to us fatal to his idea of St Paul's development, for we can find no further evidence to support it.

pleted salvation) is nearer than when we believed. The night has advanced, the day is at hand" (Rom. xiii. 11, 12).[1] Undoubtedly, in *Colossians* and *Ephesians*, the outlines of his expectation are far more vague than in the earlier letters. The term ἐλπίς often exhausts his Eschatology (*e.g.*, Col. i. 5, i. 23; Eph. i. 18, iv. 4). Still, the expression παραστῆσαι in Col. i. 22, "to *present* you holy and blameless and without reproach before Him," the same word used of the apostle himself in i. 28, "that we may present every man perfect in Christ," together with the striking statement in iii. 4, "when Christ shall be made manifest, who is our Life, then you also will be made manifest with Him in glory," remind us that his early conviction continues to weigh with him. In *Philippians* it is of importance to notice the blending of the two diverging elements in his outlook. By this time, in his Roman prison, he feels no certainty and no desire of surviving to the great crisis of the Lord's appearing: "I am constrained between the two alternatives, having the desire to depart and be with Christ, for that is very much better" (Phil. i. 23). He speaks of his converts at Philippi as "being a cause of glorying" to him "in the day of Christ," and thus testifying to the efficacy of his labours. But immediately he goes on to contemplate the possibility of "being poured out as a libation upon the sacrifice and service" of their faith, a contingency which he can meet with joy, although it means death for him (ii.

[1] At the same time, in *Romans* also, the possibility of dying before the Parousia is by no means excluded: *cf.* xiv. 8, "For whether we live, we live unto the Lord; and whether we die, we die unto the Lord; whether we live therefore, or die, we are the Lord's."

16, 17). And in the magnificent statement of his own Christian experience in chap. iii., he uses these remarkable words: "If perchance I may attain unto the resurrection from the dead" (iii. 11). It seems evident from the context that here he has in view a personal possession of the life-giving power of the risen Lord, whereby he also may share in the Resurrection, thus obviously accepting the probability of death before the Parousia. Yet, side by side with these possibilities for himself, he has high hopes of a different kind for his readers. He is assured that God who began His good work in them "will finish it up to the day of Jesus Christ" (Phil. i. 6). From St Paul's standpoint these words must almost certainly mean a process carried on in their lifetime. He prays that they may be pure, and kept from giving offence in the day of Christ (i. 10). Nevertheless, if he seems to separate himself in some places from his expectations for *them*, there is no such distinction drawn in that most memorable passage where he exclaims: "Our commonwealth is in heaven, from whence also we eagerly expect the Saviour, the Lord Jesus Christ, who shall transform the body of our humiliation that it may be conformed to the body of His glory, according to the energy whereby He is able even to subdue all things to Himself" (Phil. iii. 20, 21). And in the closing chapter of the Epistle, in an exhortation to reasonableness and calmness of spirit, he declares to them, "the Lord is near" (Phil. iv. 5; see a similar setting for the thought in James v. 8, 9).[1]

[1] In spite of his idea of a development in St Paul's eschatological conceptions, Holtzmann frankly admits his enduring expectation of a speedy end of the world (*N.T. Theol.* ii. p. 188).

Having now the evidence in considerable fulness before us, let us attempt to answer the question proposed at the outset: For what reason does St Paul lay so remarkable an emphasis upon the conception of the Parousia? Here, as in all investigations of the teaching of the Epistles, an important caution has to be noted. Certain truths, and certain special aspects of these truths, come into prominence simply because they are problems of peculiar interest to the Christian communities addressed. Thus, as we have hinted, the large place given to the Parousia in the First and Second Epistles to the Thessalonians is due to the perplexing questions which centred around it for the minds of the converts in that Church. For precisely the same reason, we have the elaborate discussion of the Resurrection in 1 Cor. xv. At the same time, the phenomena we have observed throughout his Epistles are enough to suggest that the Parousia must have occupied an important place both in the thought and the teaching of St Paul. And I believe that we are put upon the right track for ascertaining the significance of this fact, when we look carefully into its character and setting in those letters in which it bulks most largely, namely, 1 and 2 *Thessalonians.* For there we are at once impressed by the noteworthy parallelism between the language of the apostle and many passages in the Synoptic Gospels. Take a typical example. In the second chapter of 2 Thessalonians, St Paul warns his friends against the panic which had seized them as to the immediate approach of the Parousia, and points out certain conditions which he believes must be fulfilled, ere this tremendous crisis can break in upon the present order. "We beseech you, brethren, concerning the Parousia of our Lord Jesus Christ and our gathering together (ἐπισυναγωγῆς) to Him, that ye be not quickly shaken from your mind nor perturbed" (θροεῖσθαι) (2 Thess. ii. 1, 2). Compare with this, Mark xiii. 27: "Then shall He send forth His angels, and shall gather together (ἐπισυνάξει) the elect from the four winds" (parallel in Matt. xxiv. 31). Further, in Mark xiii. 7 (parallel in Matt. xxiv. 6) we read: "But when ye hear of wars and rumours of wars, be not perturbed (θροεῖσθε): these must happen, but the end is not yet." The apostle goes on in verse 3 to warn them against deception (*cf.* Mark xiii. 5, "Take heed lest any one deceive you"; Matt. xxiv. 4), and to announce the revelation of the "man of lawlessness" (ὁ ἄνθρωπος τῆς ἀνομίας). In Matt. xxiv. 12 the same expression is found: "On account of the multiplying of lawlessness (διὰ τὸ πληθυνθῆναι τὴν ἀνομίαν), the love of many shall grow cold." In his description of the "man of lawlessness," St Paul speaks of him as "sitting in the temple of God, giving himself out to be God" (verse 4). We may compare Matt. xxiv. 15: "When, therefore, ye see the abomination of desolation, predicted by Daniel the prophet, standing in the holy place" (Mark xiii. 14, "standing where it ought not"). The presence (παρουσία) of the lawless one is depicted in verse 9 as being "according to the working of Satan, with all power and lying signs and wonders, and with all injurious deceit for those who are perishing." The parallel in Mark xiii. 22 is noteworthy: "There shall rise up false Christs and false prophets, and shall work signs and wonders, to deceive, if possible, the elect" (parallel in Matt. xxiv. 4).

The above are striking instances of verbal agree

ment between St Paul and the Synoptic tradition of our Lord's eschatological discourse. But there is far more to be noted than a group of verbal coincidences. The more closely we examine the eschatological sayings of Jesus, especially as these are reported in Mark xiii. with its parallels, Matt. xxiv. and Luke xxi., the better can we appreciate St Paul's emphasis upon the Parousia. But at this point we are confronted by one of the most perplexing problems of interpretation which the New Testament presents. It is well known that many scholars, following, with various modifications, Weiffenbach (*Der Wiederkunftsgedanke Jesu*, 1873), have regarded the discourse on the Last Things, related in Mark xiii. and its parallels, as a combination of at least two separate sources. One of these is held to be an authentic tradition of the words of Jesus. The other, consisting of verses 7-9*a*, 14-20, 24-27, 30-31, is considered, on this hypothesis, to be a Jewish-Christian Apocalypse, composed not long before the Fall of Jerusalem. Some plausible arguments may be adduced for the theory. But definite reconstructions of this kind appear to us highly precarious. Ingenuity can always rearrange a text to suit its preconceptions. (J. Weiss, *e.g.*, makes the Apocalypse consist of verses 8, 14-15, 17-20, 23*b*-27; see *S.K.*, 1892, p. 246 ff.) The same section can be adapted to fit various critical schemes. Thus Haupt (*Die eschatol. Aussagen Jesu*, pp. 25-34), following a similar method, reaches a different, and in our judgment, equally specious analysis of this discourse of Jesus. It would be unwarrantable to preclude processes of redaction or interpolation in the composition of the Gospels, but hypotheses carried out with such precision as the above, assume an acquaintance with the conditions under which ancient documents took shape, or came to embody traditions, which has no foundation in fact. The apocalyptic elements in the passage may readily be accounted for by the influence of Old Testament prophecy, more especially of a book like *Daniel*, with which Jesus was certainly acquainted, and which provided a symbolism more or less familiar to His hearers (see Stevens, *N.T. Theol.* pp. 156, 157; Beyschlag, *N.T. Theol.* i. p. 188, *et al.*). There is nothing improbable, however, in the supposition that this mysterious discourse consists of kindred sayings of Jesus grouped together in the earliest documents—a phenomenon natural in itself, and usually assumed in the case of the Sermon on the Mount, as reported in *Matthew*, and elsewhere.[1] Such an hypothesis would account for the fact that here we seem to find references to at least two groups of events; the Destruction of Jerusalem, and the Parousia in the strict sense of the term. Cognate words of our Lord are to be found in Mark viii. 38 ix. 1 (parallel are Matt. xvi. 27, 28; Luke ix. 26, 27), and Luke xii. 36-46 (parallel in Matt. xxiv. 43-51).

It is quite impossible to determine whether any of these predictions had been committed to writing by the time St Paul wrote his earliest Epistles. But whether that be so or not, many of them, at least, must have formed part of the oral tradition with which the Christians of that age would become acquainted sooner or later. Certain ideas must have come to be regarded as fundamental. Jesus had often spoken to His disciples, in one form or other, of His own

[1] See Weisse, *Die Evangelienfrage*, pp. 167-170; Haupt, *op. cit.*, p. 24.

Parousia.[1] It was to be a coming in glory (see Matt. xxv. 31; and compare Mark xiii. 26, Matt. xxiv. 30, Luke xxi. 27). It was to be a sudden event: like the lightning-flash darting across the sky from east to west (Matt. xxiv. 27; Luke xvii. 24). There was therefore a danger that it should overtake them unawares. "Observe, then," He warns them, using a familiar illustration, "that if the master of the house had known in what watch the thief was coming, he would have watched, and not suffered his house to be broken through. For this cause, be ye also ready, for at an hour when ye think not, the Son of Man cometh" (Matt. xxiv. 43, 44; parallel in Luke xii. 39, 40). And then, changing the figure, He pronounces that servant blessed whom his master, when he returns, shall find busy with his appointed task. "But if that servant shall say in his heart, My lord delays his return; and shall begin to beat his fellow-servants . . . and to eat and drink with the drunken, the lord of that servant shall come in a day when he expects him not, and at an hour of which he knows not, and shall cleave him in twain, and appoint his portion with the hypocrites" (Matt. xxiv. 46-51; parallel in Luke xii. 43-46). Of

[1] Teichmann fails to find a basis for the Parousia-expectations of the early Christians in the words of Jesus. He supposes that Jesus Himself was not convinced of His own second coming. On a par with this hypothesis is the argument he uses to establish it, which consists in a quotation of Matt. xxvii. 46; Mark xv. 34; Luke xvii. 20 f. The former two passages give the word on the Cross: "My God, My God, why hast Thou forsaken Me." The latter is the well-known saying: "The Kingdom of God cometh not with observation" (*op. cit.*, p. 12, note). For the real facts of the case, we need only refer, *e.g.*, to Haupt, *op. cit.*, pp. 119-121; and (from a different standpoint) to Holtzmann, *N.T. Theol.* i. p. 312.

similar import are the parables of the Ten Virgins and the Talents (Matt. xxv. 1-13, 14-30). In the former, the emphasis is laid on the necessity of preparation for a sudden and incalculable event. This is, to a large extent, true also of the latter, only the efforts put forth by the servants are more prominent than the master's return, which, however, still remains the decisive moment in the whole picture. It is noteworthy that in this parable the expression occurs: "*After a long time* the lord of those servants cometh, and reckoneth with them" (ver. 19). Many interpreters have taken for granted that an integral part of Jesus' conception of His Parousia was the expectation of its nearness (so, *e.g.*, Holtzmann, *N.T. Theol.* i. p. 312). Various passages, certainly, can be quoted in favour of this impression. But if His utterances, as a whole, on this mysterious question, are viewed in their mutual relations, it will be evident, we believe, that to concentrate attention on the greater or lesser *nearness* of the Parousia is not Jesus' purpose. Rather, to quote a very apt remark from J. Weiss (*Predigt Jesu vom Reiche Gottes*, p. 69), "The essential point in the preaching of Jesus (*i.e.* concerning the Kingdom of God) is not the greater or lesser nearness of the crisis, but the thought that the Kingdom of God now comes with absolute certainty. The crisis is inevitable; salvation no more a dream but an undoubted reality." (So also, in essence, Baldensperger, *Selbstbewusstsein Jesu*,[1] p. 148: "The nearness of the Parousia is, in a certain sense, only another concrete, intelligible expression for its absolute certainty.") This is a true appreciation of the balance of His thought, and it completely accords with the remarkable statement in Mark xiii. 32 (parallel in Matt. xxiv. 36): "Concerning that day or hour knoweth no one, not even the angels in heaven, nor the Son, only the Father." And on this statement follows the direct warning: "Watch, therefore, for ye know not when the lord of the house cometh" (Mark xiii. 35; parallel in Matt. xxiv. 42). The Coming, moreover, of the Son of Man, was to be the signal for Judgment. This idea is indicated in the dealing of the master with his servants in the Parable of the Talents. A vivid pictorial description of the scene is given in Matt. xxv. 31-46. It reveals some remarkable transformations of the Old Testament "Day of the Lord," its ancient prototype. Jesus, the Son of Man, is judge. We have no more pictures of noise and battle. It is essentially a judgment of individuals according to their conduct. It is an ethical verdict upon the manner in which they have used their opportunities.[1] But certain conditions must be fulfilled before the arrival of the crisis is possible. "The Gospel must first be preached to all the nations" (Mark xiii. 10). Compare Matt. xxiv. 14: "This Gospel of the Kingdom shall be preached throughout the whole world for a testimony to all the nations, and then shall come the end." Further, there must be a period of fierce opposition and cruel persecution for the followers of Jesus, in which their endurance shall be put to a severe strain (Mark xiii. 9*b*, 11-13; parallel are Matt. xxiv. 9-13, Luke xxi. 12-19). Deceivers also will arise, with pretentious claims, attempting to seduce even Christian disciples, who must keep unceasingly

[1] See an interesting paragraph in Briggs, *The Messiah of the Gospels*, pp. 311, 312.

on their guard (Mark xiii. 21-23; parallel in Matt. xxiv. 23-26), lest they renounce their loyalty and deny their Lord. It is little wonder that our Lord's predictions of the destruction of Jerusalem should have been blended in the Synoptic tradition with His utterances concerning the Parousia and accompanying Judgment. For to the first generations of Christians, more especially those who were Jews, this overwhelming event appeared as an appalling proof of the Divine sentence of doom, pronounced on the guilty nation which had crucified the Messiah of God. There can be no doubt that it is often an exceedingly delicate operation to separate between Jesus' utterances regarding the Parousia and those which concern what He frequently designates the "coming" of the Kingdom of God. At various points the two conceptions seem to merge into one. So largely is this the case, that here and there even the Parousia itself partakes to some extent of the nature of a process, with preparatory elements in it. Instructive, in this connection, are the words of Jesus to the high priest: "From this time forward (ἀπ' ἄρτι) ye shall see the Son of Man sitting on the right hand of power, and coming on the clouds of heaven" (Matt. xxvi. 64). And we can by no means summarily dismiss that interpretation of the perplexing words in Mark ix. 1 (parallel in Luke ix. 27), "Verily I say unto you, That there be some of them that stand here, which shall not taste of death, till they have seen the Kingdom of God come with power," which sees in them a forecast of the remarkable events of the day of Pentecost (so, *e.g.*, Beet, *Last Things*, p. 45). Many scholars, indeed, taking these words in their Matthæan form ("Verily I say unto you, There be some standing here, which shall not taste of death, till they see the Son of Man coming in his Kingdom"), regard them as direct evidence that Jesus expected to return within that generation. Although we are unable to assent to that hypothesis, it must be noted that, in its barest form, it by no means involves the consequences which are frequently deduced from it. Thus Prof. Huxley argues: "If he (*i.e.* Jesus) believed and taught that (*i.e.* his speedy return), then assuredly he was under an illusion, and he is responsible for that which the mere effluxion of time has demonstrated to be a prodigious error" (*Collected Essays*, vol. v. p. 303). Such a statement reveals a complete misunderstanding of the inherent nature of prophecy. Unless the process of history be conceived as wholly mechanical, all the details of a prophetic forecast must necessarily be conditioned by the actual factors operative in the process. The Parousia of Jesus had, for Him, a vital relation to the whole redemptive purpose of God. But He openly disclaimed a full knowledge of the *external* bearings of that purpose (Mark xiii. 32). These, from the very nature of the case, must be more or less contingent. For human wills are concerned in the great development of history as well as the Divine. God operates by means of second causes. That Jesus was fully alive to this aspect of the situation, is abundantly clear from His express teaching as sketched above.

We are now in a better position to understand the ideas concerning the Parousia which prevailed in early Christian circles, when the Epistles were written. They were based, as we have endeavoured to show, on various remarkable utterances of Jesus,[1]

[1] It is important to note that the circle of events which St Paul

and these came more prominently into the foreground of Christian thought, owing to the experiences through which the group of disciples had passed. Their Master had been crucified. That was a paralysing blow to their high hopes. But He had vanquished death, and His resurrection was the pledge that His claims were true, and their faith wholly justified. Yet they must have felt from the outset that His saving purpose could not end with His exaltation. The Kingdom of God, whose foundation He had laid, must grow until it should reach its full development. This was a truth He had often taught them in His parables. A time must come when the development was complete, and the Divine intention realised. Then the Lord must return and vindicate His claims and dominion before a wondering humanity. The day of universal reckoning would be the final decision for all men. It was the end of the present Æon, the ushering-in of the future eternal world.

This view of the events which should inaugurate the perfected rule of God received immense support among the early Christians from the prophetic pictures of the future in the Old Testament. Without entering into any detailed examination of the various books and the varying aspects of the subject which they present,[1] we must call attention to the

groups round the Parousia are no mechanical reproduction of current Judaistic ideas, but all take their colour from his own experience of the risen Jesus. See, *e.g.*, Stähelin, *Jahrb. f. deutsche Theol.*, 1874, p. 218.

[1] A conception peculiar to the later prophetic writers, and notably the Book of Joel, is that of the "Day of the Lord," not as a single event, but rather as "a series of Divine acts." This modification, which no doubt owes its origin to the facts of

dominating conception of the *Day of the Lord.* Perhaps the expression originated, as some scholars (*e.g.*, W. R. Smith, *Prophets of Israel*, p. 397) suggest, in phrases like the "day of Midian" (Isa. ix. 4), the day made famous by a victory of Israel over her enemies. In any case, it has come to stand for that era or crisis in which Jehovah will manifest Himself to the world. To His faithful people it will be a day of great joy. "Let the heavens be glad, and let the earth rejoice . . . let the field exult, and all that is therein: then shall the trees of the wood sing for joy before the Lord, for He cometh: for He cometh to judge the earth" (Ps. xcvi. 11-13). In this coming, Jehovah will vindicate His chosen nation. His true reign will begin. "The Lord alone shall be exalted in that day. And the idols shall utterly pass away" (Isa. ii. 17, 18). It is the beginning of a great redemption for Jerusalem. "O thou that tellest good tidings to Jerusalem, lift up thy voice with strength: lift it up, be not afraid: say unto the cities of Judah, Behold your God. Behold, the Lord God will come as a mighty one, and His arm shall rule for Him: behold His reward is with Him, and His recompense before Him" (Isa. xl. 9, 10).

But there is another side to the picture. It is a time of terror for the enemies of the people of Jehovah. "Multitudes, multitudes in the valley of decision, for the day of the Lord is near in the valley of decision. The sun and the moon are darkened, and the stars

their personal experience, is of paramount importance for the New Testament view of the Parousia. See Cheyne, *Origin of Psalter*, p. 380, note x. Prof. Charles gives a good classification of the various prophetic conceptions of the "Day of the Lord" in *E.B.* ii. coll. 1348-1353.

withdraw their shining. And the Lord shall roar from Zion, and utter His voice from Jerusalem, and the heaven and the earth shall shake, but the Lord will be a refuge unto His people, and a stronghold to the children of Israel" (Joel iii. 14-16). "Behold the Lord will come with fire, and His chariots shall be like whirlwinds: to render His anger with fury, and His rebuke with flames of fire" (Isa. lxvi. 15). "Behold, one like a son of man came with the clouds of heaven . . . and there was given him dominion and glory and a kingdom, that all people, nations, and languages should serve him" (Dan. vii. 13, 14). But if it is a day of judgment for the heathen, Israel shall not wholly escape. For in Israel there are many who are not true worshippers of Jehovah. "I will turn my hand upon thee, and throughly purge away thy dross" (Isa. i. 25). "And it shall come to pass at that time that I will search Jerusalem with candles. . . . And I will bring distress upon them, that they shall walk like blind men, because they have sinned against the Lord" (Zeph. i. 12, 17). The very fact that it was an entrance of Jehovah into the course of the world-order, imparted to the Day a wide significance. It was a crisis which should inaugurate a new condition of things. It involved a transformation of the material universe. "Behold I create new heavens and a new earth" (Isa. lxv. 17). "The wilderness and the solitary place shall be glad: and the desert shall rejoice and blossom as the rose" (Isa. xxxv. 1). From being a day, it expands into an era. That era is often regarded as the Messianic age. To the prophets, as Dr A. B. Davidson used to point out, it is entirely homogeneous. There are no incidents within it.

It is the ideal period, in which all the moral principles which have emerged in history are at length finally perfected.

It is needless to say that the conception of the Day of the Lord, in one form or other, continues to hold its place in Judaistic literature. Thus, in Sibyl. Orac. iii. 796 ff., a detailed description is given of the signs which presage the end of all things. This is identical with the establishment of a Divine kingdom "for all times, over all men," which will be an era of peace (Sibyl. Orac. iii. 767 ff.). The idea is specially prominent in the Book of Enoch. Its very first chapter depicts the Judgment. "The great holy One shall go forth from his dwelling, and the God of the world (or the Æon, virtually = the eternal God) shall come from thence to Mount Sinai, and He shall be visible with His hosts, and shall appear in the strength of His might from the heaven of heavens. Then shall all men be afraid . . . and great fear and anguish shall seize them to the ends of the earth. The high mountains shall be shaken, they shall fall and pass away, the high hills shall sink and melt in the flame as wax before fire. The earth shall be rent in pieces, and everything upon it shall perish, and a judgment shall take place upon all. But with the righteous shall He make peace, and protect the elect. Grace shall rule over them, and they shall all belong to God. They shall have His good pleasure and be blessed, and the light of God shall appear to them. And behold, He comes with myriads of saints, to hold judgment upon all, and He shall destroy all the ungodly, and shall correct all flesh on account of all the ungodly acts which ungodly sinners committed" (Enoch i. 3 f.). In the Book of Similitudes (Enoch chaps. xxxvii.-lxxi.) the descriptions are still more remarkable, as here the Messiah is a central figure. Thus, in chap. xlv. 3 f., we read: "On that day shall mine Elect sit on the throne of glory, and shall deal with a selected portion of their (*i.e.* men's) deeds. Their spirit shall be strengthened within them when they see mine Elect, and those who have implored my holy name. On that day will I cause mine Elect one to dwell in their midst, and I will transform heaven, and make it for an everlasting blessing and light. I will transform the earth, and make it a blessing, and cause mine elect ones to dwell upon it: but those who commit sin and misdeeds shall not enter it. For I have beheld my righteous ones, and satisfied them with salvation, and set them before me. But for sinners I have the judgment in store, to extirpate them from the surface of the earth." With this we may compare lxix. 27: "He (*i.e.* the Son of Man) sat on the throne of his glory, and the sum of judgment was committed to him, the Son of Man, and he causes the sinners and those who have beguiled the world, to disappear and to be destroyed from off the face of the earth." Our last example is from Apoc. of Bar. lxxii. 2 ff., "After the miraculous signs, of which thou wast told before, when the peoples are set in confusion and the time of my Messiah is come, then shall he summon all peoples, and some he shall preserve in life, and some he shall slay . . . (lxxiii. 1). And after he has humbled all that is in the world, and has sat down for ever in peace on the throne of his kingdom, then gladness shall be revealed, and rest shall appear." An elaborate picture follows of the blessedness of the Messianic kingdom. Instances might be multiplied from the apocalyptic writings to show the position which this group of conceptions occupied throughout the whole course of Jewish religious thought, and it is natural to find them prominently represented in the literature of the Synagogue (for examples, see Weber, *op. cit.*, pp. 371, 375-380). But enough has been said to indicate their paramount importance for the theology of Judaism (see the important section in Volz, *op. cit.*, pp. 257-270).

To show how powerfully these prophetic anticipations affected St Paul, we have to turn not only to his thought but even to his language. Parallel, *e.g.*, to the description of the Parousia in 1 Thess. iv. 16-17, is Joel ii. 1, 11 (LXX.): *σαλπίσατε σάλπιγγι ἐν Σειών, κηρύξατε ἐν ὄρει ἁγίῳ μου . . . διότι πάρεστιν ἡμέρα κυρίου, ὅτι ἐγγύς . . . καὶ κύριος δώσει φωνὴν αὐτοῦ πρὸ προσώπου δυνάμεως αὐτοῦ, ὅτι πολλή ἐστιν σφόδρα ἡ παρεμβολὴ αὐτοῦ*: "Blow with the trumpet in Zion, make proclamation in My holy mountain . . . because the day of the Lord is at hand, for it is near . . . and the Lord shall put forth His voice before the face of His power, for very great is His camp." With this may be compared some remarkable resemblances from the account of the Theophany at Sinai, given in Exod. xix.: *e.g.*, verse 16, *καὶ ἐγίνοντο φωναὶ καὶ ἀστραπαὶ καὶ νεφέλη γνοφώδης ἐπ' ὄρους Σεινά, φωνὴ τῆς σάλπιγγος ἤχει μέγα . . .*; verse 17, *καὶ ἐξήγαγεν Μωυσῆς τὸν λαὸν εἰς συνάντησιν τοῦ θεοῦ . . .*; verse 18, *τὸ δὲ ὄρος τὸ Σινὰ ἐκαπνίζετο ὅλον διὰ τὸ καταβεβηκέναι ἐπ' αὐτὸ τὸν θεὸν ἐν πυρί*: "And there were voices and lightning flashes and a misty cloud on Mount Sinai; the sound of a trumpet blared loudly . . . And Moses led forth the people to meet God . . . Now the mountain Sinai gave forth smoke everywhere, because God had descended upon it in fire." In 2 Thess. i. 7-10, we have a mosaic of reminiscences from the prophets: *e.g.*, Zech. xiv. 5, *ἥξει κύριος ὁ θεός μου, καὶ πάντες οἱ ἅγιοι μετ᾽ αὐτοῦ*: "The Lord my God shall come, and all His holy ones with Him" (*cf.* 2 Thess. i. 7); Isa. lxvi. 15, *ἰδοὺ γὰρ κύριος ὡς πῦρ ἥξει . . . ἀποδοῦναι ἐν θυμῷ ἐκδίκησιν αὐτοῦ καὶ ἀποσκορακισμὸν αὐτοῦ ἐν φλογὶ πυρός*: "For behold the Lord shall come as fire, with wrath, to render His vengeance and His rejection with a flame of fire"; Jer. x. 25, *ἔκχεον τὸν θυμόν σου ἐπὶ ἔθνη τὰ μὴ εἰδότα σε*: "Pour out thy wrath upon the nations which know thee not" (*cf.* 2 Thess. i. 8); Isa. ii. 10, *εἰσέλθετε εἰς τὰς πέτρας . . . ἀπὸ προσώπου τοῦ φόβου κυρίου καὶ ἀπὸ τῆς δόξης τῆς ἰσχύος αὐτοῦ*: "Enter into the rocks . . . from the presence of the terror of the Lord, and from the glory of His power" (*cf.* 2 Thess. i. 9); Isa. xlix. 3, *δοῦλός μου εἶ σύ, Ἰσραήλ, καὶ ἐν σοὶ ἐνδοξασθήσομαι*: "Thou art my servant, Israel, and in thee will I be glorified" (*cf.* 2 Thess. i. 10). In 2 Thess. ii. 4 ff., a comparison with the Book of Daniel yields most important results. As a parallel to the description of the "man of lawlessness" (ver. 4), we may quote Dan. xi. 36, *καὶ ὑψωθήσεται ὁ βασιλεὺς καὶ μεγαλυνθήσεται ἐπὶ πάντα θεόν, καὶ λαλήσει ὑπέρογκα, καὶ κατευθυνεῖ μέχρις οὗ συντελεσθῇ ἡ ὀργή*: "And the king shall be exalted, and shall be magnified against every god, and shall speak swelling words, and shall experience prosperity until the wrath be fulfilled"; (*cf.* Ezek. xxviii. 2, where the ruler of Tyre says: *θεός εἰμι ἐγώ*). In Dan. vii. 27, the last king that shall arise, *λόγους πρὸς τὸν ὕψιστον λαλήσει*, "shall speak words against the Highest." In Dan. viii. 23-25, a king is described who shall come forth, *πληρουμένων τῶν ἁμαρτιῶν αὐτῶν*, "when their sins have reached a climax" (*cf.* 1 Thess. ii. 16, *εἰς τὸ ἀναπληρῶσαι αὐτῶν τὰς ἁμαρτίας πάντοτε*); several of his characteristics correspond to St Paul's delineations in the passage before us. And the whole paragraph, Dan. xi. 30-40, abounds in traits which are more or less combined in the apostle's description (especially ver. 4). For ver. 8 we may refer to Isa. xi. 4, *ἐν πνεύματι διὰ χειλέων ἀνελεῖ ἀσεβῆ*: "By his breath (or spirit), through his lips, he shall destroy the ungodly," a passage which depicts the operations of Messiah. And we must not omit the remarkable parallel in Enoch lxii. 2 ff., "The Lord of Spirits seated him (*i.e.*, Messiah) on the throne of His glory, and the spirit of righteousness was poured out upon him, and the word of his mouth slew all the sinners, and all the unrighteous were destroyed before his face. And there shall stand up in that day all the kings, and the mighty, and the exalted, and those who hold the earth, and they shall see and recognise him, how he sits on the throne of his glory, and righteousness is judged before him, and no lying word is spoken before them. Then shall pain come upon them as a woman in travail. . . . And one portion of them shall look on the other, and they shall be terrified, and their countenance shall fall, and pain shall seize them, when they see that Son of Man sitting on the throne of his glory."[1] The associated picture of Judgment in 1 Cor. iii. 13-15, recalls Zech. xiii. 9, *διάξω τὸ τρίτον διὰ πυρός, καὶ πυρώσω αὐτοὺς ὡς πυροῦται τὸ ἀργύριον, καὶ δοκιμῶ αὐτοὺς*

[1] *Cf.* Ps. Sol. xvii. 41, *ἐλέγξαι ἄρχοντας καὶ ἐξᾶραι ἁμαρτωλοὺς ἐν ἰσχύι λόγου*; Job iv. 9, *ἀπὸ δὲ πνεύματος ὀργῆς αὐτοῦ* (*i.e.* *κυρίου*) *ἀφανισθήσονται*.

ὡς δοκιμάζεται τὸ χρυσίον: "I will bring the third part through the fire, and will refine them as silver is refined, and will test them as gold is tested." The same imagery is to be found in Mal. iii. 3, and a most striking parallel occurs in Testament of Abrah. xciii. 10, δοκιμάζει τὰ τῶν ἀνθρώπων ἔργα διὰ πυρός· καὶ εἴ τινος τὸ ἔργον κατακαύσει τὸ πῦρ, εὐθὺς λαμβάνει αὐτὸν ὁ ἄγγελος τῆς κρίσεως καὶ ἀποφέρει αὐτὸν εἰς τὸν τόπον τῶν ἁμαρτωλῶν, πικρότατον κολαστήριον· εἴ τινος δὲ τὸ ἔργον τὸ πῦρ δοκιμάσει καὶ μὴ ἅψεται αὐτοῦ, οὗτος δικαιοῦται: "He tests the works of men by fire; and if any man's work is consumed by the fire, straightway the angel of judgment taketh him and carrieth him away into the place of sinners, a most bitter abode of punishment; but if the fire shall test any man's work, and shall not touch it, he is justified." The description of retribution in Rom. ii. 5-9 has a marked Old Testament background. With verses 5-7 we may compare Ps. cx. 5, κύριος ἐκ δεξιῶν σου συνέθλασεν ἐν ἡμέρᾳ ὀργῆς αὐτοῦ βασιλεῖς: "The Lord on thy right hand broke in pieces kings in the day of His wrath"; Prov. xxiv. 12, κύριος καρδίας πάντων γινώσκει . . . ὃς ἀποδίδωσιν ἑκάστῳ κατὰ τὰ ἔργα αὐτοῦ: "The Lord knoweth the hearts of all . . . who rendereth to every man according to his works"; Jer. xvii. 10, ἐγὼ κύριος ἐτάζων καρδίας καὶ δοκιμάζων νεφρούς, τοῦ δοῦναι ἑκάστῳ κατὰ τὰς ὁδοὺς αὐτοῦ: "I, the Lord, am He that searcheth hearts and testeth reins, to give to each according to his ways." The penalties with which the unrighteous are visited, we find foreshadowed in such passages as Isa. viii. 22, καὶ εἰς τὴν γῆν κάτω ἐμβλέψονται· καὶ ἰδοὺ ἀπορία στενὴ καὶ σκότος, θλίψις καὶ στενοχωρία καὶ σκότος ὥστε μὴ βλέπειν: "And they shall look down towards the ground, and behold grievous perplexity and darkness, tribulation and straits and darkness, so that men cannot see." The examples quoted will suffice to reveal the religious environment in which St Paul's *pictures* of the Parousia and the Judgment took shape. One important caution for exegesis may be noted. It is evident that he has lavishly appropriated the vivid metaphors of the prophets just as they stand. It is altogether illegitimate, although the practice is quite common, to interpret with a prosaic literalism in the New Testament those bold poetic images, so dear to the Eastern mind, which readers of the Old Testament like St Paul knew how to estimate in their true significance.

But further, we may expect that the apostle's *conceptions* of these all-important events will also be regulated by the Old Testament delineations. But before we endeavour to examine his ideas of the Parousia and the Judgment, it is worth while observing that the expectations he seems to have had of their imminence, must have been, in a large measure, stimulated by the prophetic teaching. We have seen that various mysterious predictions of Jesus might naturally lead to the hope that His Second Advent was not far distant. And the rapid progress of the Gospel through his own labours and those of his fellow-apostles would suggest to St Paul a speedy preparation of mankind for the Coming of the Lord. The hope thus kindled must have been powerfully fanned by the influence of Old Testament prophecy with its eager expectancy. It has already been observed that when the prophets saw a quickening of the currents of Providence in any direction, they looked upon that as prefiguring the Day of the Lord. It seems to us that St Paul occupied precisely the same position. There were various reasons why he should take this attitude.

To begin with, there was his own religious experience. By means of his contact with the risen Lord, he knows himself to be a partaker of those high spiritual privileges which the prophets had seen afar off and had dimly foreshadowed, as ushering in the new dispensation.[1] He felt as if he stood at the close of one Age (*αἰών*) and at the beginning of another. That other, the era of the Spirit, had already begun to project itself into human life. He can speak of himself as belonging to those "on whom the ends of the ages have come" (*εἰς οὓς τὰ τέλη τῶν αἰώνων κατήντηκεν*, 1 Cor. x. 11). The present is the age which is evil (*τοῦ αἰῶνος τοῦ ἐνεστῶτος πονηροῦ*, Gal. i. 4). But it is passing away (*παράγει γὰρ τὸ σχῆμα τοῦ κόσμου τούτου*, 1 Cor. vii. 31). The future, *ὁ αἰὼν ὁ μέλλων*, is that in which the Kingdom of God must prevail. It will be inaugurated by a crisis like the Day of the Lord. That Day is for the Christian apostle necessarily transformed into the Parousia of Christ, who is the vicegerent of the Father, to whom He has committed all judgment. But besides, the period in which St Paul wrote his Epistles was characterised by a thrill of expectancy. "The numerous popular tumults of a politico-religious kind" (we quote the words of Schürer, *H.J.P.*, ii. 2, p. 149) "which took place in the time of the Roman procurators, give sufficient evidence of the feverish tension with which a miraculous intervention of God in

[1] See especially, Gunkel, *Wirkungen d. heiligen Geistes b. P.* [2] p. 65.

history and the appearance of His kingdom on earth were expected." And finally, the circumstances which attended St Paul's own work as a missionary were in themselves prophetic, for just as the prophets, above all Ezekiel and Daniel, look for the crisis as the culmination of a movement in which evil has reached a height,[1] so the apostle, more especially in his earlier Epistles,[2] discerns the ripening of forces of wickedness, which, he believes, presages the end. This conviction is most vividly disclosed in 1 Thess. ii. 15-16, where he describes the Jews as "those who killed the Lord Jesus and the prophets, and bitterly persecuted us, and please not God, and are opposed

[1] In Judaistic literature this notion, it is interesting to observe, appears most prominently in 4 Ezra and the Apocalypse of Baruch, both of them works belonging, in all probability, to the half-century in which St Paul wrote his epistles. See, *e.g.*, 4 Ezra v. 1-13, vi. 11-26, ix. 3-4; Apoc. Bar. xlviii. 25-41, and esp. lxx. Drummond refers to Sotah ix. 15, Synhed. 97a, from the Mishnah-literature (*Jewish Messiah*, p. 209).

[2] Beyschlag considers that "according to the later and maturer view of the apostle, it is not so much the final culmination of the evil and obduracy of mankind as the victory of the Gospel and the conversion of the world which calls down from heaven the exalted Christ, and brings in His visible dominion of the world" (*N.T. Theol.* ii. p. 260). So also Titius (p. 48), who makes this a distinguishing feature between St Paul and Jewish Apocalyptic. As a matter of fact, we must conceive both ideas as blended together in his thought all along. Certainly the culmination of evil appears to impress him peculiarly at the time when the letters to the Thessalonians were written. The same phenomenon is found in Judaistic literature. The closing period witnesses an abnormal outbreak of evil, *e.g.* Jub. xxiii. 14 calls the generation then living "the evil generation"; Sibyl. Orac. v. 74 speaks of "the last time in which there shall be utterly depraved men"; 4 Ezra v. 1 foretells days in which "the realm of truth shall be hidden, and the land of faith without fruit" (see Volz, *op. cit.*, pp. 179-180).

to all men,[1] preventing us from speaking to the Gentiles that they might be saved, in order to fill up the measure of their sin always. But the wrath (ἡ ὀργή) has come upon them to the uttermost." It is easy, bearing these words in mind, to discover why the Parousia so impresses the apostle at this stage in his activity. The iniquity of his own fellow countrymen is rampant. It takes the most daring form it has ever assumed in prompting the persecution of those who preach the Messiah of God to the heathen. This is an appalling provocation of the Divine judgment. "The wrath" (ἡ ὀργή), the peculiar eschatological visitation of the Divine retribution,[2] is about to sweep down upon them. This will be the first act in the new order of things. The Parousia, the Judgment, the Resurrection of those who have fallen asleep in Jesus—all these tremendous events belong to the same experience.[3] The foregoing suggestions give a clue to the meaning of St Paul's vivid expectations, wherever they occur in his writings. It is not that he possesses any time-schema. He never professes, any

[1] *Cf.* the remarkable parallels from classical writers in T. Reinach's *Textes . . . relatifs au Judaisme*, *e.g.* pp. 284, 295, 303 ff., which disclose the hatred excited by the Jews.

[2] See B. Weiss, *N.T. Theol.* i. pp. 305-306.

[3] Stevens aptly summarises the essence of the related conceptions in the following sentence: "As the kernel of the teaching about the Parousia is the assurance of the triumph of Christ's kingdom, and that concerning the Resurrection is the certainty of immortality, so the teaching concerning Judgment centres in the principle that human life and action bring forth fruit after their kind, and that every man shall receive from God his just recompense of reward" (*A. J. Th.*, Oct. 1902, p. 677). For a fine poetic rendering of St Paul's expectations, see F. W. H. Myers' *St Paul*, pp. 10, 11.

more than his Master, to know when the Parousia will take place. When it does come, it will be sudden, "like a thief in the night" (1 Thess. v. 2).[1] But at times, when the attitude of God's foes appears peculiarly defiant, when the work and saving purpose of God seem to be hindered by a daring outbreak of iniquity, he feels compelled to foreshadow that climax of human history at which the authority of the exalted Messiah asserts itself, and Christ shall appear to vanquish all wickedness, to vindicate the righteous will of God, and to establish finally the Kingdom which shall endure for ever. From the standpoint of the believer, the yearning which underlies the expectation of the Parousia may be fitly expressed in the words of Psalm lxxx. 3: "Cause Thy face to shine, and we shall be saved."

Let us now look more in detail at his conception of the Parousia. Not much requires to be said about the term παρουσία. In the LXX. the noun seems almost without exception to mean "arrival," although there are several instances of the verb in the sense of "being present." In the New Testament the noun usually seems to have the idea of "arrival" in it,

[1] *Cf.* 2 Thess. ii. 1-2, and Heinrici on 1 Cor. xv. 20-22. The question as to when the End will come is a pressing one for apocalyptic literature, *e.g.*: Apoc. Bar. xxiv. 4, "What will happen to our enemies I know not, and when thou wilt visit thy works"; 4 Ezra vi. 59, "If the world has been created on our account, wherefore have we not this our world in possession? How long is it to remain thus?" Sibyl. Orac. iii. 55: "When will that day come?" The most divergent answers are found (see Volz, *op. cit.*, pp. 162 ff.). St Paul's feeling is echoed in such a passage as Apoc. Bar. xxi. 8: "Who . . . alone knowest the consummation of the times before they come." Volz notes that in Rabbinic Judaism the less confident mood is more common than in Apocalyptic, p. 171.

although there are one or two undoubted examples of the simple meaning "presence" (2 Cor. x. 10; Phil. ii. 12; perhaps 2 Thess. ii. 8).[1] The difference of signification is of comparatively little importance, as either would suit the conception. For the arrival of Christ in visible guise on the scene of earthly history, is, after all, only the unveiling of One who is never truly absent from the fortunes of His followers. That this very idea was before the apostle's mind, is proved by several passages where he definitely speaks of the "unveiling" of Christ.[2] See, *e.g.*: 1 Cor. i. 7, "Awaiting the unveiling (ἀποκάλυψιν) of our Lord Jesus Christ"; 2 Thess. i. 7, "To you, who are in tribulation, rest with us at the unveiling (ἀποκαλύψει) of our Lord Jesus from heaven with the angels of His power"; Rom. ii. 5, "The day of the unveiling of the righteous judgment of God." The expression occurs three times in the same sense in 1 Peter (i. 7, i. 13, iv. 13). In Rom. viii. 19, St Paul has the remarkable statement that "the eager expectation of the creation earnestly looks for the unveiling of the sons of God." Hort, who justly traces back the apostolic usage to the words of Jesus Himself in Luke xvii. 30: "Similarly shall it be on the day when the Son of

[1] Bruston interprets the term παρουσία of the "presence" of Christ in heaven. According to his exposition of St Paul's teaching, each believer at death is ushered into the "presence" of the glorified Christ. The final crisis is the unveiling of Christ's presence along with the saints who are in His fellowship before the gaze of the living. His efforts to attain these results by exegesis of the Epistles are more quaint than convincing. (See *Revue de Théologie et de Philos.*, 1895, p. 486 ff.).

[2] *Cf.* 4 Ezra vii. 28: *Revelabitur enim filius meus Messias* (so Gunkel: *Jesus*=Christian correction) *cum his qui cum eo, et jocundabit qui relicti sunt annis quadringentis.*

Man is revealed" (ᾗ ἡμέρᾳ ὁ υἱὸς τοῦ ἀνθρώπου ἀποκαλύπτεται), observes that there is nothing in any of the passages, "apart from the figurative language of 2 Thess., to show that the revelation here spoken of is to be limited to a sudden preternatural theophany. It may be a long and varying process, though ending in a climax. Essentially, it is simply the removal of the veils which hide the unseen Lord, by whatever means they are withdrawn" (on 1 Peter i. 7). For St Paul, at least, the climax holds the chief interest. He believes in a definite moment when the veils are to be withdrawn.

Nevertheless, in marked contrast with the prophetic descriptions of the Day of the Lord, the apostle scarcely ever paints a picture of the Parousia. The only real instance occurs in the earliest of his letters, 1 Thess. iv. 16-18. There he depicts the Lord as descending from heaven with a commanding word (κελεύσματι), with the voice of the archangel and the trumpet of God.[1] Both dead and living shall be

[1] Teichmann discusses elaborately the details of the κέλευσμα, the φωνή, and the σάλπιγξ, summing up the whole event as follows: "While Christ is on His way from heaven to earth, He commands (κελεύσματι) the dead, who have been wakened from their slumber by the call of the archangel and the blowing of the trumpet of God, now in actual reality to arise" (*op. cit.*, pp. 22, 23). He criticises Kabisch for identifying κέλευσμα, φωνὴ ἀρχαγγέλου, and σάλπιγξ θεοῦ. Surely the latter is nearer the truth. It is highly improbable that St Paul ever worked out the picture in its minutiæ. He is simply making use of the traditional imagery belonging to a Theophany. See Exod. xix. 16 ff. (to which reference has already been made). We may here refer to the noteworthy parallel to this appearance of Christ for judgment and the resurrection of the dead which is found in the Persian religion. See Darmesteter, *Ormazd et Ahriman*, p. 227: "The day of great decision stands in close connection with Soshyos,

snatched up together in the clouds, to meet the Lord in the air. It is of little value to inquire into the precise significance of the words εἰς ἀέρα. As Stähelin notes (*op. cit.*, pp. 229-230), they emphasise the *ideal* character of the whole transaction, which takes place in a region exalted above this earth. Similarly, the clouds (ἐν νεφέλαις) are viewed in their common Biblical significance as the mediating space between heaven and earth, which forms, as it were, the pathway into the unseen world (*cf.* Acts i. 9: ἐπήρθη, καὶ νεφέλη ὑπέλαβεν αὐτὸν ἀπὸ τῶν ὀφθαλμῶν αὐτῶν; Rev. xi. 12: ἀνέβησαν εἰς τὸν οὐρανὸν ἐν τῇ νεφέλῃ, see Stähelin, *op. cit.*, p. 225). The immediate goal of this meeting with Christ is left indefinite. We cannot decide whether, in St Paul's view, the ἀπάντησις was for the purpose of escorting the Lord back to earth (so Schmiedel on 1 Thess. iv. 13 f., and, with reserve, Stähelin, *op. cit.*, p. 228) in accordance with the old prophetic anticipations, or whether it was the prelude to their accompanying Him to heaven, although this hypothesis would appear more congruous with the general direction of the apostle's thought. In passages where we might expect the use of vivid imagery, such as 1 Cor. xv., it is entirely absent. One or two touches, indeed, are added in other places to the picture described above. Thus, in 2 Thess. i. 8, the revelation of the Lord Jesus is said to be with the might (δυνάμεως) of His angels, in a fiery flame, (ἐν πυρὶ φλογός).[1] Fire was a characteristic symbol

the Messiah of Parsism, whose function is to awake the dead, to bring immortality into the world, and to endure the last decisive struggle with Angra Mainyu." See also Söderblom, *op. cit.*, p. 224.

[1] Kabisch baselessly supposes that fire, which he describes

of Old Testament Theophanies, see Exod. iii. 2, xix. 18; Ps. xviii. 9-15; Ezek. i. 13; Deut. iv. 24, etc. Again, in 1 Cor. vi. 2, 3, he speaks of the saints as judging the world, apparently indicating thereby that they should form the retinue of the returning Lord. *Cf.* Rev. ii. 26, 27, xx. 4; Wisd. iii. 8 (*κρινοῦσιν* [*i.e.*, *οἱ δίκαιοι*] *ἔθνη καὶ κρατήσουσιν λαῶν*); Dan. vii. 27; Matt. xix. 28.[1]

This lack of pictorial drapery is another reminder of the remarkable sobriety and self-restraint of the apostle in dealing with those eschatological events which gave free play to the most extravagant fancies of Jewish apocalyptic writers. Evidently, apart from Old Testament reminiscences, St Paul was not concerned about framing an imaginary scene, in which the events of the Day of the Lord should group themselves harmoniously. Probably the reason is, that, as Titius puts it, "he does not possess a definite programme of the course of the apocalyptic development" (p. 152). In all likelihood, the longer he lived

here as "pneumatic," "the effect of the spiritual substance of the exalted Christ" (!), will be the instrument of judgment on the ungodly (p. 246). This crude materialism continually mars a discussion which is full of suggestion for Pauline Eschatology.

[1] See Weiss, *ad loc.*: "As they (the disciples) stood next to Jesus in His earthly activity, so will they have the most intimate share in the honour of the exalted Messiah; and as they preached the Gospel to the twelve tribes (*cf.* x. 5, 6), they will pronounce their judgment according as they have received or refused this offer of salvation." Parallels in Judaistic literature are to be found in Enoch i. 9 (already quoted); 4 Ezra xiii. 52: "As no one can investigate or know by experience that which is in the depths of the sea, so no one of the inhabitants of earth can behold my Son or His companions (Gunkel interprets as ≐ 'angels') until the hour of His Day" (*cf.* vii. 28). *Cf.* Volz, *Jüd. Eschatol.* p. 33.

and knew his Lord, the less interest did he feel in forecasts of occurrences for which there was no human standard of comparison.

The Coming or Unveiling of the exalted Lord, in close agreement with Old Testament teaching, is, in one aspect of it, for *judgment.* This conception, as it appears in St Paul's writings, must now be examined with care. Various designations of the crisis occur in the Epistles. In 1 Thess. i. 10, it is called "the coming wrath" (ἡ ὀργὴ ἡ ἐρχομένη); in Rom. ii. 5, "the day of wrath and of the revelation of the righteous judgment of God"; in Rom. ii. 16, "the day when God judgeth the hidden things of men according to my Gospel." In 2 Cor. v. 10, he declares that "we must all be made manifest before the judgment-seat of Christ"; in Rom. xiv. 10, "we shall all appear at the judgment-seat of God"; and he continues, "It is written, As I live, saith the Lord, every knee shall bow to Me, and every tongue shall give honour (ἐξομολογήσεται) to God." (*Cf.* Enoch xlviii. 5: "All who dwell on earth shall fall down and bow the knee before Him, and shall bless and laud and celebrate with song the Lord of Spirits"; also lxii. 6, 9, 10, lxiii.) In 1 Cor. iii. 13, the apostle speaks of the event as "the day" (*cf.* 2 Thess. i. 10, "that day"). Perhaps its most characteristic title for him is "the day of our Lord Jesus Christ" (1 Cor. i. 8), "the day of Christ Jesus" (Phil. i. 6), or simply, "the day of Christ' (Phil. ii. 16, i. 10).[1] These designations at once

[1] We have an instance of that almost wilful misapprehension of St Paul's thought which shows itself here and there in Kabisch's treatment of Pauline Eschatology, in the emphasis which he lays upon ἡμέρα κυρίου as the "*time of light*" as opposed to the era of darkness (p. 236).

reveal the intimate connection of the apostle's idea of judgment with the prophetic conception of the "Day of the Lord." Only, on the one hand, the horizon has immensely widened. On the other, the somewhat vague pictures of God's judgment which the prophets clothe in various forms, have given place to the definite intervention of the exalted Lord, Jesus Christ, armed with complete authority. Here it is plain that St Paul has taken his stand on the teaching of Jesus Himself. For there can be no doubt whatever that one of the lofty claims which our Lord put forward with emphasis and frequency, was His position as the Judge of the final destinies of mankind. It will suffice to refer to such familiar passages as Matt. vii. 22, 23, xiii. 41 f., xxv. 31 f. This was the point, we may say, at which the foundations of a distinctly Christian Eschatology were laid. There was nothing to correspond to it in Judaism. There could not be, for the Jews had never conceived of a Messiah who should pass through a career of earthly activity, a career checked by death, and then return as the medium of God's final purpose for the universe. The truth took firm hold of the apostles. Again and again, in the history of their labours, we find it set in the forefront. See Acts x. 42, xvii. 31, xxiv. 25. This was inevitable. For the proclamation of judgment must ever be one of the most powerful weapons in the hands of the missionary. It is one of those appeals which first find an echo in the burdened conscience. When, as in their preaching, it was a judgment wielded by that Saviour whom they knew, its solemnity and terror must be tempered by the pity of eternal love.[1]

[1] Wernle, who is rightly alive to the importance of the

The judgment of Christ is destined for Jews and heathen alike. St Paul has passed far beyond a purified theocracy. This broader outlook, as we have seen, had already established itself in Judaism. It was bound to accompany the emergence into prominence of the influential eschatological doctrine of the two Æons. The very statement of such a conception implies its universal bearing. The Judgment, which marks the transition between the old Æon and the new, would be meaningless unless it embraced all mankind.[1] "The day of judgment will be the end of this period (and the beginning) of the future immortal period in which corruption has passed away" (4 Ezra vii. 113). It is final, for it inaugurates the end of the present. It is the inevitable preparation for the pure and perfected Kingdom of God.[2] But even if this stage in the conception had not been reached in Judaism,

judgment in missionary preaching, misconceives both the facts and the apostle's position when he writes: "The preaching of judgment has only this aim: it does not attempt to make men better, but to make believers. By this preaching of judgment, Paul draws heathen to Christianity: that is different from giving Christians in the Church comfort as regards their sins" (*Der Christ u. die Sünde bei Paulus*, p. 99). It is this isolating of the various elements of the Christian Gospel in a mechanical fashion which leads to the discovery of contradictions in Paulinism, where there are none. St Paul, no more than the modern intelligent Christian, looks upon the Christian life as a tightly-shut compartment into which the believer enters, and which he can never leave. The reminder of judgment is quite as necessary in the ordinary work of the Church, as in making appeals to those who are still outside.

[1] *Cf.* Bousset, *Religion d. Judenthums*, p. 246.

[2] This aspect of the judgment is specially prominent in the second example quoted from Matthew above.

the world-central position of the exalted Christ for St Paul would necessarily have involved its formulation. He is the Saviour and Lord of all. He is "the Image of the invisible God, the First-born of all creation. . . . All things were created by Him, and for Him: and He is before all things, and by Him all things consist" (Col. i. 15, 17). His Gospel is the winnowing-fan which sifts humanity. Men's attitude to Him and to the revelation of God which He has given, is the touchstone of their eternal destiny.

There are several features of St Paul's conception of judgment which claim special attention. Here, as in the case of the Parousia, there is an almost complete lack of scenery. We seem to pass into a new atmosphere, when we turn from the exuberant and often bizarre fantasies of the Jewish apocalyptic writers (*e.g.*, Enoch, Slavon. Enoch, Apoc. Bar., even 4 Ezra) to the solemn, restrained, and genuinely ethical statements of the apostle, whose mind appears to be wholly concentrated on the spiritual issues. No less marked is the contrast between the comparative *prominence* assigned to this conception in the Pauline Epistles and the pseudepigraphal literature. In the latter group of writings, it stands in the forefront. These authors delight to linger over its circumstances. Such a predilection, no doubt, is partly due to the fact that their faith largely consists in the conviction of Divine retribution: that the condemnation of the ungodly (more especially the foes of Israel) and the vindication of the righteous (more especially Israelites) absorb their interest in the future of the Kingdom of God. It is true that in the later apocalyptic books, as, *e.g.*, Jubilees, the idea of the Judgment falls into the background owing to the belief that reward or punishment is meted out immediately after death (see Clemen, *Niedergefahren zu d. Toten*, p. 149). This applies in particular to the writings of Hellenistic Judaism. In the Wisdom of Solomon, indeed, mention is made of a day of judgment (*ἡμέρα διαγνώσεως, ἐξέτασις, ἐπισκοπὴ ψυχῶν*, this latter term *ἐπισκοπή*, with the verb *ἐπισκέψασθαι*, Latin, *visitare* being a sort of technical expression in apocalyptic literature for the return of God to judgment; *cf.* Ps. Sol. xv. 12; Apoc. Bar. lxxxiii. 2; Enoch lx. 6); but it is exceedingly difficult to combine it with the conception of retribution for the individual immediately after death, a conception dominant in this branch of Jewish thought, which did not admit a resurrection of the dead.[1] But even in 4 Ezra, which probably belongs to the last quarter of the first century A.D., and so ranks among the latest products of its class, room is left for a final allotment of penalties and rewards at the End.

Probably St Paul's *comparative* reticence as to the Judgment, and the lack of elaborate treatment of the event in his letters, should be connected with the nature of his conception of salvation. The sinner who is justified by faith, receives already a new standing before God. "There is, therefore, now (*νῦν*) no condemnation (*κατάκριμα*) to those that are in Christ Jesus, who walk not after the flesh but after the Spirit" (Rom. viii. 1). They already belong to the class designated as *οἱ σωζόμενοι* (1 Cor. i. 18;

[1] See Bousset, *op. cit.*, p. 282. It is of interest to note that, in later Jewish Apocalyptic, the chief feature connected with the Judgment is the practical issue, that the ungodly reap their punishment, and the pious their reward. See Volz, *op. cit.*, p. 85.

2 Cor. ii. 15). There awaits them the final salvation, ἡ σωτηρία. See, *e.g.*, Phil. ii. 12, τὴν ἑαυτῶν σωτηρίαν κατεργάζεσθε; Rom. i. 16, δύναμις γὰρ θεοῦ ἐστιν εἰς σωτηρίαν; Phil. i. 28, ἥτις ἐστὶν αὐτοῖς ἔνδειξις ἀπωλείας, ὑμῶν δὲ σωτηρίας. The converse of σωτηρία is invariably ἀπώλεια, and there are those who belong already to οἱ ἀπολλύμενοι. Their end (τέλος) is ἀπώλεια (Phil. iii. 19). They have rejected the gospel of Jesus Christ. They have despised the riches of God's goodness and forbearance and long-suffering, and hence, in accordance with their hardness and impenitence of heart, they treasure up for themselves wrath in view of the day of wrath, and revelation of the righteous judgment of God (Rom. ii. 4-8).

It is, perhaps, difficult to realise how the apostle would adjust this conception of salvation and all that it involves to the more traditional idea of a judgment-day, when each shall be rewarded according to his deeds. For, obviously, in a very real sense, God's judgment on the believer, according to St Paul's view, has already been pronounced in the act of justification. He has received the forgiveness of his sins in Jesus Christ. How can there be any further place for acquittal or condemnation? So also, on the other hand, those who have refused to surrender to the love of God, established in the Cross of Christ, have thereby, in the apostle's estimation, pronounced their own judgment. "If our Gospel be hid, it is hid to them that are lost: in whom the god of this world hath blinded the minds of them which believe not, lest the light of the glorious Gospel of Christ, who is the Image of God, should shine unto them" (2 Cor. iv. 3, 4). The problem is, to find some mediation between that aspect of St Paul's thought which may be called retribution, which seems to look exclusively to God's final verdict on human conduct, and the other, which we know as justification, of whose effects we are conscious already in the present. This difficulty has led to misapprehensions of St Paul's conception. Thus Reuss asserts that the final Judgment is a purely Jewish-Christian idea, "having no natural link with the evangelical doctrine of Paul." For, from the fact of union with Christ, it follows that judgment takes place on this side of the grave (*Histoire de la Théol. Chrét.* ii. p. 221). Teichmann considers that St Paul has two parallel but irreconcilable ideas of judgment, the one ethical, the other belonging to the close of history (*op. cit.*, pp. 81-83). For Christians, he holds, the latter must be done away with, for in their case St Paul leaves out of account all human action. Everything, with them, rests on faith and the bestowal of the Holy Spirit. There is no room for a final judgment as to their deeds (p. 103). These are examples of a type of criticism which is constantly applied to the apostle's doctrine. And at first sight it seems plausible enough. Yet this apparent incongruity of thought, on which so much stress has been laid, really pervades all Christian experience. A lively faith assures believers that God has begun His good work in them; nevertheless, most of them must tremble as they anticipate, in their inmost self-knowledge, the verdict of Him who is the Searcher of hearts. Not only so, but justification has no meaning, cannot be understood, apart from its practical results. No one was ever more fully alive to this than St Paul himself. The sixth, seventh, and eighth chapters of Romans are sufficient proof of it. Those who have been fully justified must, from the nature of the case, walk after the Spirit, and not after the flesh. To continue heedlessly in sin, is to make void the grace of God. "How shall we, that are dead to sin (*i.e.* have broken our connection with our sinful environment in Christ Jesus), live any longer therein?" (Rom. vi. 2). "No," says the apostle, and he is speaking to believers, "if ye live after the flesh, ye shall die" (Rom. viii. 13). So that there is no real contradiction between that group of ideas which centre round justification, and a statement like Gal. vi. 8: "Whatsoever a man soweth, that shall he also reap; for he that soweth to his own flesh shall of the flesh reap corruption (or destruction, φθοράν), but he that soweth to the Spirit shall of the Spirit reap life everlasting." The forgiven man must live as one who is under the profoundest obligations to the grace of God, and the only fulfilment of such obligations is a life of righteousness. That life, which is the sowing to the Spirit, is possible solely through the Spirit's aid, and His aid is given exclusively to those who abide in fellowship with Christ (Rom. viii. 8-10). Now, as we have hinted above, believers will always be conscious of their utterly imperfect service. The clearer their knowledge of God, the more glaring must appear to them the contrast between what they are and what they might have been. Hence the final verdict of God upon their completed lives is for them no mere dramatic scene, belonging to a stage of reflection which is now antiquated. It meets a craving of human conscience which can find full satisfaction in no other direction. Accordingly, it is altogether untrue to the workings of the spirit of a Christian to say that St Paul has clung by force of tradition to the Old Testament conception of the

Day of the Lord, while his real idea of judgment bears no relation to it. The same kind of profound paradox runs through all his deepest thoughts. For example, he can say in one place (Rom. viii. 16), "The Spirit beareth witness with our spirit that we are children of God"; and yet in another (Phil. iii. 11), "If haply I may attain unto the resurrection from the dead"; (see 1 Cor. iv. 4; and *cf.* the utterance of Jochanan b. Sakkai, *Tanchuma*, *Schofetim*, sect. 7, qu. by Volz, *op. cit.*, p. 118, "Woe to us in the day of judgment, woe to us in the day of correction"). In an exultant mood he can exclaim (Rom. viii. 33), "Who shall lay anything to the charge of God's elect?"; but at a later time (Phil. ii. 12), "With fear and trembling, work out your own salvation to the end" (κατεργάζεσθε). And all who, like the apostle, set the loftiest spiritual ideals before them, while never distrusting the grace of God, which is able to keep them from falling, will ever distrust themselves, lest in the end they should prove unworthy of God's high calling in Christ Jesus.

It does not appear as if St Paul had worked out in any detail the actual events and processes of the final Judgment. If we view this solemn crisis, however, in close connection with the rest of his teaching, it is plain that the judgment of the σωζόμενοι will be their admission into the heritage of glory. That is to say, he regards it as the decisive confirmation of that earlier acceptance of them in Christ, the confirmation which absolutely fixes their eternal destiny.[1] They

[1] *Cf.* Clemen, *Niedergefahren zu d. Toten*, p. 143; Titius, p. 152; also Castelli, *J.Q.R.*, i. p. 343. Charles puts the facts strikingly: "(Paul) teaches that at the consummation of the universe, all rational beings will receive their due unto the full.

shall obtain "everlasting life" (Rom. ii. 7, vi. 23; Gal. vi. 8).[1] For the ἀπολλύμενοι, judgment will mean the experience of the ὀργή of God. Its effect is exclusion from the Kingdom of God. Such exclusion is nothing else than ἀπώλεια.

Perhaps one reason why St Paul speaks so seldom in detail regarding the Judgment, and never apparently fixes a definite place for it in the sequence of the Last Things,[2] may be found in the fact that he seems usually to have the *living* in view. As we have noted, he does not expect that the End is far distant. Whether he survives to that day or not, he deems it probable that many of his brethren will. So that such questions as the relation of an Intermediate State, or of the Resurrection, to the Judgment, do not come prominently within his horizon.[3] He writes concerning the Day of the Lord, not with a theoretical but with a practical interest. He desires to set its grave issues before members of those Christian communities which are dear to him, men and women who may themselves experience the Parousia. Hence, he treats the Judgment altogether from the side of its

According to the doctrine of the kingdom, individual members cannot reach that consummation apart from the consummation of the blessedness of all" (*Eschatology*, p. 399). This brings out an element in the conception which St Paul does not explicitly emphasise, but which, even from his relation to the Old Testament, not to speak of the teaching of Jesus, must have been tacitly present to his mind.

[1] These passages are most instructive for the light they shed upon St Paul's twofold conception of Judgment. This twofold conception, in a more elementary form, is also apparent in the literature of Judaism; see Volz, *op. cit.*, pp. 111-115.

[2] See Heinrici on 1 Cor. xv. 22.

[3] *Cf.* Wernle, *Anfänge*, etc., p. 174; Orr, *Christian View*, p. 335 f.

spiritual significance, refraining from all curious speculations as to its method and guise. Moreover, in a number of important passages, he is thinking exclusively of Christians. It is so, for example, in 2 Cor. v. 9, 10: "Wherefore also we make it our ambition, whether present or absent, to be well pleasing to Him. For all of us must be made manifest (φανερωθῆναι, shown in our true colours) before the judgment seat of Christ, that each may receive the things done in the body, according to what he did, whether good or worthless" (φαῦλον). The context of this passage makes it clear that he has believers in his mind. It is the last clause alone which might suggest, and has suggested, the opposite. But, as it happens, we find an entirely relevant parallel in 1 Cor. iii. 12-16. In this section of the Epistle he is dealing with the work of Christian teachers. He himself had laid the foundation. But the crucial point is, What kind of building is being erected upon it? "Let each," he says, "take heed how he raises a building upon it" (ἐποικοδομεῖ, verse 10). But, be that as it may, "if any one builds up upon the foundation (τὸν θεμέλιον = Ἰησοῦς Χριστός) gold, silver, precious stones, wood, hay, stubble, the work of each shall be made manifest (φανερὸν γενήσεται): for the day shall declare it, because by fire (ἐν πυρί) it is laid bare (ἀποκαλύπτεται), and the fire itself shall test each man's work of what quality (ὁποῖον) it is. If any man's work, which he built up, shall remain, he shall receive a reward; if any man's work shall be consumed, he shall be punished (ζημιωθήσεται), but he himself shall be saved, yet in such a way as by fire." He recognises the many imperfections in the service and activities of Christian workers. These will be made manifest in the day of judgment. God's welcome to them must necessarily be affected by the greater or less degree of unworthiness (φαῦλον) which the sum of their life discloses, so that, even within the sphere of salvation, men shall receive according to the things done in the body. St Paul accepts, that is to say, the conclusion which commends itself to every reasonable mind—a conclusion authenticated by our Lord Himself in the parables of the Talents and the Pounds—that in the future consummated Kingdom of God, each will receive that portion for which his spiritual capacities have fitted him. This truth has not received the emphasis in New Testament theology to which it is entitled. "It is neither according to Scripture, nor to moral instinct, to depict the Final Judgment as implying that all in whom the same *set* of character exists receive an equal reward or penalty. It is strange how much the doctrine of a destiny proportionate to the measure of fidelity or failure, so perpetually on our Lord's lips, has become a 'lost theological principle.' It must be recovered, if we are to bring the fundamental conceptions of a final Judgment and a final Kingdom of righteousness into relation with the moral facts of life" (Forrest, *Christ of History*, etc., p. 367).[1]

[1] *Cf.* Cone, *New World*, 1895, p. 299; and for a fine imaginative rendering of the thought, Dante's *Paradiso*, xxxii. 50-58. Degrees of bliss form a prominent doctrine in the Persian religion. The highest blessedness is to reach the "House of Hymns" (garôtmân): the next highest condition is called the "best existence," and is divided into the "space of the sun," that "of the moon," and that "of the stars." These are attained according as certain special virtues have been practised (see Söderblom, *op, cit.*, p. 128). For numerous examples in Jewish literature, more especially the Rabbinic, see Volz, *op. cit.*, pp. 366, 367

From these passages and from others, notably, *e.g.*, 1 Cor. iv. 5, "Do not come to any judgment (*i.e.* on St Paul and his work) before the time, until the Lord come, who shall bring to light the hidden things of darkness, and shall reveal the schemes of many hearts" (*cf.* the exact parallel in Rom. ii. 16, "the day when God shall judge the secrets of men by Jesus Christ according to my Gospel"), it is evident that the idea which stands out most sharply before him in connection with the *process* of judgment, is the revelation of the secrets of human souls to themselves and probably to others, the testing of human character by a severe experience, which he symbolises by fire. These ideas have their anticipations in the Old Testament and in the literature of Judaism. As to the revealing of the hidden realities of human character, we may quote Prov. xxiv. 12 (LXX.), "The Lord knoweth the hearts of all . . . who shall render to every man according to his deeds"; Eccl. xii. 14, "God shall bring every work into judgment with every secret thing, whether it be good or whether it be evil." The same thought appears in such passages as Sirach i. 39, "The Lord shall reveal thy secrets, and in the midst of the assembly (συναγωγῆς) shall cast thee down"; Apoc. Bar. lxxxiii. 1 ff., "The Most High shall assuredly hasten the times, and He shall assuredly bring on His hours. And He shall assuredly judge those who are in His world, and shall visit in truth all things by means of all their hidden works. And He shall assuredly examine the secret thoughts, and that which is laid up in the secret chambers of all the members of man, and shall make them manifest in the sight of all, with reproof." *Cf.* the Arabic poet Zuhair: "Whatever men seek to hide from God, He knoweth: it is reserved, laid up in writing, and kept in store against the day of reckoning" (qu. by Bevan, *Daniel*, p. 123). The idea occurs repeatedly in Jewish literature, *e.g.*, Enoch xlix. 4, ix. 5; Slav. Enoch xlvi. 3: "When God shall send a great light, by means of that there shall be judgment to the just and unjust, and nothing shall be concealed." The closely-related conception of a testing as by fire is foreshadowed by similar expressions in the prophets, *e.g.*, Zech. xiii. 9, "I will bring the third part through the fire, and will refine them (πυρώσω in LXX.) as silver is refined, and will try them as gold is tried"; Mal. iii. 2, 3, "But who may abide the day of His coming (=the Day of the Lord), and who shall stand when He appears? for He is like a refiner's fire (πῦρ χωνευτηρίου), and like fuller's soap: and He shall sit as a refiner and purifier of silver; and He shall purify the sons of Levi, and purge them as gold and silver."[1] The thought which underlies

[1] See also the remarkable passage already quoted from Testament of Abraham xciii. 10, and a very materialistic picture in Sibyl. Orac. iii. 80-91; and *cf.* the most striking parallel of the ordeal by fire in the Persian religion, "The two blessings (*i.e.* salvation and immortality) mayest thou give (in harmony) with the holy spirit, O Mazda Ahura, by means of the decision with fire" (Yasna xlvii. 6). "The last judgment . . . will dispense to men reward and punishment. Then the earth will be purified by the fiery metal-stream. All men shall enter the fire-stream, which is felt by the pious like a bath in tepid milk, by the wicked as a frightful torture . . . With the tribulation of earth, the fire devours also the hell of Ahriman and the serpent" (F. Justi, *Preussische Jahrbücher*, Bd. 88, Hft. 1, p. 242; *cf.* Böklen, *op. cit.*, pp. 119, 121). The idea of fire as a purifying agent occurs in the Alexandrian Fathers—*e.g.* Clem. Alex., *Strom.* vii. 6, p. 851: φαμὲν δ' ἡμεῖς ἁγιάζειν τὸ πῦρ, οὐ τὰ κρέα, ἀλλὰ τὰς ἁμαρτωλοὺς ψυχάς· πῦρ οὐ τὸ παμφάγον καὶ βάναυσον, ἀλλὰ τὸ φρό-

those statements of St Paul which we have quoted, is entirely in accord with much recent philosophical speculation on the ultimate issues of life.[1] No future life can be conceived without the consciousness of self-identity. But this consciousness must depend on memory. Is there not profound truth in the idea that the self-identity of a personality fully realised will rest upon a memory wholly unclouded, in which all past experience, and every part of it, is grasped, as it were, in one perception. Would not such a perception in itself prove a tremendous factor in the process of retribution?[2]

We must defer to a later chapter the consideration of St Paul's teaching on future bliss and future punishment. And the relation of the Parousia and the Judgment to the Resurrection can be more conveniently treated when that central province of his Eschatology is under review. But it is necessary, before quitting the subject of the Parousia itself, to examine the difficult passage which deals with the mysterious figure of the "man of lawlessness" (2 Thess. ii. 3-12). Considerable light has been shed upon this whole conception by recent studies in the history of religion. Of these we shall endeavour to make use, but we must first form as clear an idea as possible of St Paul's statement in 2 Thess. ii. The statement is not made for its own sake, but to correct the erroneous notion prevalent at Thessalonica that

νιμον λέγοντες τὸ διϊκνούμενον διὰ ψυχῆς . . . τὸ πῦρ; also Origen, *c. Celsum* iv. 21: *οὐκ ἀρνούμεθα οὖν τὸ καθάρσιον πῦρ, καὶ τὴν τοῦ κόσμου φθορὰν ἐπὶ καθαιρέσει τῆς κακίας καὶ ἀνακαινώσει τοῦ παντός.*

[1] See, *e.g.*, F. C. S. Schiller, *Riddles of the Sphinx*, pp. 399, 400.

[2] For a very concise and well-balanced summary of St Paul's conception of Judgment, see Heinrici on 2 Cor. v. 10.

the Parousia was to take place immediately. The apostle declares that certain events must precede it. The first of these he names the "apostasy" (ἡ ἀποστασία). Apparently coincident with the "apostasy," or closely subsequent to it, is the revelation (ἀποκαλυφθῇ) of the "man of lawlessness" (ὁ ἄνθρωπος τῆς ἀνομίας), "the son of destruction, who opposes and raises himself up against every one called God, or object of reverence (σέβασμα), so as to take his seat in the temple of God, giving forth (ἀποδεικνύντα ἑαυτόν) that he is God." But this revelation is for the present hindered. "Ye know the restraining force" (τὸ κατέχον). Already, indeed, "the mystery of lawlessness" (τὸ μυστήριον τῆς ἀνομίας) is in operation. "Only, the restrainer is now (present), until he be taken out of the way (ἐκ μέσου γένηται). And then shall be revealed the lawless one, whom the Lord Jesus shall slay by the breath of His mouth (τῷ πνεύματι τοῦ στόματος αὐτοῦ), and destroy by the radiance (ἐπιφανείᾳ) of His Parousia; whose whole coming (or appearance, παρουσία) is according to the power of Satan, sheer force (so Weizsäcker, admirably), signs and wonders of lying, sheer deception of unrighteousness for the lost, for the reason that they did not receive the love of the truth to their salvation. Therefore God sends them the power of deception that they should believe falsehood, so that they all might be judged who did not believe the truth, but had their pleasure in unrighteousness."

In examining this description, certain preliminary points may be noted. The dimness and vagueness in the outlines of the figure here presented may be partly explained by St Paul's statement in verse 5: "Do ye not remember that while I was yet with you

I spoke to you of these things?" There is no need for him to do more than recall to their minds the remarkable picture whose details he must have explained to them orally in his preaching at Thessalonica. This is no doubt a consideration which may often serve to explain perplexing allusions in the apostolic writers. Further, as we have already discovered, a number of features in the description have noteworthy parallels in the Book of Daniel, a writing of extraordinary significance and importance for the early Christian Church. These parallels are echoed in the New Testament in the great eschatological discourse of Matt. xxiv. (parallel in Mark xiii.), in 1 John ii. 18 f., iv. 3, and in Rev. xiii. (especially verses 4-7, 13-15).[1] Can we find any clue to the genesis of this conception of a Person in whom the forces of evil are concentrated, rising up in blasphemy, seducing men by deceit, giving himself out as the antagonist of the true God? Several recent investigators have come forward with attempted solutions of the problem. W. Bousset, in particular, who has made a careful and exhaustive study of the subject (*Der Antichrist*, Göttingen, 1895; E. Tr. by A. H. Keane, *The Antichrist Legend*, 1896), endeavours to trace the conception through a long tradition, back to the old Babylonian myth of the Dragon which stormed the abode of God. The next phase he finds in the wicked angel of Judaism, Belial[2] (or Beliar), who becomes the ruler of the

[1] Holtzmann exaggerates when he says that there is no real parallel to our passage in the New Testament except Rev. xiii. 5-8, 12-17, xvi. 9-11 (*N.T. Theol.* ii. p. 192).

[2] M. Friedländer attempts to prove that in the last pre-Christian century Beliar was the demonic embodiment of an

ethereal region (*cf.* "The prince of the power of the air, the spirit that now worketh in the children of disobedience," Eph. ii. 2), and thus a rival to the Divine power. The tradition, which culminates in the conception of Antichrist, he regards as an esoteric doctrine handed down orally in Judaism. Various traits derived from contemporary circumstances are added from time to time to the hateful figure, which is the incarnation of insolent wickedness. Thus, in the epoch of Daniel, the blasphemy and cruelty of Antiochus Epiphanes supply some prominent features. While, for the minds of the early Christians, it is natural that this demoniac power, which was opposed to God and all goodness, should be transformed into the idea of a false Messiah, who arises out of Judaism, which had rejected and crucified the true Christ, and appears among the Jews in Jerusalem, doing wonderful works

antinomian spirit which pervaded a very powerful Jewish sect, designated מִינִים in the Talmud. He lays great stress on the character of Beliar as the seducer, from the LXX. translation of "children of Belial," by ἄνδρες παράνομοι in Deut. xiii. 13, and compares Judg. xix. 22, xx. 13; Prov. vi. 12; 2 Sam. xxiii. 5-7. As we approach the Christian era, he holds, Beliar grows beyond the range of anything human, until at length he represents Satan in human form (*cf.* Sibyl. Orac. iii. 63-75). Along these lines he comes to be the prototype of Antichrist (*Der Antichrist in d. vorchristlichen jüdischen Quellen*, Gött., 1901). There are probably true elements in this hypothesis, but its basis seems decidedly questionable. *Cf.* Volz, *op. cit.*, p. 77, who, among various instances of renegade Jews designated "sons of Belial," quotes *Kidduschin*, 66a, where an evil adviser, who stirs up the Maccabæan princes against the Pharisees, is called a Belial. This application of the name to Jewish apostates corroborates the view of ὁ ἄνομος which has been taken in the text.

by the help of Satan, and ultimately seating himself n the temple of God. Bousset goes the length of saying, that in all probability "man of lawlessness" is a translation of the Hebrew *Belial*[1] (for his theory, see *The Antichrist Legend*, especially pp. 30, 128, 137, 144, 155, 165, 166, 182).[2]

There is probably a mixture of fact and mere hypothesis in these statements. The notion of an esoteric, eschatological tradition handed down orally in Judaism, is a pretty theory, but where are we to find a sure basis for it? We are by no means certain that clear traces of it are to be discerned in Rev. xi., in the Beast that comes up out of the abyss and makes war with the two witnesses, and kills them.[3] For symbolic figures of this description (having their basis, no doubt, in popular mythology) occur in the most arbitrary fashion throughout the whole province of apocalyptic literature. Compare the various Beasts of Daniel, the symbolic oxen and heifers and sheep of Enoch (lxxxv.-xc.), and the three-headed

[1] *Cf.* the preceding note.

[2] Gunkel agrees with him as regards an eschatological tradition which goes back to the primitive Babylonian conception of the conflict between order and chaos, symbolised by the struggle between Marduk, the supreme god of Babylon, and Tiamat, the dragon of the abyss. "The ἄνομος-expectation of 2 Thessalonians," he says, "is not the arbitrary invention of an individual, but only the expression of a belief which had arisen throughout a long history, and was at that time widely circulated . . . Since Daniel (xi. 36), it is declared that this culmination of evil (expected by Judaism) would be embodied in a man who insolently violates everything sacred, even the temple of God in Jerusalem. *Cf.* also 3 Macc. i., Ps. Sol. i." (*Schöpfung und Chaos*, p. 221).

[3] M. R. James (in his article on "Man of Sin," *H.D.B.*) agrees with Bousset in this identification.

eagle rising out of the sea and the roaring lion of the forest in 4 Ezra (xi., xii.). To emphasise the fact that the scene of these occurrences (in Rev. xi.) is Jerusalem (so Bousset, p. 20), contributes little to the matter in hand. For in the Apocalypse (in accordance with its Old Testament background) Jerusalem is necessarily a central point in the drama of history. Bousset makes reference to the eschatological discourse of Jesus in Matt. xxiv., assuming that "the distinctly apocalyptic part is a fragment of foreign origin introduced amid genuine utterances of the Lord" (p. 23). This is an assumption which we have already seen grave reasons to doubt. But after making it, he finds it needful to apply 2 Thess. ii. to explain the passage. In our judgment, it seems much more probable (and we think that our investigation so far goes to prove it) that echoes of a genuine tradition of Jesus' words are to be found in the statements of St Paul. But we are astonished to find that the hypothesis of an oral, esoteric teaching is mainly based on eschatological commentaries of the Fathers, such as Hippolytus, Irenæus, and Victorinus of Pettau. This is, at best, a precarious foundation on which to rest. The mere figure of Antichrist, perhaps mainly derived from 2 Thess. ii., and viewed in the light of (*a*) the sayings of Jesus as to false Christs and false prophets, (*b*) the references in the Johannine Epistles to deceivers (who are called ἀντίχριστοι), (*c*) the mysterious Beasts of the Apocalypse (largely reflecting the appalling impression of Nero's cruelties), (*d*) the picture of Antiochus Epiphanes in Dan. xi., and (*e*) Ezekiel's descriptions of the attacks of Gog upon the chosen people (chaps. xxxviii., xxxix.), was sufficient in itself to inflame the imaginations of spiritualising commentators, and to produce a whole apparatus of accompanying details which require no link of connection with an earlier esoteric tradition. At the same time, without attempting any elaborate discussion of the Antichrist-doctrine, we can certainly gather from an examination of the passage in 2 Thess. ii. that the idea is not one which sprang up in a moment, or as the result of the speculations of any single individual. Thus in Ezek. xxxviii. (already cited), we find the conception of a final assault of a heathen prince upon the people of God. "It shall come to pass in the *latter days* that I will bring thee against my land, that the nations may know thee, when I shall be sanctified in thee, O Gog, before their eyes (verse 16). . . . Thou shalt fall upon the mountains of Israel, thou and all thy hordes, and the peoples that are with thee: I will give thee unto the ravenous birds of every sort, and to the beasts of the field to be devoured" (xxxix. 4, R.V.).[1] This conception may have been allied with some popular tradition, but it would be unwise to

[1] *Cf.* Apoc. Bar. xli.: "The last ruler of that time shall be left alive, when the multitudes of his hosts are destroyed, and shall be bound with chains. And they shall take him up to Mount Zion, and my Messiah shall convict him of his insolent deeds, and he shall gather and set before him all the deeds of his hosts. And afterwards he shall put him to death." Bousset's remarkable quotation from Sibyl. Orac. iii. 46 ff. is regarded by Jülicher, on good grounds, as of Christian and not Jewish origin, and as referring to Simon Magus (*Th. L.Z.*, 1896, Sp. 379). The enormous literature which sprang up in the early Christian centuries round the name and fortunes of Simon Magus is, in itself, a proof of the inherent tendency to speculations of the Antichrist type in connection with a far-reaching religious movement. The same phenomena are to be found in the heretical books of the Middle Ages,

dogmatise. In Dan. vii., we find something of a parallel picture. The seer has the vision of the fourth Beast "dreadful and terrible . . . it devoured and brake in pieces and stamped the residue with the feet of it. . . . I beheld till the thrones were cast down, and the Ancient of Days did sit. . . . His throne was like the fiery flame, and His wheels as burning fire. . . . I beheld them because of the voice of the great words which the horn spake: I beheld even till the beast was slain, and his body destroyed and given to the burning flame" (verses 7, 9, 11). Here, again, there is the destruction at the end of time of a brutal and boastful force which has risen against the Most High. Its destruction prepares the way for the possession of the kingdom by the saints of the Most High (verse 22). In Dan. xi. there is that portrayal of a profane and blasphemous king, with which, as we have seen, St Paul is familiar. "His heart shall be against the holy covenant. . . . Such as do wickedly against the covenant shall he pervert by flatteries. . . . And the king shall do according to his will; and he shall exalt himself, and magnify himself above every god, and shall speak marvellous things against the God of gods: and he shall prosper till the indignation be accomplished: for that which is determined shall be done" (verses 28, 32, 36). Probably most of these traits belong to Antiochus Epiphanes, whom the seer may have regarded as fulfilling some terrible expectation associated with the End. In any case, bearing in mind all that we have already demonstrated as to St Paul's relation to the prophetic teaching, it seems clear enough to us that in passages such as those above, we come upon the more immediate background of the apostle's thought. Only, the conception of a final struggle between God and evil,[1] we might almost say, between God and the Devil,[2] before the end, is of course determined and coloured by the circumstances and experiences of his own time. Thus, in Ezekiel, the conflict is between the heathen prince Gog and Jehovah Himself. In Daniel, it is the God of gods (*i.e.* the God of Israel, see Bevan, *ad. loc.*) whose indignation shall be visited upon the impious and insolent king of the north. The figure of Antichrist has not yet taken definite shape, for there is no mention of a Messiah as occupying a central place in the culminating collision between good and evil. But for the first Christian circles, of necessity, all the events of the End have a Messianic bearing. For them the cause of God has its supreme representative in the Christ of God. Now, plainly, Jesus Himself had

[1] This dominating idea of the Persian religion finds expression in a vaguer, and also in a more precise form. Thus, as a rule, we find merely the general expectation that the powers of evil will be vanquished, and will vanish, no surmises being made as to their definite fate. Thus, Yasna xxx. 10: "Then shall be beaten down, then shall be broken the army of the Druj." But at times, more definite statements are made: *e.g.*, Bundehesh xxx. 31 f., "Thereafter the snake Gôkîhar is consumed in the molten metal" (Böklen, *op. cit.*, p. 128; *cf.* Hübschmann, *Jahrb. f. prot. Theol.*, 1879, p. 226). This latter idea belongs to the same type of conceptions as the Jewish Antichrist; *cf.* the conception of Azi Dahâka, originally a mythical monster, who appears at the End, as the incarnation of evil, and is slain by a hero who rises from the dead. He is placed in Babylon (Söderblom, *op. cit.*, p. 258, note).

[2] *Cf.* Bousset (*Religion d. Judenthums*, p. 486): "The figure of Antichrist is . . . in all probability, nothing more than an anthropomorphising of the Devil."

given grave and frequent warnings against false Christs and false prophets who should strive to deceive their fellows (*e.g.*, Matt. vii. 15, xxiv. 4 f; Luke xvii. 21, 23, etc.). As a matter of history, the Jewish nation had rejected the true Messiah. What could be more natural than that the apostle, his mind steeped in the prophetic delineations of the future, delineations which would receive a new significance and importance in the light of those predictions of Jesus which had been reported to him, should expect the appearance of a false Messiah, whose very coming and influence should be a judgment upon the Jewish nation for their daring opposition to the redemptive purpose of God? Obviously, he would be inclined to attribute to such a figure, whose outlines remained still vague and obscure, any features of surpassing ungodliness which might impress themselves on his mind at the time. We are therefore disposed to believe that the remarkable description, for example, which occurs in 2 Thess. ii. 4 (*ὁ ἀντικείμενος καὶ ὑπεραιρόμενος ἐπὶ πάντα λεγόμενον θεὸν ἢ σέβασμα ὥστε αὐτὸν εἰς τὸν ναὸν τοῦ θεοῦ καθίσαι, ἀποδεικνύντα ἑαυτὸν ὅτι ἐστὶν θεός*), while closely related to Dan. xi. 36, is directly connected with the sacrilegious conduct of the demented Roman Emperor Caligula, who, from his enthusiasm in propagating the cult of the Cæsars, went the length of attempting to place a statue of himself in the Temple at Jerusalem. To every devout Jew, and to the Christians also, who believed that they stood in the true succession of the chosen people, such an action revealed an almost incredible depth of daring impiety.[1] It is probably

[1] So also Schmiedel on 2 Thess. ii. 1-12; Findlay, art. "Paul" in *H.D.B.*

impossible to trace all the various elements which may have contributed to St Paul's mysterious conception of the "man of lawlessness." Certainly it is a gross exaggeration when Reuss speaks of the "celebrated passage on Antichrist, in which he (*i.e.* St Paul) repeats word for word, although with an appearance of mystery, the theory drawn by the Rabbis from the Book of Daniel" (*Histoire de la Théol. Chrét.* ii. p. 211). This is an instance of a type of inaccuracy of which the author is often guilty. As a matter of fact, our authorities for the Rabbinic theory are later by several centuries than the writings of St Paul. Hence, extreme caution is needful in discussing the influence of the Synagogue-theology on his conceptions. Even when we do examine the "theory" about which Reuss speaks so confidently, we find a crucial difference between it and the statements of the apostle. "Throughout the Talmudic literature," says Weber, "we meet the idea that the Roman dominion must be stamped out if the Messianic kingdom is to be erected. Thus, in the days of Messiah, there shall stand at the head of this kingdom a powerful ruler, who unites in himself all enmity against God and hatred against God's people. He is called Armilus,[1] and is the רשׁיעא *κατ᾽ ἐξοχήν*. . . . This Armilus, the last and greatest oppressor of the community, shall the Messiah slay by the word of his mouth and the breath of his lips (Targ. of Jonathan on Isa. xi. 4)" (*Lehren d. Talmud*, p. 349). As we shall see in a moment, this attitude by no means tallies with that of St Paul towards the Roman Empire. Yet, as might

[1] Supposed by some scholars to be a corruption or reminiscence of Romulus.

be expected, there are undoubted affinities between the apostle's view and the tradition of the Synagogue. But whatever may have been the exact lines along which St Paul reached the thought of a combination of evil in that strange figure, designated by him the "man of lawlessness," it appears to us that the description given sheds some valuable light on the manner in which he expected his conception to be realised. It is apparent that he has no definite historical personage in view. So much seems to be implied in the use of the term ἀποκαλύπτειν (verses 3, 6, 8) to denote his appearance on the scene of action. We are led to infer from the term, that the principle embodied bulks more largely before his mind than the person in whom it finds expression. Further, his ἀποκάλυψις is connected with an event which St Paul names ἡ ἀποστασία, "the apostasy." This can only mean a revolt against God. Therefore it must take place among the people who acknowledge the true God, *i.e.* the Jews.[1] But the title given to the leader of the revolt corroborates our hypothesis. His characteristic is ἀνομία, lawlessness. He is ὁ ἄνομος, the lawless man. He is untrue to the highest tradition of the race. Defying the law, he defies the God who has promulgated it. Now we saw at an earlier stage that the apostle was led to his expectation of the speedy coming of the End by the aggravated sinfulness of the Jews. They had committed the unspeakable crime of crucifying the promised Messiah. Not content with this, they instigated and carried on a most relentless persecution of those who bore testimony to the Resurrection of

[1] So also Weiss, *N.T. Theol.* i. pp. 307, 308; Charles, *Eschatology*, p. 381, note 1: Bousset, *Antichrist*, passim.

the Crucified (1 Thess. ii. 14-16). These facts explain his assertion that the "mystery of lawlessness is already in operation" (2 Thess. ii. 7). His life is embittered by their unscrupulous machinations. He feels that they are completing the full tale of their iniquities (πληρουμένων τῶν ἁμαρτιῶν). The Divine wrath is accumulating upon them. It only requires the final culmination of evil in the ἄνομος, the "son of destruction," to usher in the last act in the drama of human history, the Parousia of the Messiah, the destruction of the supreme foe of God and godliness.

But the final outburst of impiety (to proceed from within Judaism, *ut sup.*) was, for the present, being hindered. There was a restraining force which interfered, τὸ κατέχον or ὁ κατέχων. Until this ceased to act, the closing catastrophe would be averted.[1] We agree with those scholars who recognise in this preventing power the Roman Empire and its government. It is evident, both from his Epistles and from Acts, that St Paul experienced and valued a certain protection on the part of the Roman authorities. Christianity had not reached the formidable dimensions to which it attained fifty years later. The disputes it occasioned appeared in the eyes of the Roman officials to turn exclusively on questions of Jewish law and custom. The obscurity of the sect of the Nazarenes told in the apostle's favour. Probably more frequently than our documents inform us, the secular arm intervened to shield him from the fanatical rage of his fellow-countrymen. Could anything be more intelli-

[1] *Cf.* Bousset (*Antichrist*, p. 123): "The mention of one distinct premonitory sign occurs in nearly all the sources. The end is at hand when the Roman Empire perishes."

gible than that St Paul should see in this impartial State the main bulwark against the forces of injustice and impiety which menaced his work at every turn? To us, looking back along the course of history, and able to estimate the true proportions of empires and kingdoms, it may appear altogether incongruous to bring two such unequal magnitudes as Rome and Judaism into a relation of this kind. To the apostle, nurtured in the magnificent traditions of his country and his race, the nation to whom belonged the promises of God overshadowed all others. Although he did not survive to see it, the last awful struggle round the walls of the holy city must have appeared to the eye-witnesses a struggle for life or death, involving the triumph or the doom of one of the opposing forces. It is of interest in this connection to note that long after the destruction of Jerusalem, the leader of the fierce Jewish insurrection against Hadrian in 132 A.D., Simon Bar-Cochba (Num. xxiv. 17), was greeted by the famous Rabbi Akiba as the King Messiah, and in this rôle attracted great masses of adherents. Thus the expectation of a false Messiah, who should by delusive signs and wonders produce an impression on his fellow-countrymen, was in no sense an unreasonable one.

The place assigned by St Paul to the Roman power in the development of the events of the End, supplies a needful caution in our estimate of his expectation of the Parousia. Apart from this, indeed, he distinctly declares to the Thessalonians that the Day of the Lord is not imminent (ἐνέστηκεν). But his reference to the restraint of the Imperial government suggests that the apostle must have been prepared, even in those early days, to allow the intervention of a lengthened period ere the End should break in. For assuredly, at the time when he wrote, there was little to presage any speedy collapse of the mightiest Empire of the world.

From our point of view, we may be surprised that the apostle laid so strong an emphasis on an event which, in reality, was so far distant. But he never professed any minute knowledge as to times and seasons. His judgment was mainly formed by observation of the spiritual processes advancing in mankind. At times it appeared to him as if the world must soon be ready for Christ. At times it seemed as if the ripening of evil demanded the Judgment of the Messiah. But we never find him lamenting the delay of the End. Even when his thoughts of the Parousia are most vivid, he never undervalues the ethical significance of his present opportunity. In truth, it may be said that the early Christian belief in the nearness of the Second Advent was one of the most momentous and inspiring influences for holiness in the primitive Church. It was a call to watchfulness and prayer, a call to strenuous effort and solemn preparation.[1] Perhaps it did more than any other impulse to raise the life of the young Christian community to a lofty level, and to keep it there. For they lived in the expectation of Christ, their returning Lord, as those who must buy up the time.[2]

[1] See especially 1 Thess. v. 23. The verse is an indication of how the apostle dealt with the expectation.

[2] Sanday and Headlam suggestively note how the Parousia-belief preserved the elasticity of Christianity, as the apostles, from its influence, "never realised that they were building up a Church to last through the ages. . . . They never wrote or legislated except so far as existing needs demanded . . . They never admonished or planned with a view to the remote future." —*Commentary on Romans*, p. 380.

CHAPTER V

ST PAUL'S CONCEPTION OF THE RESURRECTION

NO other conception of his Eschatology has received such elaborate treatment at the hands of St Paul as that of the Resurrection. Yet perhaps in no province is there more room left for the raising of perplexing questions. In one aspect of it, the full delineation of the event and process which he has given, is due to the pressure of circumstances. In the course of his missionary labours, more especially in the province of Achaia, that subject of his teaching which proved the chief stumbling-block to his quick-witted and combative Greek audiences was the Resurrection of the dead. It was not that their minds were prejudiced against the idea of a life after death. Owing to Platonic and other influences, this conception had long been familiar in intellectual circles. No doubt, by the middle of the first century A.D., it must have filtered down into popular belief as, at least, a speculation worthy of attention. Indeed, we have good evidence for its widespread diffusion in many interesting sepulchral inscriptions (see Lehrs, *Vorstellungen d. Griechen über das Fortleben nach d. Tode*). Its influence would be stimulated by that strong impulse of ethical aspiration which marked the opening centuries of our era. In all probability, the formulation of the doctrine of immortality by Plato himself, owed as much to the intense *moral* interest which formed part of his conviction of future retribution, as to his metaphysical speculations on the nature of the soul (see Zeller, *Platonism*, p. 404). That element weighed powerfully with the Stoics, who held an unrivalled position as religious teachers in the era with which we are concerned. But a belief in immortality was a different thing from a belief in resurrection. The latter would be usually regarded as a grotesque superstition, tenable only by barbarian peoples. Diogenes Laertius, in the preface to his great collection of the doctrines of the philosophers, seems to look at it from this standpoint when he refers to the notion ἀναβιώσεσθαι κατὰ τοὺς Μάγους . . . τοὺς ἀνθρώπους καὶ ἔσεσθαι ἀθανάτους. The notion of a higher *organism* (σῶμα) was that which repelled the Hellenic mind. It was altogether contrary to their dualistic view of human nature (*e.g.* the Platonic).[1]

Those philosophers, also, who attempted to surmount this dualism by a higher synthesis were apt

[1] "As long as we have this body, and an evil of that sort is mingled with our souls, we shall never fully gain what we desire; and that is the truth. . . . It (*i.e.* the body) fills us with passions and desires and fears, and all manner of phantoms, and much foolishness. . . . In truth, we have learned that if we are to have any pure knowledge, we must be free from the body; the soul in herself must behold things as they are" (*Phædo*, 66, B, C, D). At the same time, it should be noted that some eminent interpreters of Plato's doctrine of immortality (*e.g.*, Susemihl, *Genetische Entwicklung d. Platonischen Philosophie*, i. p. 461) explain it as implying that absolute incorporeality can never be reached, and that in the future life man will possess a higher kind of body, having a closer conformity to the soul which sways it.

in the process to lose any true conception of *personality* as surviving death. Probably the majority of Greek thinkers would have assented to the definition of Chrysippus (Nemes. *de nat. hom.* p. 81): ὁ θάνατός ἐστι χωρισμὸς ψυχῆς ἀπὸ σώματος—"Death is the separation of soul from body." How powerfully this idea worked, may be realised from the fact that Jewish thinkers who came under the influences of Hellenism, no longer shared with their contemporaries the doctrine of a personal resurrection, but conceived of a purely spiritual immortality, which they sought to express in terms akin to Plato. Thus Philo: ὅρος ἀθανάτου βίου κάλλιστος οὗτος, ἔρωτι καὶ φιλίᾳ θεοῦ ἀσάρκῳ καὶ ἀσωμάτῳ κατεσχῆσθαι (*De Fuga et Invent.* iii. 122, C. W.): "This is the noblest definition of an immortal life, to be possessed by a fleshless and bodiless love and friendship for God." Compare his definition of death: χωρισμὸν καὶ διάζευξιν ἀπὸ σώματος (*De Abrahamo*, iv. 56, C. W.). The same idea is found in Wisdom, which affirms of the pious dead (iii. 1), δικαίων δὲ ψυχαὶ ἐν χειρὶ θεοῦ, καὶ οὐ μὴ ἅψηται αὐτῶν βάσανος[1]: "Now the souls of the righteous are in the hand of God, and torment shall not touch them"; *cf.* 4 Macc. xiii. 13-15, ἑαυτούς, ἔλεγον, τῷ θεῷ ἀφιερώσομεν ἐξ ὅλης τῆς καρδίας τῷ δόντι τὰς ψυχάς, καὶ χρήσωμεν τῇ περὶ τὸν νόμον φυλακῇ τὰ σώματα. μὴ φοβηθῶμεν τὸν δοκοῦντα ἀποκτενεῖν. μέγας γὰρ ψυχῆς ἀγὼν καὶ κίνδυνος ἐν αἰωνίῳ βασάνῳ κείμενος τοῖς παραβᾶσιν τὴν ἐντολὴν τοῦ θεοῦ[2]: "'With our whole heart,' they said,

[1] Also ix. 15: φθαρτὸν γὰρ σῶμα βαρύνει ψυχήν, καὶ βρίθει τὸ γεῶδες σκῆνος νοῦν πολυφρόντιδα.

[2] See Grimm on 4 Maccabees, p. 289. Heinrici gives an interesting summary of related Pagan ideas as contrasted with the resurrection-doctrine of St Paul. We condense it here. (1) Simple returning of the soul into its abandoned earthly

'we will consecrate ourselves to the God who gave our souls, and let us offer our bodies as a defence of the law. Let us not fear him who supposes that he can slay us. For grievous is the soul-conflict and peril which is reserved in eternal torment for those who have transgressed the commandment of God.'"

There was no place for a resurrection in Greek habits of thought as to the Last Things. Hence, although, in accepting the Christian Gospel, they had also accepted the fact that Jesus Christ was risen from the dead, the Corinthian Christians, *e.g.*, were inclined to regard His experience as abnormal, an event on a par with the miraculous process of the Incarnation, but by no means regulative for the Christian brotherhood as a whole. So the apostle is obliged to set forth in detail the position at which he has arrived, largely as an inference from his own experience of Christ risen. It is impossible to say whether the content of his famous exposition in 1 Cor. xv. had for long been a possession of his thought, or whether the objections raised by his opponents at Athens, Corinth, and elsewhere, have for the first time compelled him to draw out into clearness conceptions which merely lay in germ within his mind. It is conceivable that the question asked by the perplexed Corinthians, in the letter to which we have St Paul's reply, was the main

shell. So Plato of the Pamphylian Er, *Repub.* x. 614 f.; *cf.* Pliny, *Hist. Nat.* vi. 55, *Similis . . . de adservandis corporibus hominum et reviviscendi promissa Democrito vanitas, qui non revixit ipse.* (2) Periodic wanderings of souls through the temporal life; so Pythagoras. (3) Secret doctrines of the Orphics, who promised the initiated immortality and a pre-eminent place in Elysium (*cf.* Welcker, *Griech. Götterlehre*, ii. pp. 514 f., 561 f.; Heinrici, 1 *Cor.* pp. 466, 467).

reason which led him to formulate in its minutiæ his doctrine of the *σῶμα πνευματικόν*. Yet it seems to us more probable that he had reached his position gradually, as the result of prolonged reflection. We know what gave the impulse to such reflection. St Paul, indeed, as a Pharisee, was perfectly familiar with the idea of resurrection. In discussing the apocalyptic literature of Judaism, we have observed how the doctrine took shape and gained currency. There is abundant evidence from the Gospels, Acts, Josephus,[1] and the Talmudic treatises, that the notion was prevalent in Pharisaic circles. "Gamaliel proved the Resurrection from the Bible in answer to the challenge of the Sadducees, by pointing to passages from the three portions of Scripture (*i.e.*, Law, Prophets, and Hagiographa), namely, Deut. xxxi. 16, Isa. xxvi. 19, Cant. vii. 10; and when they did not allow these proofs, convinced them by Deut. i. 8, or according to others, Deut. iv. 4 (Sanh. 90b)" (Bacher, *Agada d. Tannaiten*, i. p. 87). But in the religious thought of the Synagogue it had remained somewhat of a mechanical event, an adjunct of the great Judgment. By many it was regarded as a privilege of the righteous Israelite, by a smaller number as universal, thus becoming a more or less unrelated item among the circumstances of the End, whose ethical significance could scarcely be estimated, inasmuch as there seemed to be no basis for it in the phenomena of the earthly, personal life. Indeed, if we may judge by the

[1] *Antiq.* xviii. 1. 3, *ἀθανατόν τε ἰσχὺν ταῖς ψυχαῖς πίστις αὐτοῖς εἶναι καὶ ὑπὸ χθονὸς δικαιώσεις τε καὶ τιμὰς οἷς ἀρετῆς ἢ κακίας ἐπιτήδευσις ἐν τῷ βίῳ γέγονεν, καὶ ταῖς μὲν εἱργμὸν ἀΐδιον προτίθεσθαι, ταῖς δὲ ῥᾳστώνην τοῦ ἀναβιοῦν*; *B.J.*, ii. 8. 14, *ψυχήν τε πᾶσαν μὲν ἄφθαρτον, μεταβαίνειν δὲ εἰς ἕτερον σῶμα τὴν τῶν ἀγαθῶν μόνην, τὰς δὲ τῶν φαύλων ἀϊδίῳ τιμωρίᾳ κολάζεσθαι.*

Talmudic literature, there seems to have been little that was spiritual about the conception. It was a restoration from Sheol, by the power of Messiah, to a temporal life. And "the future body, as to material and organisation, was conceived as essentially of the same quality as the present" (so Weber, *Lehren d. Talmud*, p. 353). This view is corroborated by the Apocalypse of Baruch, *e.g.* chap. l. 2: "For assuredly the earth gives back at that time the dead which it now receives, in order to preserve them, without altering anything in their appearance; but as it has received them, so it gives them back, and as I have committed them to it, so it causes them to rise."[1]

At no point in his conceptions of the Last Things has St Paul produced so remarkable a transformation as in his doctrine of the Resurrection. We need not even here, indeed, expect a complete, rounded-off system of ideas. Gaps remain at various points. The apostle claims no completeness for his views. "At the present my knowledge is a fragment; at that time I shall know as completely as I am known" (1 Cor. xiii. 12.) Some of the traditional conceptions lie, as it were, side by side in his mind with those which he has attained through the creative power of his Christ-possessed spirit. He is not concerned about their mutual adjustment. But the whole trend of his spiritual life, the whole genesis of his Christian experience, compels him to place the fact and the significance of the Resurrection in the foreground. We have seen in a former chapter how this man yearned for fulness and certainty of life. Death, as

[1] In Enoch cviii. 11, on the other hand, we find a parallel view to that of St Paul.

he originally conceived it, was unrelieved horror. The Pharisaic idea of resurrection would probably do little to mitigate the gloom, for after all it was only an hypothesis. One might reach, no doubt, a strong degree of probability that God must be true to those who trusted and obeyed Him, that He must in the end secure their deliverance and blessedness. But how was conviction on the question to be attained? Did not the facts of the spiritual life expressly militate against such certainty? No man was ever more sensitive to a mental situation of this kind than St Paul. It was not that he doubted for a moment the righteousness of God. That was perfect, flawless. It overawed him; it presented itself to him as the highest attribute of the Divine nature. It was his own standing before the Holy One for which he feared. This status was most precarious, as he was compelled to view it. He was eager to obey the Divine will. But he felt his fleshly nature rudely thwarting him. Even if, on reviewing each day's life, he could assure himself that, on the whole, he was striving to please God, a sudden temptation, or the memory of one, intruded to shake his confidence. Then, once more, he was plunged into anxiety as to the proportion of merit and demerit in his conduct, as it lay bare to the searching gaze of the Judge.[1] Where was there a place for calm assurance regarding the final issues of his relation to God? Must he drift on to the end, tormented by anxiety as to the Divine verdict on his career, with no sure foundation for the hope of eternal blessedness? These, doubtless, were the questions which surged within him when he met the risen

[1] See Weber, *Lehren d. Talmud*, pp. 271-273.

Christ. This meeting brought him a wonderful solution of his various perplexities.

To begin with, Jesus of Nazareth must be what He claimed to be, the promised Messiah of God, in whom all the hopes of Israel were to be realised. The disgrace and scandal of the Cross were swallowed up in the glory of the Resurrection. Nay, rather, they enhanced its glory. For the shame and desolation of Calvary, in the light of all that followed, were no meaningless tragedy. "God was in Christ," even Christ the crucified, "reconciling the world unto Himself." "He was delivered up for our transgressions, and was raised for our justifying" (Rom. iv. 25). As risen, He proved Himself to be in closest contact with God. For it was by virtue of the Spirit of holiness, the Spirit which is God's, that He rose from the dead, and "was declared (or, determined, defined, ὁρισθέντος) the Son of God in power" (Rom. i. 4). Necessarily, when viewed in its full range and significance, the Resurrection of Christ must usher in a new world of spiritual experiences. As risen, the exalted Lord did not remain in solitary isolation from humanity. Precisely the reverse was the case. His rising inaugurated the dispensation of the Holy Spirit. The marvellous, Divine gift was the response to faith in Him who had broken the bonds of death. The risen Christ became the source of a mighty diffusion of spiritual power, of spiritual life, among His believing followers. They came into actual touch with the Divine.

St Paul speaks of that which he has experienced. Since that day on the Damascus road, he has become a new man (καινὴ κτίσις). The sight he received of the risen Lord has kindled faith and conviction within him: not mere conviction of a truth which may be expressed in the words, "Jesus of Nazareth is not dead, but alive"; but devotion to the living Person whom he has seen and come to know in His true character as Saviour: such devotion, that there grows up a communion between them, a fellowship of spirit with spirit: so true a union, that the apostle can only say that he possesses the Spirit (πνεῦμα) of Jesus Christ, that the actual life which he now lives as a human being, that life in its unity and entirety, depends not on him or on anything that originates with him, but rests in the power and life of Christ, depends on his faith in the Son of God, who had loved him and given Himself for him. We are in danger of repeating ourselves, in thus laying fresh emphasis on St Paul's conception of the new life; but we must follow this course even at the risk of such repetition, for we have here the unmistakable basis of his doctrine of the Resurrection.

We can now see how he reached the goal of his yearnings, absolute certainty as to eternal life, and the kind of certainty for which he craved, one which bore upon human existence as a unity, and did not involve its disintegration into soul and body. The new life which St Paul knows he has received from the risen Christ, is one which embraces the entire personality. Greek thinkers could picture with complete satisfaction an immortality of the soul, of the disembodied spirit. In all probability the apostle was more or less acquainted with the Jewish-Alexandrian literature, particularly the Hellenistic Wisdom of Solomon, in which the Greek conception of immortality is adopted, and fused with an Eschatology which, in many respects, remains Judaistic.

Teichmann adduces various parallels to prove a close kinship between this book and St Paul (pp. 69-71). There may be some affinities on such points as the conception of σοφία in Wisdom as compared with the πνεῦμα-doctrine of the apostle, but even these may be grossly exaggerated. And Teichmann has yielded to the temptation (see, *e.g.*, p. 74, an extraordinary overstatement).[1] The question before us provides a test. So far from being content with the Hellenistic idea of immortality, the apostle remains wholly loyal to the genuine Hebrew tradition. The Old Testament never regards the bodily organism in itself as the principle of evil. The notion of the body as the prison of the soul (σῶμα σῆμα) is wholly alien to it. For, as Prof. Robertson Smith points out, "a religion which lays so much stress on man's vocation to lordship over the creation (Gen. i., Ps. viii.) necessarily recognises the bodily organism through which this is realised as something more than a seat of low desires. Not the soul, but the soul equipped with a body, constitutes man as God created him, and as He desires to restore him" (*Expos.* I. iv. p. 352). We can see how direct a bearing this view must have on St Paul's conception: how it opens to him a vista for all creation; how it enlarges his idea of the future life of man, and gives a profounder meaning to the thought of resurrection. It is the entire person, who is to rise to a new life; πνεῦμα (or ψυχή), apart from σῶμα, is meaningless, a barren formula. And the

[1] Grafe's estimate of the relationship between St Paul and Wisdom is much more careful (*Abhandlungen . . . Weizsäcker gewidmet*, pp. 253-286, esp. the closing pp.). But even his results have to be accepted with reservation; see, *e.g.*, Gunkel, *Wirkungen d. heiligen Geistes*, [2] pp. 79-81; Titius, p. 245.

condition of the exalted Christ, as he conceives it, confirms him in his position. The objective impression which St Paul has received of his Lord is manifestly that which he would describe as a σῶμα πνευματικόν. In our judgment, his doctrine of the resurrection "body" is proof positive of that. The organism is removed from earthly and fleshly limitations. It is wholly subordinate to and under control of the πνεῦμα. How this difference affected his perception of the risen One, the apostle does not attempt to delineate. But enough is said to indicate that one effect upon him at least was that of brightness, of light. Whether that description is employed merely as a symbol or picture, we cannot tell. Perhaps, too, it is difficult to say how far we can be helped in representing to ourselves St Paul's conception by the narratives of the appearances of Jesus to the disciples after His resurrection. Those appearances took place under mysterious conditions. Obviously they were altogether occasional and unexpected, yet they were given to companies as well as to individuals. This fact is noteworthy. Further, the disciples had some difficulty in recognising their Master. Even after they had seen Him once or twice, their perplexity remained. He had undergone a certain transformation. In traditions so divergent as the Synoptic and the Johannine, attention is directed to His power of presenting or withdrawing Himself suddenly.[1] The descriptions given

[1] Cf., *e.g.*, M'Connell (*Evolution of Immortality*, p. 162): "We seem . . . to be in the presence of something which is both material and immaterial, something which is cognisable by the senses, and which, at the same time, plays fast and loose with sense-perceptions."

are remarkable for their sobriety and restraint. One is never conscious of any bizarre element in perusing them. Yet we find nothing parallel to them in the rest of the New Testament. They are confined to our Lord's post-resurrection existence. But they appear to us, in not a few points, to adjust themselves with remarkable accuracy to St Paul's idea of the *σῶμα πνευματικόν*.

But let us endeavour to come closer to the apostle's doctrine, and attempt to realise how he conceived the process and the event of Resurrection. Whatever may have been his former view of the matter, it is plain that we must seek the basis of his final conception in the Resurrection of Jesus Christ Himself and all its consequences. Not that this will carry us the whole way. For we find little trace in the Epistles of any reflection upon the inner spiritual movements of the life of Jesus. We have no hints as to the silent history of the three days between the Cross and the Resurrection.[1] Further, the process of super-physical activity in the existence of the exalted Christ must be on a different level from that which belongs to His followers, just because of His position as *κύριος*. It is rather the fundamental principles and the final issues of his doctrine that we must seek in his conception of the Resurrection of Jesus Christ, than any details or precise stages in that experience, such as appeal to our inquisitive minds as we ponder the fact of resurrection for ourselves. Nor must we neglect the consideration that, as the apostle reflected on the

[1] "There is nothing in this paragraph (*i.e.* Rom. x. 5-10) beyond the most general statement that Christ was in the world of the dead, and was raised from it by God" (Salmond, *Christian Doctrine of Immortality*, p. 525).

momentous crisis which had occurred in his own life through the power of the risen Lord, he would necessarily interpret it in the light of the teaching of Jesus. We have already noted in chap. ii. the remarkable parallels between 1 Cor. xv. and the narrative of our Lord's discussion with the Sadducees in Mark xii. 18 f., Luke xx. 27 f. Jesus had spoken of the future life of the risen as being *ὡς ἄγγελοι* (Luke xx. 36—*ἰσάγγελοι*). Now St Paul can connect his personal experience not only with the evidence of his fellow-apostles, but also with the authoritative statements of the Lord Himself. The phenomenon of the journey to Damascus at least helps him to apprehend what *ἰσάγγελος* really involves. And from whichever of the two standpoints he regards the resurrection-life, he must be conscious of the extraordinary transformation which is wrought. Just as his impression of the risen Lord, which formed the turning-point in his career, was an altogether unique and solitary event in his experience, so must we regard the Resurrection of believers as entirely of its own kind, an event which cannot be measured by any human criteria. This conception he must have felt to be fully confirmed by the actual sayings of Jesus, several of which are full of suggestion in their bearing on the question before us. Thus, for example, in Matt. xix. 28, He speaks of the future condition of glory as the *παλινγενεσία*, which virtually means a new order of existence, a re-creation of all things. And intimately related is the noteworthy phrase occurring in Luke xx. 36, where the risen are called *τῆς ἀναστάσεως υἱοί*, "sons of the resurrection," a phrase which certainly implies a fresh commencement of being, their entrance into a sphere in which their whole nature is transfigured. Hence, as Haupt points out (*op. cit.*, p. 91), *ἀνάστασις*, in Luke xx. 35, is used as a synonym for *αἰὼν ἐκεῖνος*, and is practically equivalent to the inauguration of a supra-earthly condition of life—substantially, the perfected Kingdom of God. A remarkable extension of the thought which we have been considering, is to be found in St Paul's description of Christ in Coloss. i. 18 as *πρωτότοκος ἐκ τῶν νεκρῶν*: "the First-born from the dead." The expression is of course to be read in the light of a preceding verse (15), which describes Him as the *εἰκὼν τοῦ θεοῦ τοῦ ἀοράτου, πρωτότοκος πάσης κτίσεως*, "the Image of the invisible God, the First-born of all creation." The idea is expanded by verse 16, *τὰ πάντα δι' αὐτοῦ καὶ εἰς αὐτὸν ἔκτισται*: "All things have been created through Him, and with a view to Him." It is further illumined by the statement of Rom. viii. 29, *προώρισεν [αὐτοὺς] συμμόρφους τῆς εἰκόνος τοῦ υἱοῦ αὐτοῦ, εἰς τὸ εἶναι αὐτὸν πρωτότοκον ἐν πολλοῖς ἀδελφοῖς*: "He predestinated them to be conformed to the image of His Son, in order to His being First-born among many brethren." The same thought is expressed by a different metaphor in 1 Cor. xv. 20, where Christ as risen is named *ἀπαρχὴ τῶν κεκοιμημένων*, "the First-fruits of them who have fallen asleep." Here the risen believers are looked upon as a new family, a new class or lineage, if we may so say, in the human race. And as He who heads the line is the Image of God, the Instrument and Ideal of creation, this new spiritual progeny of His for the first time fulfils the original purpose of creation: they are re-created through Him in that image of God which mankind lost or made of none effect by disobedience.[1] Hence, the Resurrection, of which His is the type and norm and pledge, initiates that glorious era which is decisive for the whole universe, in which God sees His aim attaining complete realisation.

It may be said that for St Paul, resurrection, final salvation (σωτηρία), eternal life, are all designations of the same great hope viewed from divergent standpoints. The statement of this fact at once discloses the foundation of the apostle's doctrine. Whatever steps he had taken or omitted to take to reconcile his present position with that which he held as a Pharisee, his supreme interest in the Resurrection is due to the place which it occupies in the culmination of the development of the Christian man. For St Paul, Christianity is *the condition of being in Christ* (ἐν Χριστῷ). The implications of that condition, indeed, are many, and we cannot dwell upon them now. At all events, it involves possession of the πνεῦμα, the Divine Spirit, the Spirit of Christ, the πνεῦμα ἅγιον. The important consideration to keep before us here is that the πνεῦμα is a regenerative principle or power for the *whole* existence, for the personal life as a unity. What effect, then, does the apostle conceive the indwelling of the Divine πνεῦμα to produce upon the nature of the individual? It is one of gradual but complete transformation. It is a metamorphosis into

[1] In the Avesta, the resurrection is also associated with a saviour, Astvatereta, born of a virgin and the seed of Zarathustra. He achieves the resurrection with six companions. "Saosyant and his auxiliaries are all servants of the Lord, so that we may quite well say that the resurrection is wrought by the power of the Lord, or by the Amesa Spentas (Yast 19, 22)" (Söderblom, *op. cit.*, p. 261).

the same likeness as Christ, from glory to glory (2 Cor. iii. 18). The "glory" which he here speaks of can be no mere outward semblance, as some have held. The context, especially verses 15, 16, shows clearly that he is thinking of inward transformation and illumination in the first instance; nor can any other meaning be assigned to the clause which qualifies the verse referred to above, "we all with unveiled face reflecting the glory of the Lord," for the unveiled face is really equivalent to the unveiled heart of verse 16. But how, we may ask, does this process affect the bodily nature, or what relation does it bear to our present material constitution? Professors Tait and Balfour Stewart, in their ingenious treatise on the *Unseen Universe*, assuming the possession of "a frame or rudiments of a frame connecting us with the invisible universe, which we may call the spiritual body," proceed to speculate in these terms: "Each thought . . . is accompanied by certain molecular motions . . . in the brain: and parts of these are stored up in that organ . . . to produce . . . physical memory. Other parts . . . are . . . communicated to the spiritual or invisible body, and are there stored up, forming a memory which may be made use of when that body is free to exercise its functions . . . We can . . . well imagine that, after death, when the spiritual body is free to exercise its functions, it may be replete with energy and have eminently the power of action in the present, retaining also, as we have shown above, a hold upon the past, . . . and thus preserving the two essential requisites of a continuous, intelligent existence" (p. 200). It would be absurd to look for any similar attempt on the part of St Paul to investigate scientifically the process by which he conceives the regenerated spirit, or the spirit-possessed personality, to dominate the purely material elements in the nature. Yet from hints he lets fall we can catch some of the outlines of his thoughts. "Flesh and blood cannot inherit the Kingdom of God," he asserts (1 Cor. xv. 50), "nor does corruption inherit incorruption." Here is one of the apostle's axioms. Flesh is, of course, the material substance of the earthly life: the blood was regarded by the ancients as containing in itself the vital principle. *Cf.* Sirach xiv. 18: οὕτως γενεὰ σαρκὸς καὶ αἵματος, ἡ μὲν τελευτᾷ, ἑτέρα δὲ γεννᾶται. The outward man perishes: the inward man (ὁ ἔσω ἄνθρωπος) is renewed from day to day (2 Cor. iv. 16). And for St Paul ὁ ἔσω ἄνθρωπος signifies that side of human nature which is sensitive to Divine influences: that side on which the Holy Spirit operates. The renewal here spoken of (ἀνακαινοῦται) cannot be analysed further than as the effect of the Spirit's operation.[1] But plainly, in St Paul's view, the present material body has nothing to do with the Resurrection or the future Kingdom of God, although this by no means involves the absence of all that corresponds to the bodily organism of the earthly life.[2]

[1] "The crucial question then is, When and under what conditions does the spirit begin to establish a nexus with a physical basis of life which may be more abiding . . . We want the continuous life of the individual . . . Where . . . does personality begin? . . . Only at the point where the sense of relationship with other personalities begins. But this is the place where the moral faculty (=Pauline νοῦς) emerges . . . Until moral sensibility becomes self-conscious . . . there is . . . no personality to be immortal" (M'Connell, *op. cit.*, pp. 179, 180).

[2] Must it not be an organism modelled after the earthly type

The precise question which the apostle sets himself to answer in detail in the famous resurrection-passage is that which asks, "With what kind of body do they come?"—*i.e.* at the Resurrection (I Cor. xv. 35). It is quite possible, as Heinrici suggests (*Comment. on* I *Cor.*, p. 469), that the difficulty may have been raised by the Apollos-party at Corinth. For Apollos, as trained in the schools of Alexandria, would naturally have become familiar with the idea of a purely spiritual immortality. This the Corinthian Christians would

rather than that foreshadowed by St Paul, that T. H. Green has in view when he speaks of "a renewed embodiment" being "but a return to that condition in which we are parts of nature, a condition from which the moral life is already a partial deliverance?" The σῶμα which the apostle conceives of is "the organism for the self-realising of a spiritual power" (so Schmiedel, Holtzmann's *Hand-Commentar*, p. 125), "the organ of the will's self-expression" (Titius, p. 63), a neutral conception. It is only a part of nature, in so far as nature is a direct expression of the Divine purpose. But it is wholly removed from the present, earthly order of existence. Cf. *Paradise Lost*, Bk. v. 469-484:—

"O Adam, one Almighty is from whom
All things proceed, and up to him return,
If not depraved from good, created all,
Such to perfection, one first matter all,
Indued with various forms, various degrees
Of substance, and in things that live of life;
But more refined, more spiritous, and pure,
As nearer to him placed or nearer tending,
Each in their several active spheres assigned,
Till body up to spirit work, in bounds
Proportioned to each kind. So from the root
Springs lighter the green stalk, from thence the leaves
More aëry, last the bright consummate flower,
Spirits odorous breathes: flowers and their fruit
Man's nourishment, by gradual scale sublimed
To vital spirits aspire."

be bound to admit. Indeed, from their own special circumstances, they must have been powerfully influenced in its favour. For their charismatic endowment was unique, and the doctrine of the πνεῦμα, which was the foundation of a practical belief in immortality, must have had an unusual prominence among them. In any case, the question sprang from a very natural perplexity. It is interesting to find echoes of it in various directions. It appears to have been a frequent subject of discussion in the schools of the Synagogue. There, strongly realistic conceptions prevailed, in marked contrast to the view of the Christian teacher. Thus, *e.g.*, the school of Schammai concluded from the reviving of the bones (Ezek. xxxvii.) that it would take place in the reverse order from the formation of the child in the mother's womb; the school of Hillel taught that the new formation of the rising person corresponded entirely to the formation of the growing man, proving this from Job xiv. 10 f., where the verbs in the future really point to that which is future (Bacher, *op. cit.*, i. p. 19). So also, in answer to a question of the Emperor Hadrian regarding the resurrection of the body, R. Josua b. Chananja replied that the new body would be constituted out of an almond-shaped bone in the vertebral column; for this, as he showed by experiments, was indestructible (Bacher, *op. cit.*, i. pp. 178, 179). In the apocalyptic literature, also, the problem presents itself. "In what form shall they go on living who are in life at Thy day? Or how can their subsequent glory at that time continue? Shall they in some way at that time put on their present form, and be clad with those limbs which are bound with bands, which are now in sin, and by which sins are committed? Or dost Thou transform in some way those who have been in the world, just like the world itself?" (Apoc. Bar. xlix. 2, 3).

St Paul's elaborate answer to the question is characteristic of his whole treatment of eschatological subjects. He dwells with insistence on points which we might pass over, while many aspects of the inquiry which would appeal to us for discussion, he barely touches.[1] Yet his answer and the background of thought which it presupposes are very remarkable. His elucidation of the problem starts with the well-known analogy to the sowing of seed, an illustration which, as purely analogical, must not be unduly pressed. Here, in all likelihood, he could count upon his readers' sympathy. For the growth of the seed supplied one of the most powerful and impressive symbols in the popular religion. In the mystic rites of Eleusis, the conception of a life beyond death was dimly foreshadowed by scenes based upon the silent and wonderful processes of vegetation, as they unfolded themselves in the progress of the seasons.[2] The Stoics, also, were accus-

[1] *Cf.* the silence of Jesus on similar matters of the End; and see Haupt, *op. cit.*, p. 92 ff.

[2] See Heinrici on 1 Cor. xv. 36. Rohde, *Psyche*, [2] Bd. i. p. 288 ff., holds, however, that there was little connection between the Eleusinian mysteries and the events of harvest, etc. The relationship he considers to have been greatly exaggerated. "After Sôshyans comes, they prepare the raising of the dead, as it says that Zaratûst asked of Aûharmazd this: 'Whence does a body form again which the wind has carried and the water conveyed? and how does the resurrection occur? Aûharmazd answered thus . . . When by me corn was created, so that, scattered about in the earth, it grew again and returned with increase; . . . when that which was not was thus

tomed to dilate upon the seed, with its mysterious hidden potency, which gradually developed into a perfected organism. Their interest in its growth was heightened by their notion that its essence was spirit, which they conceived as breath or air (πνεῦμα), and air for them was identical with the Logos, the rational principle pervading the universe (see Drummond's *Philo*, i. pp. 83 f., 102). From these facts we can gather the relevance of St Paul's illustration to the audience he has in view. Perhaps, indeed, he had learned something of its use from the Rabbinic schools, for in *Sanhedr.* 90 b., R. Meir is reported as saying: "The corn of wheat is entrusted naked to the earth, and comes again to life with a multitude of clothing: shall the pious who are buried in their garments not also rise clothed?" (see Bacher, *op. cit.*, ii. pp. 68, 69). Again we are struck by the advance the apostle has made beyond his early environment.

"What thou sowest is not made alive except it die" (1 Cor. xv. 36).[1] The seed deposited in the earth will not put forth a living stalk or ear until its present phase of existence dissolves or disappears, to make room for existence of a fuller and more advantageous kind. The seed does not really die, because the germ of life is already there and only demands a favourable environment in which to develop, according to the law of its being. But it must die to its existing condition

produced, why is it not possible to produce again that which was'?" (West's transl. of *Bundehesh*, chap. xxx., qu. by Söderblom, 226, 227).

[1] *Cf.* John xii. 24: "Verily, verily, I say unto you, Except a grain of wheat fall into the ground and die, it abideth by itself alone; but if it die, it bringeth forth much fruit."

as bare, unsown grain, else its life can never burst the enclosing shell and come to maturity. "And what thou sowest, not the body (σῶμα) which is to be dost thou sow, but a bare grain (γυμνὸς κόκκος), it may be of wheat or any other: but God giveth it a body according as He willed (καθὼς ἠθέλησεν), and to each seed a body of its own" (verses 37, 38). The question we should naturally ask at this point is, How would St Paul, in his thought, connect the γυμνὸς κόκκος with its future σῶμα? What, for him, is the organic link between them? His answer is extraordinarily typical. It is the only one we can expect him to give, and it is given in the clause immediately following: "The sovereign power of God." "He giveth it a body according as He willed" (ἠθέλησεν, "the aorist denotes the final act of God's will, determining the constitution of nature," so Edwards *ad loc.* admirably). No theory can be founded on such a statement. It does not imply any unique act of creation. It is wholly irrelevant to deduce from it, as Teichmann is inclined to do, that St Paul held the pre-existence of resurrection-bodies in heaven (p. 53, note 1). The conception is entirely true to the Hebrew standpoint. For to them "God was all in all. Events were all His work, and all immediately His work. All the changes on the earth in history and life were but the effects of an unseen power operating within all things" (Davidson, *Expos.* v. i. p. 327). The apostle's outlook is excellently illustrated by Gen. i. 11: "And God said, Let the earth bring forth grass, the herb yielding seed, and the fruit tree yielding fruit after his kind, whose seed is in itself, upon the earth; and it was so" (καὶ ἐγένετο οὕτως, in the Bible which St Paul used). The last clause is a sufficient rationale of the process for the apostle. The crucial matter for him at this point consists in each seed having a body peculiar (ἴδιον) to itself. This body will be the one best fitted to fulfil the functions of the life which informs it. Through it that life will find its most appropriate and effective expression. St Paul is well aware that the difficulty which perplexes his Corinthian friends turns upon the revivifying of the present material body, the σῶμα σάρκινον. This, as we have seen, was the current popular idea among the Jews, and possibly those Jewish teachers, so inimical to St Paul, who found their way to Corinth, may have insisted on the doctrine in its grossest form. "You must not imagine," he proceeds to argue in verse 39 f., "that there is no other kind of σῶμα but that consisting of σάρξ, which you possess. Just as there are marked differences as regards the flesh of various members of the animal creation, so there are divergent groups of σώματα." It is quite possible that here he may have in his mind the statement of Gen. i. 26: "Let us make man in our image, after our likeness, and let them rule the fish of the sea, and the fowl of the air, and the cattle, and all the earth, and every creeping thing that creepeth upon the earth." In any case, a remarkable instance of difference may be seen in the contrast between heavenly bodies (σώματα ἐπουράνια) and earthly bodies (σώματα ἐπίγεια). His thoughts have already begun to turn in the direction of the σώματα πνευματικά which occupy the central position in his conception. The course which he follows gives an instructive glimpse into the workings of his thought. We have already seen that the impression left upon him by his contact with the risen Christ was that of a bright radiance. The term which expresses this impression, although there are, as we shall find, deeper elements lying within it, is almost invariably *δόξα*, "glory" (as our version always translates it, but involving the idea of "brightness"). How, then, is he to give his readers a vivid picture of his own mental conception of the *σῶμα πνευματικόν*, the "spiritual" or "glorified" body which will be possessed by the believer when he is conformed to the body of the glory of Christ? (Phil. iii. 21). He can point them to the heavenly bodies, as we still call them. They, in their beauty and brilliance most strikingly picture the future semblance of redeemed believers. In various passages of the Old Testament the stars are spoken of as living, personal agents. Some of these, indeed, are poetical as, *e.g.*, Judg. v. 20 ("The stars in their courses fought against Sisera"), and Job xxxviii. 7 ("The morning stars sang together, and all the sons of God shouted for joy"). But others can scarcely be so described. Thus, in 1 Kings xxii. 19, the prophet Micaiah says: "I saw the Lord sitting on His throne, and all the hosts of heaven standing by Him on His right hand and on His left." In Deut. iv. 19, there seems to be the idea that the peoples of the earth are assigned to their rule or guardianship. A similar conception is perhaps implied in Isa. xx. 46 (see Gunkel, *Schöpfung u. Chaos*, p. 9). And we may compare Isa. xiv. 12, 13: "How art thou fallen from heaven, O Lucifer, son of the morning . . . for thou hast said in thine heart, I will ascend into heaven, I will exalt my throne above the stars of God." In the vision of Daniel (viii. 9-11), the little horn "waxed great, even to the host of heaven; and it cast down some of the host and of the stars to the ground, and stamped upon them. Yea, he magnified himself even to the prince of the host." There is the same personification in Enoch lxxxii. 9 f.: "This is the law of the stars . . . these are the names of their leaders." Similarly, in Rev. ix. 1, we read of "a star falling from heaven to earth, and there was given to him the key of the pit of the abyss." The poet recalls the ancient idea, when he puts these words in the mouth of Beatrice:—

> "Cause too thou find'st for doubt
> In that it seems
> That spirits to the stars, as Plato deemed, return."
>
> *Paradiso*, iv. 23-25.[1]

It would be hazardous to say that St Paul attributed any personal life to the heavenly bodies. But, from the evidence adduced above, we can see how closely they were associated for the Hebrew mind with the conception of the Divine power. Hence, whether personified in the strict sense or not, they would naturally present themselves as witnesses for a purer and more glorious kind of existence than could

[1] Plato looks upon the stars as living beings, "whose souls must be higher and diviner than human souls, in proportion as their bodies are brighter and fairer than ours." See, *e.g.*, *Timæus*, 40 D: τὰ περὶ θεῶν ὁρατῶν καὶ γεννητῶν. These θεοὶ ὁρατοὶ καὶ γεννητοὶ are none other than the stars. Probably this Platonic idea was the basis of Philo's opinion that the stars were animated beings, who mediated between God and earthly creatures. Volz points out, as one of the elements in the Judaistic conception of the final Judgment, that the stars lose their power. Hitherto they were frequently regarded as spirits competing with God (*op. cit.*, p. 263).

be inferred from mere earthly phenomena. The total impression they make, St Paul goes on to show, is quite distinct from that made by earthly bodies (verse 40). Yet even they are not monotonously uniform. "There is one kind of glory (δόξα) of the sun, and another of the moon, and another of the stars, for star differeth from star in glory" (verse 41).[1]

These words are used with an important purpose in view. While the σῶμα of the believer is to be changed from σάρξ, which by its very essence decays, into δόξα,[2] which is a Divine element, the individuality which has been exhibited by the σῶμα σάρκινον will by no means disappear.[3] The σώματα πνευματικά in

[1] *Cf.* (Plato) *Epinomis*, 986 B (Stallb.): μία μὲν [δύναμις] ἡλίου, μία δὲ σελήνης· μία δὲ τῶν πλανητῶν ἄστρων. See *Paradiso*, ii. 139:—

"And as the soul, that dwells within your dust,
Through members different, yet together form'd,
In different powers resolves itself; e'en so
The intellectual efficacy unfolds
Its goodness multiplied throughout the stars;
On its own unity revolving still.
Different virtue compact different
Makes with the precious body it enlivens,
With which it knits, as life in you is knit."

[2] *Cf.* Apoc. Bar. li. 3, 9, 10: "As for the glorious appearance of those who now on the basis of My law have done righteously . . . their radiance will gleam in manifold forms. . . . And time cannot age them, for they shall dwell in the heights of that world, and be like the angels, and be comparable to the stars." See an important paragraph in Volz on the connection between the blessed (dead) and the stars, *op. cit.*, pp. 360, 361.

[3] Smyth, in observing that the matter of life is always changing, while the *form* remains identical, quotes Lotze's striking comparison of the body to the ripple round some hidden stone in a stream, a comparison which physiology shows to be true (*Old Faiths in New Lights*, p. 161).

the apostle's view will preserve their identity. As each σπέρμα has its ἴδιον σῶμα, so each renewed spiritual nature will possess its distinct and characteristic σῶμα πνευματικόν. Now, according to modern metaphysics, "all completely real Being is individual, by virtue of the fact that it is a finally determinate expression of a purpose" (J. Royce, *Conception of Immortality*, p. 33, note 3). Can we conceive such individuality apart from a distinct self-realisation of the spirit, which in turn demands some type of organism for its self-expression? Is St Paul's forecast of the σῶμα πνευματικόν, after all, a mere old-world speculation, possessing a purely historical interest for students of early religious thought? It is easy for Professor Gardner to assert that "the notion of a spiritual body, as opposed to a body of flesh and blood, is one which exists almost everywhere among peoples at a lower range of civilisation" (*Historic View of New Testament*, pp. 223-224), and to refer to Tylor's *Primitive Culture* for instances. These belong to a wholly different category from St Paul's conception. "That the apparitional human soul" says Mr Tylor, "bears the likeness of its fleshly body, is the principle implicitly accepted by all who believe it really and objectively present in dreams and visions. My own view is that nothing but dreams and visions could have ever put into men's minds such an idea as that of souls being ethereal images of bodies" (i. p. 450). And again: "To the philosophy of the lower races it is by no means necessary that the surviving soul should be provided with a new body, for it seems itself to be of a filmy or vaporous corporeal nature, capable of carrying on an independent existence like other corporeal creatures" (ii. 19). Mr Tylor quotes a saying of Swedenborg, that man's spirit is his mind, which lives after death *in complete human form* (the italics are ours). Where can we find anything corresponding to these notions in the apostle's words? Does he ever hint that his σῶμα πνευματικόν is to "bear the likeness of the fleshly body," or that it is to be of "a filmy or vaporous corporeal nature?" Or does he at any time connect with it the idea of "complete human form?" Critics of St Paul's conceptions ought first to be sure that they realise what these are, a result which can only be achieved by the study of them *in the context of his whole thought.*

The equipment of each regenerated life with a corresponding and distinctive organism (σῶμα) is the point he has reached, when he sums up his discussion in the words: "So also is the resurrection of the dead" (verse 42).[1] The next paragraph is one of considerable difficulty. The familiar words of the Burial Service, "It is sown in corruption, it

[1] Lightfoot (on Phil. iii. 11) has the extraordinary note, that "the general resurrection of the dead, whether good or bad, is ἡ ἀνάστασις τῶν νεκρῶν (*e.g.* 1 Cor. xv. 42); on the other hand, the Resurrection of Christ, and of those who rise with Christ, is generally [ἡ]. ἀνάστασις [ἡ] ἐκ νεκρῶν (Luke xx. 35; Acts iv. 2; 1 Pet. i. 3). The former includes both the ἀνάστασις ζωῆς and the ἀνάστασις κρίσεως (John v. 29); the latter is confined to the ἀνάστασις ζωῆς." But there is absolutely no evidence for this definite assertion. The passage quoted for the "general resurrection" quite plainly applies only to the resurrection of believers. How could the ungodly be described in the New Testament as rising ἐν ἀφθαρσίᾳ, ἐν δόξῃ, ἐν δυνάμει? But that is evidently the kind of resurrection the apostle is thinking of in 1 Cor. xv. 42.

is raised in incorruption; it is sown in dishonour, it is raised in glory; it is sown in weakness, it is raised in power; it is sown a natural body (σῶμα ψυχικόν), it is raised a spiritual body (σῶμα πνευματικόν)," may be interpreted in two divergent senses. Certainly our first impulse is to refer the "sowing" here spoken of to the burial in the grave after death. The emphasis seems to be laid upon the contrast between σπείρειν and ἐγείρειν. Hence the decision will turn on the scope or range which the latter verb is held to embrace. If it denote exclusively or primarily the definite experience of resurrection, then it appears to us that σπείρειν, in spite of other difficulties which may be raised, must directly describe the experience of death and its accompaniments and consequences. But many scholars (*e.g.*, Calvin, Milligan, F. Köstlin, Heinrici, Teichmann, Charles) presuppose a wider outlook on the part of the apostle. They believe he has in view, not the mere point of time occupied by the Resurrection, but the entire new resurrection-life on which the believer enters; the condition of immortality, glory, power, the life of the "spiritual organism." If that be so, σπείρειν must also have a wider significance. No doubt in both cases St Paul has prominently before him the actual experiences which mark "the transition from the earthly to the heavenly life," but he does not restrict his view to these. Thus σπείρειν will mean, to quote Charles (*Eschatology*, p. 392), "the placing the vital principle or spirit in its material environment here on earth, where, even as a seed gathers to itself a body from the matter around it, so the spirit of man fashions for itself a body out of the materials around it."[1] Milligan (*Expos.* iv. 2, p. 36) will not even allow that σῶμα is the strict subject of σπείρεται (verse 42), holding that "it is less the body alone than the body regarded as the outward organ and experience of the man that he has in his eye." We cannot admit that σῶμα in verse 44 is too far distant to allow of its being taken as the subject of σπείρεται. But it is quite possible that the apostle here thinks of σῶμα in a vague sense, such as that stated above, and it certainly will not affect his argument to accept this larger vista. To assert, however, as Milligan does (*loc. cit.*, p. 37), that the terms "dishonour" and "weakness" are too wide for suitable application to the body at the time when it is committed to the dust, is not warranted. In our judgment, it is precisely the appropriateness of these terms to the time of burial and dissolution which would justify the more restricted view of σπείρεται.

The point at which an obscure problem in the interpretation of St Paul's thought presses upon us, is found in the affirmation, "It is sown a natural (ψυχικόν) body; it is raised a spiritual (πνευματικόν) body." To begin with, it may be noted that these all-important adjectives are really the apostle's own coinage. No light can be shed on them from the Old Testament. The Greek version of it, which is so frequently helpful in the exegesis of the Pauline writings, fails us here. The terms can only be

[1] It is surely needless for Titius to hold that "Paul has found a point of departure for his appreciation of the spiritual Ego as the particular kernel of man in the Wisdom of Solomon" (p. 65). St Paul had sufficient spiritual originality, aided by profound self-knowledge gained by introspection, to discover this truth for himself.

understood from the apostle's own use of them. Do the words which have been quoted, it may be asked, in any sense elucidate St Paul's idea of *how* or *when* the great transformation takes place? Do they mean that this process is accomplished between death and resurrection? We do not believe that this precise question was before his mind at all in the present passage, nor indeed to any large extent at any time. We shall have to discuss a little further on some statements which have a bearing upon the problem, but here it would seem that he is concerned exclusively with the *contrast* between the two organisms, the "natural" and the "spiritual," more especially on the side of their genesis. Accordingly, when he goes on to state, "If there is a natural body, there is also a spiritual" (verse 44), he simply brings out definitely that which lies at the basis of his whole Christian psychology. The ψυχή, the natural principle of being, the life-force in the individual, has by God's appointment an organism corresponding to itself, the σῶμα ψυχικόν, the body whose substance is σάρξ, with all which that, in the actual condition of human nature, implies; whose end is necessarily φθορά, decay. How this body has arisen, it does not occur to him to speculate. It is due to the creative might of God. The πνεῦμα, on the other hand, the Divine gift, the power which enters human nature in response to faith, and changes it so that henceforward it is governed by a Divine principle, will be equipped with an organism corresponding to itself, the σῶμα πνευματικόν, the "body" which has no *fleshly* element inherent in it, which therefore enters upon ἀφθαρσία, incorruption, immortality, as its necessary sphere of existence.[1] Here it is worth while to emphasise the difference between St Paul's standpoint and our own. For us it would have been of profound interest had the apostle set himself to trace the nature of the process by which he conceived the σῶμα ψυχικόν to be metamorphosed into the σῶμα πνευματικόν.[2] We would fain discover what might be called his spiritual biology. St Paul is scarcely at all concerned with intervening links or stages. The broad results suffice for him. If he can go back to the causes, and then point forward to their finished effects, he has accomplished all that is of moment for the purpose he has in view. Now

[1] Titius goes beyond legitimate inference when, remarking that Porphyrius has the idea of an aëry, pneumatic body, with which the soul has clothed itself in its descent through the planetary system, he continues: "If one adds the thought that φύσις consists of damper, colder, and more solid pneuma than the ψυχή, the analogy to the Pauline conception of a pneumatic body is manifest" (p. 245, note). There is no basis for such a conclusion in the Epistles. Inasmuch as ψυχικός does *not* mean for St Paul, "composed of ψυχή," for we know that he holds the σῶμα ψυχικόν to be made of σάρξ, we have no right to argue that πνευματικόν, which is invariably its antithesis, means for him "composed of πνεῦμα." Nothing seems to us more remarkable than the sobriety and caution with which he avoids throughout any approach to such positions which he might very naturally have held. *Cf.* the strange parallel in the Persian religion, which teaches that the risen body is not identical with that of the world, but spiritualised (Söderblom, pp. 263, 264).

[2] It is mere arbitrary speculation when Kabisch affirms: "Evidently his (*i.e.* St Paul's) thought is that the πνεῦμα, even after death, remains dwelling in the shell of mortal bodies, while the soul goes into Sheol" (p. 288); and again, "Through union with Christ, not only is a body hidden within, created, which can now rule the dead body of flesh, and afterwards come forth in glory," etc. (p. 294). This is to read into the apostle's conception one's own synthesis.

that is precisely what he does. He appeals first of all (verse 45) to an authoritative statement of Scripture: [ἐγένετο][1] ὁ [πρῶτος] ἄνθρωπος ['Αδὰμ] εἰς ψυχὴν ζῶσαν. He supplies the correlative clause from his own Christian knowledge: ὁ ἔσχατος 'Αδὰμ εἰς πνεῦμα ζωοποιοῦν. It is easy for him to derive the σῶμα ψυχικόν. It is the heritage handed down from the first member of the human race, who was by nature ψυχὴ ζῶσα, "a living soul," and this as the result of the Creative inbreathing (ἐνεφύσησεν) of the breath of life (πνοὴν ζωῆς).[2] We may compare and contrast Philo's view of man's creation: πᾶς ἄνθρωπος κατὰ μὲν τὴν διάνοιαν ᾠκείωται λόγῳ θείῳ, τῆς μακαρίας φύσεως ἐκμαγεῖον ἢ ἀπόσπασμα ἢ ἀπαύγασμα γεγονώς, κατὰ δὲ τὴν τοῦ σώματος κατασκευὴν ἅπαντι τῷ κόσμῳ· συγκέκριται γὰρ ἐκ τῶν αὐτῶν, γῆς καὶ ὕδατος καὶ ἀέρος καὶ πυρός: "Every man, as regards his mind, has

[1] The bracketed words are inserted by himself.

[2] Dr Matheson's interesting comment is more suggestive independently than true to St Paul's thought. "*Man's* essence . . . was his physical being. . . ." (The breath of God's own life) "is something added to man." [St Paul could not have dissociated these two ideas.] "It is breathed only 'into his nostrils.' The idea is that of superficiality." [Not certainly from the point of view of Genesis, but only as compared with St Paul's deeper conception.] ". . . Human nature, even were it unfallen, is naturally frail. The Divine breath or spirit which is in it simply hovers over its surface. . . . According to this (*i.e.* Pauline) interpretation of Genesis . . . it is not merely from sin that man wants deliverance; it is from the incompleteness of his original nature." [St Paul would attribute the incompleteness wholly to sin.] "He wants a perfect union of body and soul. . . . The first Adam was simply a life which, in one solitary direction, blossomed into a spirit. The second Adam was from the outset a spirit which, by its power of infinite diffusiveness, has created for itself a body of natural life" (*Expos.* ii. 5, pp. 193, 194).

been brought into close affinity with the Divine Logos, being an impression, or particle, or effulgence of that blessed nature; but as regards the constitution of his body, he is related to the whole universe, for he has been compounded of the same elements, earth and water, and air and fire" (*De Opific. Mundi*, 146, C. W.; *cf.* Slav. Enoch xxx. 8, "I ordered my Wisdom to make man of seven substances . . . his spirit from My spirit, and from the wind"). It is highly suggestive by means of such a comparison to discover the divergent points which have been reached by two thinkers of Jewish birth and mental inheritance, who go back with equal reverence to the Creation-narratives of Genesis, and yet are led to base upon them superstructures of thought so foreign to each other, the one moulded by the speculations of Hellenic philosophy, the other transformed by the power of a living experience of Christ. St Paul does not here discuss the moral significance of the constitution of human nature. He does not even go so far as to assert, with the Book of Wisdom, that "God created man for immortality." He deals exclusively with what may be called the natural basis of human personality, no doubt regarding it from his normal standpoint, namely, that of one who knows what it has become. There is no trace of *πνεῦμα* there. He only finds *ψυχὴ ζῶσα*, of course regarded as the gift of God, as everything is, which exists in the physical universe. As *ψυχή* differs from *πνεῦμα*, so there must be in his mind a real emphasis on the distinction between *ζῶσα*, "living," and *ζωοποιοῦν*, "life-creating." The distinction is one which lies at the root of his whole Christian conception of existence. Life in man is only raised to its highest power, only attains its proper fulness and significance, when it is renewed, made over again by the entrance of a Divine force, none other than the Spirit, the creative energy of the Founder of the new humanity, the last Adam, Him who has regained Paradise for mankind.[1] This is the form in which St Paul clothes that idea of existence which the philosopher would designate the highest "reality." In this remarkable constitution of things, the apostle will not allow any haphazard element of arbitrariness. It is from first to last an orderly sequence, a rational expression of the will and aim of God. "Not in the first place the 'spiritual' but the 'natural,' thereafter (ἔπειτα) the 'spiritual'" (verse 46). Perhaps in laying down the sequence he is struck by the parallel between human history and the experience of the individual. But he has to go a step further in order to set forth the contrast in its full significance. It is not enough to show the origin of ψυχή and πνεῦμα. He must disclose the background of their several origins. He appeals to the same authorities as before: the Old Testament narrative of Creation on the one hand, and the facts of Christian history on the other. "The first man was out of the earth (γῆς), "earthy" (χοϊκός). This is a paraphrase of Gen. ii. 7: καὶ ἔπλασεν ὁ θεὸς τὸν ἄνθρωπον χοῦν ἀπὸ τῆς γῆς.[2] Hühn imagines that in Gen. i. 26 (P) St Paul found the creation of the heavenly Adam, in ii. 7 (J) that of the earthly,

[1] *Cf.* M'Connell (*op. cit.*, p. 145): "The transit for the individual man from this stage of being to the one which lies beyond, we believe to be a question of the vigour of moral personality."

[2] *Cf.* Wisd. xv. 11: ὅτι ἠγνόησεν τὸν πλάσαντα αὐτὸν καὶ τὸν ἐμπνεύσαντα αὐτῷ ψυχὴν ἐνεργοῦσαν καὶ ἐμφυσήσαντα πνεῦμα ζωτικόν.

in accordance with Jewish Midrashim[1] (see *Alttestamentlichen Citate. . . . im Neuen Testamente*, p. 176). There is no foundation for the hypothesis, so far as we can discover, in the passage before us. "The second man is from heaven." These further statements connect the inferiority of the mere ψυχή or natural principle of life with its derivation from χοῦς and γῆ (*cf.* Wisdom vii. 1, εἰμὶ . . . γηγενοῦς ἀπόγονος πρωτοπλάστου), the superior worth of πνεῦμα with its being a heavenly power and personality. The two types of humanity must correspond to their respective heads. "Of the same quality (οἷος) as the earthly (χοϊκός) are they who are earthly, and of the same quality as the heavenly (ἐπουράνιος) are they who are heavenly" (verse 48). Meanwhile (perhaps all along), his thoughts have risen to the Second Man as being *now* in heaven. But the two contrasted types are not fixed. This is the wonder of his Gospel. "Even as we bore the likeness (*cf.* Gen. v. 3, καὶ ἐγέννησεν κατὰ τὴν εἰδέαν αὐτοῦ καὶ κατὰ τὴν εἰκόνα αὐτοῦ) of the earthly, we shall bear (reading φορέσομεν with Weiss and W. H., *mg.*: the whole context favours the future, because he is rapidly working up to that view of the future life which he desires to set before them) also the image of the heavenly." His argument is complete. He has shown them from the analogy of the sowing of seed, that the same life-principle can clothe itself in altered bodily semblance; nay more, that the very meaning of what seems to be death in the natural world, may only be a transition to a fuller

[1] So Philo. The generic man was created first (ἐποίησεν, Gen. i. 27), subsequently the species Adam (ἔπλασεν, Gen. ii. 7). See Drummond, *Philo*, ii. p. 275.

life, clad in a more perfect organism. The transformation does not mean loss of identity. For "body" is not restricted to a single type. Even on earth there are different species of bodily organism. Still more remarkable is the contrast between earthly and heavenly bodies; and even those heavenly bodies, whose common characteristic is δόξα, are manifold in their types. Why should it be difficult, then, he asks, to comprehend the nature of the Resurrection? Not the body of flesh, the self-expression of the ψυχή, that in which man lives his natural life and in which he dies, is that which will be raised up as the organism of his future glorious existence, for it is subject to weakness and corruption. It has a merely *natural* history. It is the clothing of the common principle of life which belongs to all humanity, as descended from its first member. But that does not exhaust the possibilities of the race. There is a new humanity, which derives its life not from an earthly principle, but from a heavenly Spirit. Its Head is the exalted Lord, who took upon Him human nature, who never laid it aside, but has glorified it, and shown what it may become. He is not a disembodied spirit. He possesses a σῶμα, not of material substance, but πνευματικόν, corresponding to and expressing the life which He lives. That life is now "heavenly," and it awaits all who are His. They shall exchange the body of their humiliation for the body of His glory.[1] Yet the apostle will guard still further against misconceptions. "This,

[1] "So every spirit as it is most pure
And hath in it the more of heavenly light,
So it the fairer bodie doth procure
To habit in, and it more fairly dight
With chearefull grace and amiable sight;

I say, brethren (in case any should continue to be troubled by the old objections), that flesh and blood cannot inherit the Kingdom of God, neither does corruption inherit incorruption" (verse 50). It is easy to see how their perplexity was bound up with the notion of the resurrection of that body of flesh which they actually possessed in their human life. How much of the confusion associated with this doctrine has rested, and still rests, on the same misconception! The apostle's view, on the contrary, is one of far-reaching significance. We can scarcely formulate any idea of the future condition of the individual life, which seems so fully to satisfy the requirements of our thought. "As we progress," says Mr Schiller, "the higher intellectual and moral qualities . . . tend to predominate in consciousness over the physical functions. For the physical processes tend to become unconscious. Consciousness, therefore, is less engrossed by the mechanism of life. Hence the body itself becomes more and more fitted to be the body of a spiritual being, better and

> For of the soule the bodie forme doth take;
> For soule is forme, and doth the bodie make."
>
> Spenser: *An Hymne in Honour of Beautie.*

In the Persian religion the soul of the pious is, on entering Paradise, clad with heavenly raiments. This idea is first clearly seen in the Pehlevi-literature, but there are traces of it in the Avesta (Yast xiii. 49 f.) *Cf.* Bundehesh xxx. 28: "This, too, it says, that whoever has performed no worship . . and has bestowed no clothes as a righteous gift, is naked there" (Böklen, *op. cit.*, p. 62). So also in the Rig-Veda (x. 14, 8), the dead are bidden to "become united to a body, and clothed in a shining form" (see Fairbairn, *Studies*, p. 116). For evidence that in Jewish literature the resurrection-body is usually conceived in a materialistic fashion, see Volz, *op. cit.*, pp. 250-253.

better adapted as the vehicle of a life which is more than physical. . . . The time may come when Matter will no longer offer any obstacles to our wishes, and when, in sober truth, Man will with a word precipitate a mountain into the sea. . . . It is enough for him (*i.e.* the philosopher) to assert . . . that a will *completely* congruous with the Divine would needs have a complete control of the material" (*Riddles of the Sphinx*, pp. 301, 305). From an entirely different standpoint, we have the statement of Professors Balfour Stewart and Tait: "If we are to accept scientific principles, one of the necessary conditions of immortality is a spiritual body, but we as resolutely maintain that of the nature of this . . . we are, and must probably remain, profoundly ignorant" (*Unseen Universe*, p. 8).[1] Is it too daring to hold the conviction that St Paul has a uniquely wonderful vision of the possibilities of a perfect spiritual development, such as that outlined above? May not the *σῶμα πνευματικόν* be the final instance of the organism belonging to "a will completely congruous with the Divine?" This would be an additional corroboration of his derivation of the conception from his personal experience of contact with the risen, perfected Christ, the crown and goal of humanity. We know too little of the connection between mind (will, etc.) and body, to assert what may or may not be possible in the way of organism for the living spirit; yet it appears to us that Hebrew

[1] See also Orr, *Christian View*, p. 136: "The whole tendency of modern inquiry is to draw the two sides of man's nature—the material and the spiritual, the physical and the metaphysical, the physiological and the mental—more closely together"; and *cf.* some suggestive remarks by McTaggart, *International Journal of Ethics*, xiii. pp. 164, 165.

thought was more in accord with the sanest scientific speculation than Hellenic, in that it postulated some type of embodiment of the personality, whether now or in a future life.[1]

But the apostle has to reckon with a problem which must inevitably present itself to his readers. He and they were prepared for a speedy occurrence of the Parousia. That was the event which should usher in the Resurrection. They could now form some conception of the experience of their deceased friends. But what of themselves? How were the survivors, the living, to pass into the final Kingdom of God? This was, in some respects, the most pressing matter of all. For there can be little doubt, from all that we know of St Paul's teaching, that his thoughts dwelt more on the future condition of those living when Christ should appear, than on that of the dead.[2] There can, to his mind, be no distinction between the two groups. "We all (*i.e.* the survivors) shall be transformed" (ἀλλαγησόμεθα).[3] The transformation will be the work of

[1] It is easy, indeed, to see from the instances supplied by Greek and Roman writers that deliverance from the *present body*, in its *present* conditions, was the consideration which weighed with them in conceiving a purely spiritual immortality. *Cf.* Seneca, *Ep.* 102: *Alia origo nos exspectat, alius rerum status. . . . Detrahetur tibi haec circumjecta novissimum velamentum tui cutis, detrahetur caro et suffusus sanguis . . . detrahetur ossa nervique firmamenta fluidorum et labentium. Dies iste, quem tanquam extremum reformidas, aeterni natalis est.*

[2] There is some force in Haller's contention: "It (*i.e.* the Resurrection) was mainly (*i.e.* for St Paul) only a reviving of bodies not long dead, and thus not subjected to total dissolution" *Zeitschr. f. Th. u. K.*, 1892, p. 291).

[3] "None of the 'we all' (verse 51) shall die . . . all of the we all' shall be changed" (Milligan, *Expos.* iv. 4, p. 24).

a moment. It is the putting on by the mortal of immortality. "The dead shall rise incorruptible, and we shall be transformed" (verse 52). Naturally, he assumes that in both cases the final experience is the culmination of a preparatory process. It is not a sudden, unrelated exercise of Divine power, although Divine power is throughout at the back of it. It is the blossoming, so to speak, of the new life, the life of the *πνεῦμα* already implanted. The presence of the Divine Spirit is for the apostle a sufficient cause of all these crowning experiences. He never troubles himself with reflection on details.

We have considered St Paul's central conception at some length, but there remain various related points which call for investigation. It has been supposed by many scholars (*e.g.*, Reuss, Holtzmann, Teichmann, Pfleiderer, Cone, Clemen, Schmiedel, etc.) that, in the interval between 1 Corinthians and 2 Corinthians, St Paul advanced to a new and more spiritual view of resurrection. The passage chiefly cited in support of this theory is the important and somewhat complicated paragraph in 2 Cor. v. 1-10, notably ver. 8: "We choose rather to be absent from the body, and to be present with the Lord." This statement is held to be corroborated by such affirmations as Phil. i. 23: "Having the desire to depart and be with Christ, for that is very much better." St Paul has drifted away, we are told, from that conception of the Resurrection which he has stated in the earlier Epistles, more especially in 1 Cor. xv.[1]

[1] See Schmiedel on 2 Cor. (Holtzmann's *Hand-Commentar*, pp. 238-241); Holtzmann, *N.T. Theol.* ii. p. 193; Reuss, *Histoire de la Théol. Chrét.* ii. p. 220; Cone, *New World*, June 1895,

He now believes that *immediately after death* the soul of the Christian is clothed with its new and appropriate organism, and passes into the immediate presence of God. From this standpoint, the idea of a remarkable crisis at the end of the age becomes superfluous. The soul has already reached its fulness of glory. There is no place for any higher mode of fellowship. The hypothesis is put forward that the apostle was led to this alteration of view, as he became better acquainted with the Hellenistic literature of Alexandria (see, *e.g.*, Pfleiderer, *Urchristentum*, pp. 161, 293, 298). However attractive the conception may appear to our minds, we cannot find that the apostle reached it, at least in the clear-cut, definite shape in which it is described by the writers to whom we have referred. The hypothesis really springs from a literalistic, pedantic interpretation of St Paul's statements. It seems impossible for some exegetes to rid themselves of the notion that when this fervid, ardent missionary, glowing with intense spiritual life, sat down to write to a community of his Christian friends and converts, he could not avoid composing

p. 308; Teichmann, *op. cit.*, pp. 59, 61-67; Clemen, *Niedergefahren zu d. Toten*, p. 144; Charles, *Eschatology*, pp. 395-401. Curiously enough, in the Persian religion, which recognises a judgment at the end of the world, this judgment has been transferred at a later period to the moment which follows death. "According to the Avesta, the separation after death is accomplished by God without a judgment or any particular tribunal" (Söderblom, *op. cit.*, p. 95). Volz notes a parallel process in Jewish literature: "From Hades the path leads to Paradise and Heaven by way of the receptacles guarded by angels, and, instead of the Intermediate State before the Resurrection, there is ultimately found the immediate transference of the individual into the full blessedness of the future" (*op. cit.*, p. 146).

an outline of systematic theology. No account is taken of his varying states of feeling, no account is taken of the many-sidedness of his spiritual experience. Men forget that, in the reachings-forth of his religious faith and imagination, he must often, like Christian thinkers in all ages, overleap wide distances of time and space, must ignore definite and prosaic details, must embrace in his mind vast stretches of the spiritual world.

Probably we shall most easily appreciate his standpoint in the passages cited above, if we attempt to review the famous paragraph in 2 Cor. v. 1 ff. Let us first endeavour to trace the line of thought which was uppermost with St Paul when he wrote the verses under consideration. This is determined by the conclusion of chap. iv., which must never be separated from the opening of chap. v. In iv. 16-18, he emphasises the contrast between the weariness and trouble of the earthly life even for the Christian, and the glory which awaits him in the unseen eternal future. This contrast, it must be noted, remains vivid to his mind throughout the discussion (Volz quotes some remarkable parallels from Jewish literature, p. 156). The present and the future, the seen and the unseen—these are the opposing magnitudes round which his thoughts centre. "For we know that if our earthly house consisting in this tent[1] (the *σῶμα τῆς σαρκός*, the *σῶμα ψυχικόν*) be dissolved (*καταλυθῇ*, lit. broken up), we have a building from God, a house not made by hands,

[1] *Cf.* Wisd. ix. 15, where τὸ γεῶδες σκῆνος is used as an equivalent to σῶμα, in the preceding clause; also Isa. xxxviii. 12, "Mine habitation is removed and is carried away from me as a shepherd's tent."

eternal in the heavens." There is no reference here to the detail of time. He does not yet specify a period. The ἔχομεν ("we have") is simply equivalent to "there awaits us as a sure possession." Bousset shows a disposition to emphasise minutiæ, altogether alien to the apostle, when he supposes that, in speaking of the οἰκία ἀχειροποιητός, St Paul shares the idea (found in various religions) that the soul, ascending to heaven, receives its new body on the threshold of the eternal dwelling of God (*Archiv für Religionswissenschaft*, iv. 2, p. 144). The apostle's assertion is merely a repetition in another form of the statement in 1 Cor. xv. 38, "God giveth it a body." "And indeed for this reason (so we take ἐν τούτῳ with Heinrici) we groan (a remarkable parallel is Rom. viii. 23, 'Even we ourselves groan within ourselves, eagerly looking for our sonship, the redemption of our body,' an utterance which arises out of the precisely identical contrast of 'present sufferings' and 'future glory'), craving to put on over us (ἐπενδύσασθαι) our habitation which is from heaven (*i.e.*, 'the house not made with hands,' 'the building from God,' the σῶμα πνευματικόν), seeing that, as a matter of fact (εἴ γε καὶ, the γε and the καί must be duly emphasised), when we have put it on[1] we shall not be found naked" (*i.e.* disembodied

[1] Ἐνδυσάμενοι must be read here with ℵBCD[c], syrr., cop., etc.; for, as Heinrici most cogently shows, ἐκδυσάμενοι was introduced as a correction, when the idea which led to the addition of this clause, namely, the abolishing of the notion of a joyless vegetation of the unclothed soul in Hades, necessarily disappeared from the later Christian period which was no longer concerned with the controverting of heathen ideas.

spirits, a notion abhorrent to the Hebrew mind. It is to drag into the passage an irrelevant idea, to suppose with Charles, *Eschatology*, p. 394, and Beyschlag, *N. T. Theol.* ii. p. 270, that in using the term *γυμνοί*, he is thinking of the fate of unbelievers.) "For in truth we who are in this (lit. 'the') tent groan, being depressed, because we do not wish to strip ourselves (ἐκδύσασθαι, or 'be stripped'), but to put on (*i.e.* our habitation = the σῶμα πνευματικόν) over us (ἐπενδύσασθαι), in order that our mortality may be swallowed up by life."[1] We are inclined to believe that these words give a hint of St Paul's earnest desire and hope of surviving to the Parousia, and so escaping the terrifying experience of death. For it is difficult to suppose that ἐκδύσασθαι can mean anything else than the parting with the body of flesh. Strangely enough, we have no information as to the apostle's conception of the state after death of those who had died or should die before the Parousia. As has been already pointed out, such considerations did not appeal prominently to his mind, for he regarded

[1] Klöpper's interpretation goes beyond a legitimate exegesis of the apostle's language: "What Paul does *not* wish is that every trace of the old house should be taken from him, and that the new should simply take the place of the old. He wants to keep a germ of the old somatic organism, which would form the bond of connection between the earthly and heavenly condition of existence, and secure the continuity and identity of the old and the glorified human being" (*Jahrb. f. d. Theol.* 1862, p. 43). St Paul does not seem to have cared one whit for "traces" or "germs" of the old organism. He was impatient to be clothed with the new. He longed for this to happen without delay. If the Parousia were to come soon, and so make his transformation possible, the process must necessarily be an "overclothing" of the old by the new, although he never speculates on the *process* or method.

the End as near. Apart from the ordinary verb, ἀποθνήσκειν, the term usually employed by St Paul for the death of believers is *κοιμᾶσθαι*. Obviously it was a most appropriate word, not only as containing the consoling picture of rest, but also as lending itself to the central Christian idea of "awaking," being raised or roused to blissful fellowship with the Lord. The metaphor occurs very frequently in the Old Testament, in passages where there is no thought of a resurrection: *e.g.*, 2 Sam. vii. 12, 1 Kings ii. 10 (numerous instances in this book), etc., etc. The LXX. usually translates it by *κοιμᾶσθαι* (most often equivalent to Heb. שָׁכַב, lit. "lie down"). It is also current among the Greeks. Herkenrath, in his valuable *Studien zu d. griechischen Grabschriften* (Feldkirch, 1896), gives interesting examples of sleep as a euphemism for death in epitaphs, although these are isolated as compared with gloomier conceptions of the under-world (see esp. pp. 21, 28). It is scarcely necessary to refer to its usage in classical poetry, such as *Iliad*, xi. 341; Sophoc., *Electr.* 509. In Judaistic literature, the idea appears in a more elaborated form. This is natural, seeing that the doctrine of resurrection has now become prominent. Hence we find passages like 4 Ezra iv. 37, "He disturbs them not and wakes them not, until the appointed measure is made up"; vii. 32, "The earth shall give back those who sleep in it, and the dust those who dwell in that silence." This writer does not apply the idea of rest to the ungodly: *e.g.*, vii. 80, "Such evil souls do not enter the chambers of rest, but must at once hover about wretchedly, with constant sighs and groans." The same thought appears in the Apocalypse of Baruch: see, *e.g.*, xi.

4-5, "Our fathers laid them to sleep without pain, and the righteous—behold they slumber in the earth in peace: for they have not experienced this tribulation, and have not even heard of that which has befallen us." And in the Book of Wisdom, belonging to another branch of the literature altogether, we read (iv. 7), *δίκαιος δὲ ἐὰν φθάσῃ τελευτῆσαι, ἐν ἀναπαύσει ἔσται*: "But a righteous man, though he die before his time, shall be at rest." Probably among the early Christians the belief prevailed that every one, after death, went to Hades: *cf.* Matt. xxvii. 52, 53, xii. 40; 1 Pet. iii. 19; Eph. iv. 9 (and see Kattenbusch, *Th. L.Z.*, 1902, Sp. 14; Clemen, *Niedergefahren zu d. Toten*, pp. 143 f., 151 f. Clemen excepts from the general lot the case of certain privileged individuals, especially martyrs). Thus Irenæus, *adv. Hæres*, v. 31, 2, has the statement: *Si ergo Dominus legem mortuorum servavit, ut fieret primogenitus a mortuis et commoratus usque ad tertiam diem in inferioribus terræ.* But it would be altogether illegitimate to deduce from St Paul's use of *κοιμᾶσθαι* any imaginary hypothesis of an Intermediate State. We dare not attribute to the apostle any theory of a sleep of the soul, or of a meditative condition of calm waiting in preparation for a fuller bliss (so Matheson, *Expos.* ii. 5, pp. 197, 198; Martensen, *Dogmatics*, pp. 457-463). Nor may we infer any notion of semi-consciousness or the like. Schmiedel supposes, on the ground of the expressions *λυπῆσθε* and *μὴ ἔχοντες ἐλπίδα* in 1 Thess. iv. 13, that St Paul conceives of the Intermediate State as an unsatisfying, troubled condition (*ad loc.*). But their grief and apprehension do not refer to the Intermediate State, as is quite evident from verse 14, but to the uncertainty of resurrection at the Parousia. Simon, again, taking Phil. i. 23 as his basis, speaks of the Intermediate State as one in which we enter into closer union with Christ than was possible in this life, "a dreamy expectation of the life which will come with the day of Resurrection" (*Psychol. d. Paulus*, p. 11); but where is there any trace of this in the Epistles? Holsten imagines that the apostle regards dead believers as γυμνοί, bodiless, sleeping πνεύματα in the abyss (*Paulin. Theolog.*, p. 130). For his theory, he refers to 2 Cor. v. 3, and 1 Cor. xv. 37. If our interpretation of these passages has been correct, it is plain that this is an explanation which can only be forced upon the text. All we are justified in concluding from the writings of St Paul is, that for him death could not bring the believer into any situation which meant separation from his Lord. The fellowship was still imperfect in his view, but it was removed by an infinite gulf from the condition of those who had spurned the gift of the Divine πνεῦμα.[1] At the same time, we need not be surprised that the sensitive mind of the apostle shrank from the severing

[1] *Cf.* Heinrici on 2 Cor. v. 10: "There remains for him as for all Christians, apart from all time-considerations, the truth that leaving the body has for its direct consequence going to the Lord. Therefore he never expresses himself as to the nature of the state between death and resurrection, but only emphasises the fact that all, whether they experience the Parousia or die before it, have a share in the Resurrection and the new life." The earlier documents of the Persian religion, *e.g.*, the Gathic Hymns, have no reference to an Intermediate State. This appears much later under the designation *hamîstakân*, reserved for those in whose case the difference between good and evil is slight (Söderblom, *op. cit.*, p. 125). On "sleep"=Intermediate State in Jewish literature, see an excellent paragraph in Volz, p. 134.

of the bonds which knit the spirit and the body together. As we sought to show in a former chapter, the article of death possessed a peculiar horror for St Paul. And in view of this fact, we believe there is some warrant for supposing that, in the passage from 2 Corinthians with which we have been dealing, he does express a yearning to escape the pang of dissolution and to experience that transformation to immortality, the immortality of the *σῶμα πνευματικόν*, which is the sure heritage of those who shall meet their returning Lord (see also Heinrici on 2 Cor. v. 1 ff.). On the other hand, it may be legitimate to interpret verse 4 in a different sense. In emphasising the contrast between the present and the future, the apostle complains of the burden of the fleshly, bodily existence. But then, perhaps struck by the conception of the future life which is most familiar to his friends at Corinth, he goes on to affirm: "It is not merely to get rid of the carnal, material body we long; it is not for a condition of spiritual nakedness, a disembodied existence of the spirit: our hope, our glory, is in the new spiritual organism which we look forward to possessing." Whichever of these alternatives be truest to St Paul's thinking here, we are safe to say that it is the perfected development, expressed in the *σῶμα πνευματικόν*, which fills his mind. Hence he proceeds (2 Cor. v. 5): "He that prepared (*κατεργασάμενος*)[1] us for this very aim is God, who gave us the pledge of the Spirit. Having confidence, therefore (= on this ground, the pledge of the Spirit), always, and knowing that when at home in the body (the *σῶμα σάρκινον*) we

[1] *Cf.* Exod. xxxix. 1 (LXX.): πᾶν τὸ χρυσίον ὃ κατειργάσθη εἰς τὰ ἔργα; and see Liddell and Scott's *Lexicon*.

are absent from the Lord (for we walk by faith not by sight), we have confidence indeed, and choose rather to be absent from the body and to be at home with the Lord.[1] Wherefore also we make it our ambition, whether at home (*i.e.* in the body) or absent (*i.e.* from the body), to be well-pleasing to Him." Plainly, no theory of an altered conception of the future life of believers can be reared on these latter sentences (verses 6-8). The apostle simply reasserts his confidence (the *οἴδαμεν* of verse 1 is resumed by the *θαρροῦντες* and *θαρροῦμεν* of verses 6, 8) that the condition of the believer which is in prospect, and which is guaranteed by the pledge of the *πνεῦμα*, is infinitely preferable to that in which he is at present situated. In view of the glory in store for all who are God's, it behoves them to strive after His obedience. "For all of us (*i.e.* Christian believers) must be manifested before the judgment-seat of Christ, that each may receive the things done by the body, according to what he has done, whether good or worthless." We cannot refrain from quoting an admirable summary by Wernle, which expresses with absolute accuracy our own view of the apostle's position as represented in the passage which we have been discussing. "The man who wrote the great Resurrection-chapter in 1 Corinthians," he says, "did not possess the capacity for altering his opinions which belongs to the modern theologian. For him, his hope which he there expresses, is a truth for which he is willing to live and die. Even from his prison at Rome, he writes: 'If I may attain the

[1] *Cf.* Test. Abr. xcv. 23: *ἤγγικεν ἡμέρα ἐν ᾗ μέλλεις ἐκ τοῦ σώματος ἐκδημεῖν καὶ ἔτι ἅπαξ πρὸς τὸν κύριον ἔρχεσθαι* (qu. by Teichmann, p. 72).

resurrection from the dead.' Resurrection—Transformation—Judgment, are the absolutely fixed elements in Pauline Eschatology. . . . The yearning to die and to be with Christ is for him the same thing as the hope of resurrection. His yearning overleaps all between death and resurrection, and hurries to its goal for reunion with Jesus. [Wernle compares the attitude of the martyr Ignatius.] For religious hope, death, resurrection, coming to God, are always the same, not for Paul alone. In the same way, the passage about the dissolution of the bodily tabernacle and overclothing with the new garment refers to the transformation at the Resurrection and to nothing else. . . . At bottom, all that happens to his body before the Resurrection is quite indifferent. For he has found the consolation, 'If we live, we live unto the Lord; if we die, we die unto the Lord: therefore whether we live or die, we are the Lord's'" (*Anfänge*, pp. 175, 176). This paragraph deals directly with the important parallel in Phil. i. 23. There also St Paul contrasts his actual condition with that which awaits him. For the present, he is a prisoner in a Roman dungeon, soon to be placed upon his trial, hindered from that work which is his absorbing passion. In the future he has the inspiring prospect of a blissful fellowship with Christ which can never be broken. His thought transcends all experience of an Intermediate State, an interval between death and the full consummation of blessedness. He only sees the earthly life, on the one hand, and Christ, in whom his life is hid, on the other. What may happen between cannot interfere with his glowing conviction that his salvation is independent of death. His position is virtually in line with the pregnant words of Wisdom vi. 19, "Immortality causes to be near to God."[1]

Throughout our discussion of St Paul's conception of the Resurrection, it must have been apparent that attention has been directed exclusively to that event as it affects believers. In this we have followed closely the attitude of the apostle himself. His utterances on the Resurrection are restricted to the Christian community. Various reasons can be assigned for his procedure. To begin with, he is replying to a group of difficult questions, brought expressly before him by members of the Church at Corinth. These perplexities concern their own future. They have nothing to do with any general theory of the future condition of mankind. Indeed, such general theories never appear to have had much interest for St Paul; and a large amount of the misconception which has prevailed in all ages of the Church as to his views on the more outlying sections of Christian truth, is due to the persistent attempt to attribute to him a complete and systematised *Weltanschauung*, built up on the lines on which we construct our own, a scheme of thought in which the various problems of existence are stated, in their

[1] See also an interesting paragraph in Titius, p. 62; and *cf.* Whittier's lines:—

"And so beside the silent sea
  I wait the muffled oar;
No harm from Him can come to me
  On ocean or on shore.

"I know not where His islands lift
  Their fronded palms in air,
I only know I cannot drift
  Beyond His love and care."

(Qu. by Prof. Orr.)

mutual relationships, very much as they appeal to the modern mind. It would be going beyond our due limits to assert that the apostle never attempted to arrange the bearings of his thought in a rational and orderly fashion. But in an historical inquiry like the present, we are restricted to our evidence. We may essay to fill up the *lacunæ* which present themselves, from our own presuppositions, or from a particular modern standpoint. But we have no right to assume that St Paul would have assented to our methods. His absorbing interest is the experience of the Christian man. To his mind, that was, and continued to be, an unceasing discovery of surpassing grandeur and glory. It had not yet been toned down by the misunderstandings, the bitternesses, the worldly pressure of the centuries. The apostle felt himself to be moving in the midst of the operations of awe-inspiring and transcendent Powers. The exalted Lord, the Holy Spirit, were, for his daily experience, living Persons. And the same experiences he knew to be possible for all who were willing to surrender themselves to the sway of Christ. It was his business to press this wonderful opportunity upon Jew and Gentile alike, to win all whom he could reach to the satisfying obedience of his Lord. It need not, then, surprise us that he found little time or inclination for pushing his speculations into all the nooks and crannies of human life and destiny.[1]

[1] *Cf.* 4 Ezra viii. 35-39: "For truly I shall not trouble myself about that which sinners have prepared for themselves, about death, judgment, and destruction; but rather will I rejoice in that which the righteous have won, home-coming, redemption, and recompense." The more profound and sensitive feeling of

The question of a *general* resurrection lies outside St Paul's horizon, at least so far as definite discussions of the event are concerned. Indeed, from the very nature of his doctrine of resurrection, we can easily perceive how it must have been so. Its operating principle, its *cause*, we may go the length of saying, is the power of the new Divine life in the believer's nature—that is, the saving power of God. "If the Spirit of Him who raised Jesus from the dead dwell in you, He who raised from the dead Christ Jesus, shall also make alive your mortal bodies by His Spirit dwelling in you" (Rom. viii. 11). Plainly, therefore, the resurrection of unbelievers must proceed, in the apostle's judgment, on different lines. It cannot follow the norm of the Resurrection of Jesus Christ, which determines that of Christians. It is useless to speculate as to how he conceived of it. An instance of such speculation may be quoted from Schaeder's article, "Auferstehung d. Todten," in *Herzog*, [3] ii. p. 223: "The opinion of the apostle must have been that non-believers would rise in the same body which they formerly possessed. And then those of them who are acquitted in the Judgment, experience a transformation of their body into the spiritual body of believers already risen; the rejected, with their bodies, fall a prey to death. . . . They experience in the Resurrection the deliverance from death won for

St Paul would scarcely have permitted so blunt an utterance. Dr Denney's words are suggestive for the line of thought we have been following: "It is necessary, if we are to reflect in our minds the true proportion and balance of scriptural teaching, to escape from this preoccupation with individuals and exceptions, and to get into the centre and foreground of our thoughts —God's purpose to perfect His kingdom and glorify His people" (*Studies in Theology*, p. 246).

them by the Resurrection of Christ. But owing to their rejection in the Judgment, they must go back into death." This crude hypothesis seems amply to justify the caution expressed above. At the same time it does appear to us probable, in view of his whole conception of the End, so far as it can be pieced together, that St Paul left room for some doctrine of a *general* resurrection. Unquestionably he possessed the conception, as we have already seen, of a universal judgment (see, *e.g.*, 1 Cor. vi. 2, xi. 32; Rom. ii. 5-12). But he never works out this conception in detail. The pictorial elements which he introduces are vague and undefined. How the judgment of the ungodly, which for them is ἀπώλεια, is related in his mind to the events of the End, it is impossible to determine from the materials of the Epistles. But the fact that he does presuppose such a judgment as a definite accompaniment of the Parousia of Christ, would lead us to infer some process in the nature of a resurrection preceding it, in the case even of those who have not become partakers of the πνεῦμα. Otherwise, he must be supposed to agree with the tradition of the Talmudic literature, in holding that "he who has no future reward will also have no part in the Resurrection. He remains in death, and has been already judged in death" (Weber, *Lehren d. Talmud*, p. 373).[1] It may no doubt be said that the conception of a universal judgment, so far as its elements have an objective aspect, is simply a portion of the

[1] It is interesting to note that ἀπώλεια as a translation of אֲבַדּוֹן (Job xxvi. 6, Rev. ix. 11), is synonymous with Sheol (see Beer on Enoch li. in *Kautzsch*). On the stages in the belief in a resurrection of the ungodly, see a terse statement in Schwally, *Leben nach d. Tode*, pp. 171, 172.

popular religious consciousness of the time, which the apostle has retained, without endeavouring to adjust it to his profounder and more spiritual conceptions.[1] This is a supposition which even the soberest and most restrained Christian thought ought not to reject *à priori*. The very highest endowment of a human soul with the Divine Spirit can never turn the consciousness into an isolated automaton. Any assertions or positions resting on such an assumption, make it impossible for us to understand or appreciate the self-revelation of God, which is a process in history. But in St Paul's case, as in that of all the New Testament writers, we must be content to form our estimate of his conceptions solely from the evidence which we possess. Various problems may remain, for which we should desire to have his solution. It is safer to acquiesce in the situation with a wise suspense of judgment, than to supply plausible hypotheses of our own.[2]

[1] "It is not given to any man to see all the consequences that follow from his own thinking. He may quite conceivably hold, in the scheme of his beliefs, propositions that are inconsistent with each other" (Orr, *Christian View*, p. 43).

[2] *Cf.* the lack of adjustment between the conceptions of judgment and the future life of righteous and ungodly in Wisdom (*e.g.*, iii. 1 ff., iv. 20 ff.). "Jewish sources also show insecurity on this point. According to Josephus' representation of the Pharisees' doctrine, only the good have ῥᾳστώνη τοῦ ἀναβιοῦν, and will receive other bodies, while the bad are punished in Hades (*cf.* Dillmann, *A. T. Theol.*, p. 410 f). This evidence is confirmed by 2 Macc. vii. 9, 11, 23; xii. 43-45. . . . Ps. Sol. iii. 12, which only know a resurrection to life. Enoch lxi. 5 speaks only of a resurrection of the elect, yet in li. 1, 2 there is a general giving-forth of the dead, among whom the righteous are chosen. But the general resurrection is in xxii. 13 restricted to this extent that the ungodly, who are already sufficiently punished, are not

It is of comparatively little importance to attempt to determine the place of the Resurrection among the events of the End. In his earlier Epistles, at least, we can gain a general idea of the apostle's conception. The signal of the End is the Parousia itself, the manifestation of the Lord for judgment, and the completion of salvation. Contemporaneous with the Parousia are the Resurrection of believers and the transformation of the living (Christians), who are then *revealed* in glory along with their glorified Lord. Their judgment can only mean, as has been pointed out in a former chapter, the unfolding to themselves in the presence of Christ of the comparative worth of their life and service.

We have already referred to the frequent use of ἀποκάλυψις and ἀποκαλύπτειν in this connection. On the basis of their usage, Prof. Bruston has propounded a theory which, he believes, abolishes some of the main difficulties attending St Paul's conceptions of the Last Things. He holds that the apostle employs the verb ἐγείρειν in two different senses, "habitually, to express the revivification of the

raised (xc. 18); while renegades from Israel are cast into Gehenna (xc. 26; *cf.* xxvii. 23). On the other hand, Apoc. Bar. l., and Test. xii. Patr. xii. 10, clearly teach a general resurrection. In consequence, in 4 Ezra vii. 28-32 (*cf.* Apoc. Mosis xiii.), the event of resurrection is doubted. Obviously, this latter is the latest and most secondary idea, which one must not forthwith presuppose in Paul" (Titius, p. 51, note 1). This note is most suggestive as to the fluidity of eschatological belief, a phenomenon which is highly natural in a province where standards of comparison and the language of human life must prove inadequate. Volz notes, with reference to Rabbinic theology, that it is impossible to determine clearly whether they taught a resurrection of all men, or only of all Israel (*op. cit.*, p. 247).

believer at the moment of death, and the clothing of him in a new body, spiritual or heavenly (so, *e.g.*, in 2 Cor. v. 1 ff.; Phil. i. 23), and sometimes, more rarely, to express the appearance or manifestation of their glorified bodies to the living at the moment of the Parousia (1 Cor. xv. 23, 52; 1 Thess. iv. 16). In the later Epistles he uses precisely for this second conception the noun 'manifestation' (Rom. viii. 19), and the verb 'to appear' (Col. iii. 4)" (*Revue de Théol. et des Questions Religieuses*, Jan. 1902, p. 80). We have in this chapter attempted to show that St Paul does not set forth two contradictory conceptions of the Resurrection in these two groups of passages, but *only lays the emphasis on a different moment of thought.* Further, it is inconceivable that he should make use of the rarer and altogether abnormal sense of the crucial term ἐγείρειν, without any caution or explanation, in those passages where he is dealing expressly with difficulties which have been brought before him, and where, if anywhere, he must state his own theory. But while far from accepting Bruston's theory, we cannot help fancying that the apostle's employment of the terms ἀποκάλυψις ἀποκαλύπτειν, and φανερωθῆναι, reveals the presence of a profounder strain in his eschatological thought. It may quite well mark a process in which he begins to feel a certain inadequacy in those traditional and more external elements of Eschatology which still remained in his consciousness. This is a growth which might be expected in the maturing of his spiritual life. Possibly the very fact that he ignores all discussion or characterisation of an Intermediate State, points to the supreme importance which he assigns to the future manifestation of believers with

Christ in their σώματα πνευματικά, whatever be the stages or experiences which constitute their rising to glory. Be that as it may, it appears to us highly significant for the progress of his thought that in the Imprisonment-Epistles, which stand so late in his career, St Paul delights to sum up his outlook into the future in the simple term ἐλπίς. Perhaps, as he penetrated deeper into the relation of the believer to his Lord, the events of the Coming Æon and its inauguration paled into insignificance in the light of that perfected fellowship which was the final goal of them all. Perhaps, as he sought to fathom the treasures of wisdom and knowledge which were hidden in Christ, he felt less confidence even in the prophetic forecasts which had been a stable element in his eschatological thought. Perhaps he grew more and more to distrust the use of earthly imagery and pictures drawn from human experience, to body forth the circumstances of a life belonging to another order. Will not the Christian Church act wisely in following the example of her great spiritual teacher? "Eye hath not seen, nor ear heard, neither have entered into the heart of man, the things which God hath prepared for them that love him. But God hath revealed them unto us by his Spirit" (1 Cor. ii. 9-10). And the Spirit reveals spiritual truth, not physical or external processes. The Spirit is the Divine pledge of a future life hid with Christ in God, not the historian of a sequence of outward events framed in the setting of this temporal world. At the most, it is enough for the apostle to give his readers approximations to the great, saving, final experiences. It is enough so to present these as to inspire them with the splendid certainty of Christian hope. It will suffice for St Paul, as their spiritual father, with unfaltering faith to affirm, "Of this I am confident, that He which hath begun the good work in you will perform it until the day of Jesus Christ" (Phil. i. 6). Do Christian men require any further assurance for their future?

CHAPTER VI

ST PAUL'S CONCEPTION OF THE CONSUMMATION OF THE KINGDOM OF GOD

IN the present chapter we must attempt not so much to describe St Paul's conceptions of certain additional events of the End, as rather to gather together various hints, more or less vague, which he has thrown out in his Epistles, and from these to present as clear a view as we can reach of his foreshadowing of the final Consummation. Part of our task will be to carry a stage or two further some of the conceptions which have occupied us already, and to fill in the outline of a larger setting or background for these. And we will also endeavour to bring out into bolder relief several aspects of the Pauline Eschatology, which have hitherto only been touched in passing.

Students of New Testament theology during the past decade have grown weary of the endless, and it must be said, somewhat uninspiring, discussions which have centred round the idea of the Kingdom of God. The teaching ot Jesus has had frequently to suffer violence that it might square with the pet theory of theologians. After all, there still prevails a large divergence of opinion as to the meaning and content of this ruling thought of the Master.

Thus, *e.g.*, Ritschl defines Jesus' doctrine of the Kingdom of God as "not the common exercise of worship, but the organisation of humanity through action inspired by love."[1] Haupt, on the other hand, holds that Jesus regards the Kingdom, "not as a fellowship, but as an organism of heavenly—*i.e.* super-natural—blessings, gifts, and forces, which are to operate in humanity, and transform it into the province of the rule of God."[2] Kähler speaks of Jesus' preaching of the Kingdom as His "veiled self-assertion," as contrasted with the Gospel of Christ, which is "His revealed and fully unfolded self-assertion."[3] Orr describes it as that idea which "defines the aim and purpose of God in Creation and Redemption."[4] Whatever be its most accurate definition, in our judgment even so (apparently) rich a concept as this is far too meagre to embrace the spiritual outlook of Jesus Christ. But we willingly allow that its formulation and application have been very fruitful, both for the comprehension of the basis of Christian thought, and for the relating of Jesus' view of His Gospel to the needs of present-day religion.

In the midst of all diversities of interpretation, most competent New Testament scholars admit that Jesus' idea of the Kingdom included a distinctly eschatological element. We say "included," for it is surely a case of theorising run mad to put forward the hypothesis, which J. Weiss defends so strenuously in his *Predigt Jesu vom Reiche Gottes*, that the con-

[1] *Justification and Reconciliation*, vol. iii. (E. Tr.) p. 12.

[2] *S.K.*, 1887, p. 383.

[3] *Gehört Jesus in d. Evangelium*, p. 22.

[4] *Christian View of God and World*, p. 354.

ception of Jesus was nothing else than eschatological. Such a position can only be established by the clumsy device of arbitrarily weakening the force of those passages in the Synoptic Gospels which are its refutation. The Kingdom, in our Lord's view of it, was unquestionably the Messianic kingdom, foreshadowed from of old under various guises. But then it was Messianic in the same sense in which He was the Messiah. No unprejudiced reader of the New Testament needs to be reminded of the contrast between His conception of Himself and the Messianic forecasts dimly adumbrated in the Old Testament, and worked out in greater or less detail in Judaistic literature and the theology of the Synagogue. For Him the *religious* aspect of Messiah and His kingdom was all in all. Surrender to the gracious rule of God as Father which He proclaimed, and all the blessedness of fellowship with God which that surrender brought in its train, constituted in His view the true aim of life for individuals and for the world. On this basis, the certainty of the Kingdom was, at one stroke, dissevered from all political and national contingencies. It was a certainty planted in the religious consciousness. Hence Jesus, in the midst of humiliation and rejection, could regard the fortunes of His Kingdom with unbroken calm. For He felt the pledge of its consummation in His own experience, in that union of life with God which must be the supreme ideal for humanity. The soul which is made conscious of that life is, at the same time, made sure that God's all-embracing purpose of good must be fulfilled. The community which knows that life of God, and is ruled by it, already forms the nucleus of the

Kingdom.[1] It was this religious aspect which He pressed home upon the hearts of His disciples and those who assembled to listen to His preaching. As soon as it was appreciated and began to assert itself in human lives, He knew that the foundation of the Kingdom had been laid in the world. But inevitably, from this point of view, it must have a forward look. He plants the seed (Mark iv. 26-29). It germinates and begins to spring up. But the process, although present from the first — present in its essence and living reality—is at best but tardy. Thus the gaze of the Husbandman will always be directed to the distant end—the harvest-time—when the fruit of His toil is ripe for the ingathering, and His original aim is completely realised.

It would lead us too far afield even to attempt the

[1] Ritschl expresses, with characteristic insight, the transformation of the kingdom-idea which Jesus wrought: "While the Divine purpose in the world is bound up with the naturally conditioned unity of the Israelitish nation, the position of this nation in the world is made dependent upon legal and political conditions and material advantages, which as such are of a mundane order, and do not correspond to the supra-mundane position of the one God. Thus there was forced upon Israel the necessity of always postponing to a future, which never became present, the reconciliation between its position in the world and God. Jesus rose above this standpoint, and introduced a new religion by setting free the lordship of the supra-mundane God from national and political limitations, as well as from the expectation of material well-being, and by advancing its significance for mankind to a spiritual and ethical union, which at once corresponds to the spirituality of God, and denotes the supra-mundane end of spiritual creatures" (*Justification and Reconciliation*, vol. iii. (E. Tr.) p. 455). See also the instructive parallelism and contrast between the Synoptists and the Rabbinic writers with regard to the Kingdom of God, in Volz, *op. cit.*, pp. 299, 300.

briefest examination of the eschatological element in our Lord's conception of the Kingdom. But hints of it have already been presented. In our discussion of the Parousia, we had occasion to quote many passages from the Gospels directly bearing upon it. These prove beyond doubt that Jesus looked forward to a time, known only to the Father, when the Kingdom which he had already founded in the world should enter upon a new, which was to be the final, stage of its development. The Son of Man was to come "in the glory of His Kingdom." There was to be the inauguration of that splendid epoch which He once names the παλινγενεσία (Matt. xix. 18), "the new birth" (of things), in which His loyal followers should find a high recompense, in which fidelity to Him should rank as the most honourable distinction. Several passages, in the order in which the Synoptic Gospels place them, seem to hint that this coming epoch might be near. But the unparalleled impression made on the minds of the first generation of Christians by the destruction of Jerusalem (70 A.D.) and all the disturbances which led up to that crisis, has probably introduced complications into the eschatological discourses.

This Synoptic tradition, as we have already noted, exerted a powerful influence upon the thinking of St Paul. He could receive it, not merely as stamped with the authority of Christ Himself, but also as embodying and bringing to a fit culmination all the foreshadowings of the great prophetic men. The experiences and historical development of the people of Israel seemed, of course, to the apostle to supply the mould within which the highest spiritual life of humanity was to shape itself. No other conception could appear so truly adapted to set forth the future advance in the apprehension of God and His revelation, and in the realisation of His will in the world, as that of the Theocracy, the Divine rule of men. Only, it had to be raised above all nationalism, had to be viewed in the immense range of its significance and possibilities, had to be left unrestricted, so that it should, on the one hand, take the form of the brotherhood, the society, the Church (the side of organisation, if we may so call it); while, on the other, it stood for a Divine power, a Divine redemptive purpose, a Divine life actually working in individuals, and thus making the spiritual community possible as God's representative in the world. When we think of the largeness of scope belonging to this whole point of view, we are better able to understand the actual position of the apostle Paul.

It must appear strange, at first sight, that the central term of the Synoptic tradition, *βασιλεία τοῦ θεοῦ* (or *τῶν οὐρανῶν*), should occur, comparatively speaking, so rarely in the Pauline Epistles. When it does appear, it is generally used in a predominantly eschatological sense. Thus, in 1 Thess. ii. 12, it is directly combined with the eschatological term, *δόξα* (*τοῦ θεοῦ τοῦ καλοῦντος ὑμᾶς εἰς τὴν ἑαυτοῦ βασιλείαν καὶ δόξαν*). In 2 Thess. i. 5, it is found in the phrase, *εἰς τὸ καταξιωθῆναι ὑμᾶς τῆς βασιλείας τοῦ θεοῦ*, "that you may be deemed worthy of the Kingdom of God," a collocation which vividly reminds us of the words of Jesus in Luke xx. 35, *καταξιωθέντες τοῦ αἰῶνος ἐκείνου τυχεῖν καὶ τῆς ἀναστάσεως τῆς ἐκ νεκρῶν*, "being accounted worthy to attain the future Æon and the Resurrection from the dead," and is really a direct parallel to them.[1] We need scarcely observe that its bearing is wholly future. This may also be said of its employment in 1 Cor. xv. 24, a passage which will demand careful consideration later on. To the same category must be referred those statements of the apostle which speak of an "inheriting" of the Kingdom. Such are—1 Cor. vi. 9, "Know ye not that unrighteous men shall not inherit the Kingdom of God"; Gal. v. 21, "They that do such things shall not inherit the Kingdom of God"; Eph. v. 5, "Every fornicator, or impure person, or covetous man . . . hath not an inheritance in the Kingdom, of Christ and of God"; 1 Cor. xv. 50, "Flesh and blood cannot inherit the Kingdom of God." This last example clearly shows the sense in which St Paul uses the term, which is evidently that of the future epoch of the consummation, the era of a new and spiritual order of existence.[2] Of precisely similar significance are his words in Rom. viii. 17, although the term "Kingdom" does not occur in that context: "If children, also heirs, heirs of God, joint-heirs with Christ, if so be that we suffer with Him, that we may also be glorified with Him." This passage is so typical for another aspect of the Kingdom in St Paul's writings, that we must return to it. Meanwhile it is fair to say that no one with any true appreciation of Paulinism can restrict the apostle to the purely eschatological sense of the word, or the idea which it

[1] *Cf.* the phrase common in Rabbinic writings: "To be worthy of the future Æon" (see Dalman, *Worte Jesu*, p. 97). J. Weiss (*op. cit.*, p. 107 f.) is justified in emphasising the connection at many points between Jesus' conception of the Kingdom of God and that of the αἰὼν μέλλων.

[2] See also Wernle, *Reichsgotteshoffnung*, pp. 2, 3.

embodies. Thus, in 1 Cor. iv. 20, he declares that "the Kingdom of God is not in word, but in power," and from the context it is plain that the "power" is something not expected in the future, but now present, and capable of being put to the proof. We may compare the answer of Jesus in reply to the Pharisees who asked Him when the Kingdom of God should come: "The Kingdom of God cometh not with observation (μετὰ παρατηρήσεως, practically= 'as an event which causes a sensation'). . . . For behold the Kingdom of God is within (or, 'in the midst of,' ἐντός) you" (Luke xvii. 20, 21). This instance gives a suggestive hint as to St Paul's interpretation of the Synoptic tradition, with which he must have been familiar; and it is corroborated by such affirmations as Rom. xiv. 17, "The Kingdom of God is not eating and drinking (the questions which had stirred up controversy in the Christian brotherhood), but righteousness, and peace and joy in the Holy Spirit; for he that in this matter *serves* Christ is well-pleasing to God, and approved by men." Here it is noteworthy that membership in the Kingdom and serving Christ are deliberately identified. In Col. i. 12-14, also, he gives thanks to the Father, "who delivered us from the power of darkness, and transferred (μετέστησεν) us into the Kingdom of the Son of his love, in whom we have the redemption, the forgiveness of our sins." The Kingdom, to his mind, is obviously a realised fact, a sphere already existing. Perhaps he would call it at its present stage, more strictly, the "Kingdom of Christ;"[1] that would explain the remarkable utter-

[1] J. Weiss supposes that the idea of a βασιλεία τοῦ Χριστοῦ, as distinct from βασιλεία τοῦ θεοῦ, is "a primitive-Christian concep-

ance of 1 Cor. xv. 24, "Then the end, when He shall have delivered up the Kingdom to His God and Father."

Some scholars (*e.g.* Bornemann on 2 Thess. i. 5) endeavour to account for the comparative rarity of the *term* in the Epistles, by supposing that all the time the idea lay in the background of the apostle's thought, and that the Christian communities to which he wrote were so familiar with it from his oral teaching, and so ready to take it for granted, that it required no direct emphasis. We cannot say that such an hypothesis carries conviction. It is hard to reconcile with the method of St Paul. His favourite conceptions are not kept in the background, but have a habit of asserting themselves with remarkable prominence throughout his writings. We are far more inclined to believe that the idea of the Kingdom, which was certainly very familiar to him, has been clothed by St Paul in various guises. And these are not difficult to identify, as we shall discover. The fact must be related to the teaching of Jesus Himself. We have already pointed out that the *bare* conception of the Kingdom does not suffice to contain all the breadth and depth of the revelation

tion found in the New Testament, first in Paul, and not in the teaching of Jesus" (*op. cit.*, p. 41). This is precisely what might be expected, and is quite in line with the method of Jesus' self-revelation, as described in the Synoptists. If it were necessary, the roots of the two conceptions could be traced back to the Old Testament. The one, as Dalman points out, "attaches itself to Dan. vii. 14, 27, where the dominion is given first to the 'Son of Man,' then to the saints of the Highest. The other rests on Dan. ii. 44, according to which 'the God of heaven' will at the end set up an everlasting 'dominion,' which destroys all other dominions" (*Worte Jesu*, p. 109).

of Jesus. Again and again, for example, He uses the idea of the family to express the highest relationship between God and men. It is scarcely necessary to give instances, but we may refer to such well-known passages as Matt. vii. 9-11, xi. 25 f., v. 43-48, vi. 1-8; Luke xv. 11 f. Here it is not the relation of ruler and subjects which He has in view, but that of father and children. Titius, indeed, endeavours to show that in the East there is no sharp distinction between the State and the family, and accordingly, that when Jesus speaks of God's fatherly relation to men, the thought of the Kingdom is still implied. In proof of his position, he quotes the remarkable phrase, "the children of the Kingdom," which occurs in Matt. viii. 12, xiii. 38 (p. 32). We would not deny that there is some force in the contention. But the very fact that the kingdom-idea has to be so enlarged as to become virtually a different (although it may be a related) conception, verifies our position. The example we have chosen is most suggestive for St Paul, as revealing one of the highest aspects in which he has remodelled the kingdom-idea, possibly on the basis of the teaching of Jesus. In the words which were quoted from Rom. viii. 17, "If children, then heirs, heirs of God, joint-heirs with Christ," the apostle brings the two related thoughts into intimate connection. The position of "children of God" is attained by the reception of the Spirit. The Spirit teaches the believer in whom He dwells to cry, "Abba, Father" (ver. 15). The Spirit attests their own conviction that they are children of God (ver. 16). None other than children can inherit the future, eternal Kingdom. This passage shows how the central teaching of the apostle, his teaching on the

Spirit and the sonship (υἱοθεσία) of believers, may be directly related to the idea of the Kingdom. But a further evidence of the form in which the idea possessed him is to be found in his doctrine of the Lordship (κυριότης) of Christ. This, for St Paul, is no mere title of adoration. Its typical significance appears in the designation which he frequently gives himself in the opening sentences of his Epistles, δοῦλος Ἰησοῦ Χριστοῦ. It is shown also by such utterances as Rom. xii. 11, τῷ κυρίῳ δουλεύοντες; Col. iii. 24, τῷ κυρίῳ Χριστῷ δουλεύετε. Here we touch the very root of the matter. For the apostle, the idea of the Kingdom is really concentrated in the person of the exalted Christ. He is Lord of the realm of His δοῦλοι. They prove their membership in His Kingdom by serving Him faithfully. In the end they shall receive "the recompense of the inheritance" (ἀπὸ κυρίου ἀπολήμψεσθε τὴν ἀνταπόδοσιν τῆς κληρονομίας, Col. iii. 24, quoted above). As Feine well sums it up, "The reason why Paul did not carry on Jesus' preaching of the Kingdom is given in 2 Cor. i. 20: 'Howsoever many are the promises of God, in Him is their yea'" (*Jesus Christus u. Paulus*, p. 172).

But to realise the profoundness with which the apostle conceives the idea of the Kingdom, from the point of view which has been illustrated by our last quotations, we must refer to his far-reaching doctrine of the Body of Christ, the unity and mutual service of the members of the ἐκκλησία in the exalted Lord, their life-principle and Head.[1] New Testament theology has

[1] Thus, *e.g.*, Kaftan holds that St Paul really continues Jesus' preaching of the Kingdom, in the emphasis he lays on the fellowship of life which believers share with the glorified Christ (see *Das Wesen d. christlichen Religion*, [2] p. 253).

been too apt to lay exclusive stress on the individualism of St Paul. And truly, in his great conceptions of the genesis of the Divine life in the soul, and the liberty of the Christian man, that aspect of his thought can scarcely be over-estimated. But the liberty, based on a genuinely personal relation to Christ the Redeemer and Revealer of the Father, carries with it immense responsibilities, responsibility as regards the brethren (the members of the same elect family or society) for whom Christ died, and in mutual interaction with them, direct responsibility to the Lord Himself. Full justice must be done to those momentous passages, occurring with growing frequency as his life advances, in which the apostle earnestly reminds his readers of the duties of the "members" to the "body" (see Rom. xii.-xv. 6; 1 Cor. xii.-xiv.; Col. i. 13-23, ii. 18-19; Eph. i. 9-10, 22-23, ii. 18-22, iv. 1-24), and exults in the unifying of all jarring elements through the possession of the same Spirit in the one Lord and Head.

Throughout our discussion we have been mainly occupied with the eschatological conceptions of St Paul in their bearing upon individuals, and that aspect must at no stage be allowed to slip out of view. But we must also leave room for the broader sweep of his spiritual vision. We must avoid one-sidedness in the presentation of the apostle's thought, by emphasising the loftier flights of his religious intuition. The Pauline doctrine of the New Life and of the πνεῦμα, its creative principle, has been examined at length. We have attempted to follow the development of the πνευματικοί up to that stage at which they are raised from the dead by the power of God, through the instrumentality of the indwelling Spirit. From the time of resurrection, at all events, they possess a *σῶμα πνευματικόν*, which is the fitting organism and expression of their Divinely-imparted life. This crucial event, with all its accompaniments, is placed in intimate connection with the Parousia of the Saviour and the final Judgment of mankind. We must now inquire, What is to be the *culminating* experience, according to St Paul's view, of those who belong to Christ, who possess the pledge of the Spirit?

Their future condition is described by the apostle under various vivid pictures. One of the most significant represents them as transformed into the image (*εἰκών*) of Christ (2 Cor. iii. 18; Rom. viii. 29; *cf.* 1 John iii. 2, "It doth not yet appear what we shall be; but we know that, when He shall appear, we shall be *like* Him," *ὅμοιοι αὐτῷ*). We can discover the profound sense which belongs to this term from its use in Col. i. 15: "Who (*i.e.* Christ) is the Image (*εἰκών*) of the invisible God, the First-begotten of every creature" (or, "all creation," *πάσης κτίσεως*). Here, plainly, *εἰκών* has a *cosmic* significance. It bears a relation to the Divine purpose in the universe from the beginning. It is normative for the whole Divine self-expression which we call "creation." Not mere semblance is implied in St Paul's use of *εἰκών*, but semblance resting on identity of nature, community of being. Thus for believers the apostle expects not only fellowship with Christ, but a real assimilation to His Divine nature. That expectation is expressed in clear language by the remarkable statement of Phil. iii. 21, which asserts that Christ "shall transform the body of our humiliation (the *σῶμα σάρκινον* or *ψυχικόν*) into conformity with (*σύμμορφον*) the body of His glory (*σῶμα τῆς δόξης αὐτοῦ = σῶμα πνευματικόν*), according to the working whereby He is able even to subdue all things to Himself." In this passage, as has already been noticed, *σῶμα* does not mean mere form, but the form which corresponds to the inner principle of life, the self-realising, self-revealing nature. The same event or experience he designates in Rom. viii. 23 by the words, "the redemption of our body" (*τὴν ἀπολύτρωσιν τοῦ σώματος ἡμῶν*; *cf.* Eph. i. 14, *ἀπολύτρωσιν τῆς περιποιήσεως*, "redemption of that which has been acquired," illustrated by Acts xx. 28, *τὴν ἐκκλησίαν τοῦ θεοῦ, ἣν περιεποιήσατο διὰ τοῦ αἵματος τοῦ ἰδίου*, "which He purchased by His own blood").[1] The phrase is typical of his manner of thought. A redemption of the soul would not satisfy him. He cannot conceive a true personal life on that basis. It must be a redemption of the whole person as a unity. And he finds a basis of certainty for that high prospect in the experience of the risen Lord, who cannot be regarded as a mere disembodied, glorified Spirit, but has been exalted in the glorification of His whole nature, His Spirit (the *πνεῦμα ἁγιωσύνης*) controlling all things, and yet endowed with an organism which preserves the continuity of His human nature, and is the perfectly appropriate embodiment of His Spirit, which is the "Ego." But that is the nature in which He became

[1] Perhaps the phrase may be a reminiscence of Ps. lxxiv. 2, *μνήσθητι τῆς συναγωγῆς σου ἧς ἐκτήσω ἀπ' ἀρχῆς· ἐλυτρώσω ῥάβδον κληρονομίας σου*: "Remember Thy congregation which Thou didst purchase (Heb. קָנָה) from the beginning: Thou didst redeem the staff of Thine inheritance."

incarnate, so conferring unique dignity on human life, and claiming the creation of God for its Creator. This claim is now, in very deed, to be made good, made good in Him who is "the First-begotten among many brethren" (Rom. viii. 29). In Him human creatures are to become truly sons of God, for His Spirit which the believer receives is the "spirit of sonship" (*πνεῦμα υἱοθεσίας*, Rom. viii. 15; Gal. iv. 5, 6), which remoulds the whole nature into fitness for a place in the Divine Family.

It has been noted in a former chapter, as a fundamental axiom of eschatological thought, that "the End is to be as the Beginning." Thus, in 4 Ezra vii. 30, we read that at the opening of the new epoch "the world shall be transformed into the silence of the primitive time, for seven days, as in the beginning." One of the questions which Baruch puts to God is, "Shall the structure of the world return to its original nature?" (Apoc. Bar. iii. 7). And Enoch tells how the angel Uriel showed him all the laws of the heavenly lights and all the divisions of time, "until the new eternally-enduring creation is made" (Enoch lxxii. 1). The Christian Father, Barnabas, expresses the conception distinctly, *ἰδού, ποιῶ τὰ ἔσχατα ὡς τὰ πρῶτα* (vi. 13). It is easy to dismiss this axiom as part of an artificial scheme, devised by apocalyptic writers for the sake of securing a rounded-off completeness in their speculations on the Last Things. But the attitude of the apostle reveals the kernel of truth which lies within. Through the defacing influence of sin, humanity has failed of its high purpose in the Divine mind. It has failed to show forth the untarnished glory of its Divine source. Man's God-given power of free choice has issued in disobedience to the Highest. But that is not the conclusion of the whole matter:

> "My own hope is a sun will pierce
> The thickest cloud earth ever stretched;
> That after Last returns the First,
> Tho' a wide compass round be fetched;
> That what began best, can't end worst,
> Nor what God blessed once, prove accurst."
> (Browning, *Apparent Failure*, vii.)

The Second Adam, who is from heaven, has become the Founder of a renewed humanity—not its Founder, as standing apart from it, and looking upon His work in aloofness, but as having brought the Divine into a relation of intimacy with it, in full accord with the original purpose of God. As the *εἰκών* of the Invisible God, as having eternal relations to the Father, Christ is essentially the *πρωτότοκος πάσης κτίσεως*, "the First-begotten of every created thing," its norm and type, that which sets for it its true end, "for *in* Him were created all things in heaven and on earth . . . all things have been created through Him, and with a view to (*εἰς*) Him" (Col. i. 15, 16).[1] Here we discover what, for the apostle's mind, is His essential cosmic significance. But now this significance has been unveiled to men, can be understood by humanity in the new creation (בְּרִית חֲדָשָׁה in Rabbinic literature, see Weber, p. 382, *καινὴ κτίσις* in St Paul, *e.g.* Gal. vi. 15), of which Christ, as perfected and carrying with Him all the fruits of His redemptive work, is the life-giving principle, for He is "the beginning (*ἀρχή*, basis, precisely = our "first principle"), the First-begotten

[1] *Cf.* and contrast Philo, *De Confus. Ling.* 146, C.W.: *κἂν μηδέπω μέντοι τυγχάνῃ τις ἀξιόχρεως ὢν υἱὸς θεοῦ προσαγορεύεσθαι, σπουδαζέτω κοσμεῖσθαι κατὰ τὸν πρωτόγονον αὐτοῦ λόγον.*

(πρωτότοκος, same term as above) *from the dead* (the aspect which bulks most largely in the apostle's vision), in order that He might become (γένηται, for Christ's glorious position as exalted κύριος is always represented by St Paul as the culmination of the process which the Epistle to the Hebrews calls the τελείωσις) of the first rank (πρωτεύων) among all" (ἐν πᾶσιν, no doubt purposely left indefinite, including every province of creation), Col. i. 18. The Incarnation, the accomplishment of His redeeming purpose through death, the Resurrection, all these processes and events were needful to disclose to men the marvellous aim of God, and to begin the realisation of the aim on the stage of human history. We can discern, therefore, what lofty heights of thought lie around St Paul's conception of the future of redeemed humanity. These, indeed, are only adumbrated in such expressions as transformation into the εἰκών of Christ, conformation to the body of His glory; but in view of what he has outlined in Colossians and elsewhere, we can discover that they involve perfect assimilation to the very nature of God. That this will include a transfiguration of the material, is plain from the apostle's confident expectation of the ἀπολύτρωσις τοῦ σώματος, the redemption of the body, a redemption which, as we shall see later, extends to universal creation (Rom. viii. 18-23). Hence St Paul, in face of the marvellous vision which bursts upon his soul, gives thanks to the Father, "who hath made you capable (ἱκανώσαντι) of your share (τὴν μερίδα) in the heritage (τοῦ κλήρου)[1] of the saints in light" (ἐν φωτί), Col. i. 12.

[1] *Cf.* Enoch lxviii. 7: "For he (*i.e.* the Son of Man) shall preserve the portion of the righteous." "'To take possession

This description, which focusses in itself various hints to be found throughout the Epistles, calls now for consideration. We have had occasion in previous chapters to notice St Paul's predilection for describing the condition of future bliss by terms which imply brightness and radiance. In estimating the effect of his conversion-experience upon the shaping of his eschatological conceptions, we briefly sketched the Old Testament basis of his idea of *δόξα*, "glory"; an idea which plays so prominent a part in his forecasts of the life to come. We saw that God's revealed presence was constantly designated His "glory," as, *e.g.*, in Isaiah's vision of "the Lord sitting upon a throne, high and lifted up," the Seraphim cry to one another, "Holy, holy, holy is the Lord of Hosts; the whole earth is full of His glory" (Isa. vi. 3). Yet almost always, the overpowering sense of radiance which is created by His presence in those who realise it, is accompanied by a no less irresistible impression of His unchanging and unceasing might, the energy which is the self-expression of the living God. His whole environment is one of glory in the senses named. "They shall speak of the *glory* of Thy kingdom, and talk of Thy *power*" (Ps. cxlv. 11). "Who is this King of glory? *The Lord of Hosts*, He is the King of glory" (Ps. xxiv. 10). "Let them praise the name of the Lord . . . His glory is above the earth and heaven" (Ps. cxlviii. 13). The conception is especially prominent in Isa. xl.-lxvi., where the glory

of the future Æon' (κληρονομεῖν) is a favourite Jewish expression, whose use can be proved from the end of the first century onwards" (see Dalman, *Worte Jesu*, p. 102 f., where numerous examples and parallels are given from Old Testament and apocalyptic literature; and also Volz, p. 306).

of the Lord is virtually equivalent to His *saving* revelation (see, *e.g.*, Isa. xl. 5, lx. 1, 2). In the post-canonical literature we can trace the idea in certain concrete and closely-related forms. On the one hand, "glory" is used as a description of the Divine presence and sphere of existence. On the other, it is the designation of that future bliss which awaits the righteous, who are thus conceived as sharing in the condition of God. Examples of the former are, 4 Ezra vii. 78, "Then the spirit severs itself from the body, and returns to Him who has given it, in order to do reverence before the glory of the Highest"; *ibid.*, 91, "At first they behold with pure delight the glory of Him who takes them to Himself." Closely related is the phrase which occurs repeatedly in Enoch, "the throne of His glory," *e.g.*, lv. 4, lxi. 8. For the latter, we may refer to Apoc. Bar. xv. 8, "This world is for them trouble and labour, with much strenuousness, and that which is to come a crown with great glory"; xlviii. 49, "I will tell of their blessedness, and will not be silent in praising their glory, which is kept prepared for them"; 4 Ezra viii. 51, "Do thou rather reflect on thine own lot, and inquire into the glory which thy brethren are to inherit"; and *cf.* Enoch lviii. 3, "The righteous shall be in the light of the sun, and the elect in the light of eternal life." The Rabbinic literature contains the same line of thought. Thus in the world to come (Olam Habbâ), the righteous shall sit with crowns on their heads, and enjoy the radiance of the Shekinah (*i.e.*, the localised presence of God, an idea prevalent in the Targums). From the brightness of the Divine glory there streams forth a brilliance which the Targums and Talmud name זיו. This effulgence fills the heavenly spaces (Weber, pp. 160, 385). In the Messianic age, God's presence is shown by the glory which rests on the face of each person (*ibid.*, 304).[1] These terms implying radiance and splendour, of which "glory" is a typical instance, have taken a permanent place in the Christian vocabulary, and we all make constant use of them without realising their full content. Perhaps it belongs to the common sense of Christian experience to preserve a certain margin of vagueness and mystery in their usage. But probably we lose something by ignoring their linguistic basis, and the origin of their existence in our religious terminology. We speak of "the saints in glory." We sing—

> "Ten thousand times ten thousand,
> In sparkling raiment bright;
> The armies of the ransomed saints,
> Throng up the steeps of light."[2]

No words of the New Testament come so readily to our lips, when we speak of the future state of the redeemed, as those which place them in the environment of pure radiance. Probably, if we were asked to define more strictly what we meant—*e.g.*, by the

[1] For the equivalent in Hebrew and Jewish literature of the terms "face," "form," and "glory" of Jehovah, see Cheyne, *Origin of Psalter*, p. 431, note *p*. He refers especially to the very significant passage, Exod. xxxiii. 18 ff.

[2] *Cf.* in the Avesta, Yast xxii. 15, which describes the soul of the righteous, after death, as coming, with the fourth step it takes, into the "unending light"; while that of the ungodly (according to Yast xxii. 33) comes into the "unending darkness" (see Böklen, *op. cit.*, p. 60.) "Heaven is represented, above all, as the abode of light (Yast iii. 1; Yasna xix. 6; Vendîdâd xxii. 1), and light is used in a figurative as well as in its proper sense" (Söderblom, *op. cit.*, pp. 97, 98).

glory we assign to departed believers, we should translate it into "blessedness," "felicity," "perfect rest," and the like. But it is possible, by a study of the apostolic terms, to penetrate deeper into the conception. St Paul does not employ those expressions at random. When he speaks, as above, of "the heritage of the saints in light," he has, we believe, a more or less definite conception before his mind—that conception whose Hebrew and Jewish background we have endeavoured to fill in. But it seems to us to stand closer to the Old Testament than to Judaistic literature. The latter, when it speaks of the "glory" of God, emphasises rather what we may call the sensuous side of the idea. It thinks of the condition of radiance which characterises the Divine sphere of existence. The Old Testament keeps ever in the forefront the Divine might and energy, of which the radiance is the symbol.[1] We can easily discover St Paul's main thought by looking at one or two instances. In Col. i. 11 the phrase occurs, "strengthened with all power, according to the might of His glory." Here κράτος, "might" is singled out as the content of the δόξα of God, in its bearing upon believers. The very same idea is found most vividly in Eph. iii. 16, "That He might grant unto you to be strengthened with power, according to the riches of His glory through His Spirit in your inner man." Here there is an addition of great importance, consisting in the intimate connection indicated between δόξα and πνεῦμα. And a remarkable feature of that side of the conception is presented by Rom. vi. 4, "as Christ was raised from the dead through (διά) the glory of the Father." It is needless

[1] See Grill, *Untersuchungen*, i. p. 274.

to observe in these passages how prominently the element of might in *δόξα* discloses itself. Yet the apostle does not leave out of sight the thought of God's self-revelation, *as a revelation*, although with the utmost skill and insight, he takes care to avoid all materialistic conceptions. It is important to look at his use of *δόξα* in the third and fourth chapters of 2 Corinthians, for that is characteristic of its significance for his mind, in its related shades of meaning. He speaks in chap. iii. 7 of the "glory" of Moses' countenance as he came forth from communion with God, a glory which the children of Israel could not gaze upon; so that their leader was obliged to veil his face. But this was a *fading* reflection, and he adds the comment that the very reason why they were not to look upon that glory was its transiency (iii. 13). In contrast to that experience of Old Testament times, St Paul places the experience of the Christian dispensation in which "we all, with unveiled countenance, reflecting as in a mirror[1] (or, beholding as in a mirror) the glory of the Lord, are changed into the same image (εἰκόνα), from glory to glory, inasmuch as (this influence proceeds) from the Lord the Spirit" (iii. 18, καθάπερ ἀπὸ κυρίου πνεύματος). Quite evidently this *δόξα*, which is the aim and result of the believer's transformation even now, is the direct effect of the Spirit, is that change which the Spirit produces. It is, for the present, a process going on in the inner man (εἰς τὸν ἔσω ἄνθρωπον, Eph. iii. 16, *sup.*), that is to say, a wholly spiritual process, none other than the imparting of the life and might of God. To make

[1] The mirrors of the ancients were of metal, and so gave forth a blurred and broken image.

this doubly clear, he has inserted the word *κυρίου*, the exalted Lord. Here, plainly, there is no thought of anything sensible, any visible semblance. That is also true of his remarkable utterance in chap. iv. 3, 4: "Now if our Gospel is indeed hidden, in the case of the perishing it is hidden, in whom the God of this age blinded the thoughts of the unbelieving, so that the enlightening (*φωτισμόν*) of the Gospel of the glory of Christ (who is the *εἰκών* of God) should not irradiate (*αὐγάσαι*) them." Believers have a contrary experience. "It is the God, who said, Light shall shine out of darkness (Gen. i. 3), who shone in our hearts with a view to (*πρός*) the enlightening of the knowledge of the glory of God in the face of Christ" (iv. 6). But it must be noticed that in iii. 18 he speaks of the transformation of believers as a process which passes through various stages. It is *ἀπὸ δόξης εἰς δόξαν*.[1] The present stage is confined to what we, from the point of view of our earthly, physical existence, must call "the inner man." But, as we have seen, St Paul looks forward to a time when the conditions of life shall be altered, and the renewed spirit shall have complete control of its organism, its individualising *σῶμα*. Then it will have reached the final stage of *δόξα*. That means complete assimilation to Him whom he calls *κύριος τῆς δόξης*, "the Lord of glory." It is perhaps easier now to see why he is so fond of using Light and its associated ideas to set forth the great effects of the indwelling of the Spirit. We have had occasion repeatedly to refer to his conception of the

[1] Schmiedel (*ad loc.*) compares Ps. lxxxiv. 7: "They go from strength to strength, every one of them in Zion appeareth before God."

exalted Christ as clothed in a "body of glory" (esp. Phil. iii. 21). It has also been pointed out that the impression made upon him by the "vision" on the Damascus road was one of overpowering radiance. Hence, while great caution is needful, lest we should attribute crassly literalistic notions to St Paul for which there is no warrant, the evidence seems to justify us in affirming that he believed the *σῶμα πνευματικόν*, the organised condition of the believer as finally conformed to his Lord, to possess a character of radiance which he never attempts more closely to define, a radiance which distinguishes the self-expression, if we may say so, of the Divine *πνεῦμα*. In this way we can understand more clearly such phrases as that from which our discussion started, the description of the future condition of blessedness as "the inheritance of the saints in light." They are not wholly metaphorical, although the nature of the "glory," which is their most characteristic feature, is left entirely uninvestigated. They rest on a conception which has shaped itself in St Paul's mind (and probably the minds of other apostles)[1] as the result of personal, spiritual experiences, and in harmony with the Old Testament pictures of Theophanies (cf., *e.g.*, Ezek. i. 4 ff.; Ps. xviii. 7-13, l. 1-3, etc.), in which no symbol seemed so appropriately to set forth the combined brilliance and energy of the Divine self-manifestation as that

[1] *Cf.* the narratives of the Transfiguration of Jesus, in which occur the vivid expressions: *ἔλαμψεν τὸ πρόσωπον αὐτοῦ ὡς ὁ ἥλιος, τὰ δὲ ἱμάτια αὐτοῦ ἐγένετο λευκὰ ὡς τὸ φῶς* (Matt. xvii. 2); *τὰ ἱμάτια αὐτοῦ ἐγένετο στίλβοντα λευκὰ λίαν* (Mark ix. 3). In Luke, His raiment is described as *ἐξαστράπτων*, "coruscating," and His heavenly visitants are spoken of as *ὀφθέντες ἐν δόξῃ* (Luke ix. 29, 31).

of light or fire.[1] As the apostle pictures that future kingdom of redeemed believers, all transfigured into the likeness of their Redeemer and Head, the whole scene glows and quivers with radiant splendour.[2]

[1] In our judgment, it is needless to expect any real light on St Paul's conception of the future condition of believers from the mysterious words of 2 Cor. xii. 1-4. He himself acknowledges that the experience which he describes as ἁρπαγέντα . . . ἕως τρίτου οὐρανοῦ and ἡρπάγη εἰς τὸν παράδεισον, was an ecstatic one ("whether in the body or outside the body, I know not"). Certainly παράδεισος, in this passage, must mean, as it often does in Judaistic literature, a part of heaven itself, for the ἄρρητα ῥήματα can be none other than the words of God. *Cf.* Sibyl. Orac., *prooem.* 85, 86: ζωὴν κληρονομοῦσι, τὸν αἰῶνος χρόνον αὐτοὶ οἰκοῦντες παράδεισον ὅμως ἐριθηλέα κῆπον. Probably Paradise is here pictured as in the "third heaven" (see Gebhardt in Luthardt's *Zeitschr.*, 1886, p. 569, who gives cogent reasons for holding that St Paul here understands by "the third heaven," not the third of the Rabbinic series of seven heavens which is = the cloud-heaven, but the highest sphere of heaven in the religious sense). This is borne out by Slavon. Enoch viii. 1, 3, 8: "And these men took me from thence and brought me to the third heaven, and placed me in the midst of a garden (*cf.* κῆπον above), a place such as has never been known for the goodliness of its appearance. . . . And in the midst (there is) the tree of life, in that place in which God rests when He comes into Paradise. And I said: 'What a very blessed place is this.'" *Cf.* Enoch lx. 8: "On the east of the garden, where the elect and righteous dwell." Bousset traces the root of St Paul's ecstatic experiences to his Rabbinic past (*Archiv f. Religionswiss.* IV. ii. 144 ff.).

[2] *Cf.* Philo, *De Josepho*, 146, C. W., who describes the nature of heaven as "an eternal day without night and without shadow, for it is lighted by inextinguishable and unalterably pure radiance"; 4 Ezra vii. 42 (of Day of Judgment), "Not mid-day or night or dawn, not gleam or brightness or shining, but wholly and alone the radiance of the glory of the Most High." (See also Enoch lviii. 3 f., already quoted.) According to the Persian religion, men shall cast no shadow in heaven (see Böklen, *op. cit.*, p. 135). In a hymn of praise to Ahuza-Mazda, the

Is there an obverse side to this glorious picture? How does St Paul deal with the future condition of those who have turned a deaf ear to the appeal of the Gospel of Christ? It is of importance to notice that when he does treat of this awe-inspiring subject, he has almost exclusively before his mind those who have actually rejected the word of salvation. Indeed, the only passage where he deliberately takes a larger view is peculiarly interesting, as revealing the remarkable breadth and scope of his thought. "For whensoever the heathen, which have not the law, do by nature the things of the law, they, although not having the law, are a law unto themselves, inasmuch as they show forth the effect (τὸ ἔργον) of the law written on their hearts" (Rom. ii. 14, 15). This is an extraordinary standpoint for a man brought up in "the straitest sect of the Pharisees." In general, however, he restricts his outlook. And surely with reason, for he writes, not as a dogmatic theologian, who must handle each element in the situation, and mutually adjust them, but as a devoted missionary concerned about the special needs of some Christian community, and his letters have always to be regarded, in the first instance, as genuine missionary-documents.[1]

worshippers speak of a time when, "united with parents and family, under trees through which a green-gold light sparkles, we solemnly move with rhythmic motions" (see F. Justi, *Preuss. Jahrbücher*, lxxxviii. H. 2, p. 243). See the splendid vision of the Light of Paradise, in Dante's *Paradiso*, xxx. 100 ff. (Cary), "the yellow of the rose-perennial, which, in bright expansion, lays forth its gradual blooming, redolent of praises to the never-wintering sun."

[1] The emphasising of this fact (sometimes unduly) is one of P. Wernle's great services to the interpretation of early Christian thought.

Some exegetes have endeavoured to demonstrate, mainly on the basis of 1 Cor. xv. 21, 22, 28; Rom. v. 12-21; and the obscure passage, Eph. i. 10, that St Paul has the conception of a universal salvation. Passing by the last-cited reference in the meantime, let us attempt to reach the apostle's meaning in the other sections named. To begin with, it is of supreme importance to interpret any isolated affirmations of a writer in the light of his general view of things, so far as that can be gathered from his writings as a whole. Now, whatever difficulty there may be in mutually adjusting some of the less essential details in St Paul's religious teaching (and we have in our discussion been confronted by some of these perplexities) he is certainly not a writer who leaves his readers in doubt on the central themes of his Gospel. That Gospel is pre-eminently a setting-forth of the method of human salvation, the indispensable conditions of eternal life. These conditions have burst in upon the apostle with all the force of an epoch-making revelation. If anywhere he feels sure of his ground, it is here. Accordingly, he makes as plain as the terms he employs can make them the spiritual processes by which a human soul is justified in the sight of God, is united to the living and exalted Lord, and receives the supernatural gift of the Holy Spirit. Apart from these saving *momenta*, if we may so describe them, he has no conception of salvation at all. As to a period of probation after death, in which these redemptive opportunities, neglected during earthly existence, might again be offered and seized, he says not a single word. In fact, as we have noted, the idea of an Intermediate State is one which seems never to have appealed to him, and it is ignored as of secondary importance. Yet, if it were a condition which appeared to him in any way to make feasible the redemption of those who, in blindness, refused the grace of God while living their present life, we can scarcely conceive that so large-hearted a missionary as St Paul, who yearned with a surpassing ardour for the salvation of his fellows, should fail at least to express some faint hopes of a possible restoration of such as had died without God and without Christ in the world. Plainly, the main outlines of his doctrinal teaching leave no place for, and suggest no approximation to, a theory of universal salvation. We are quite alive to the force of such passages as Phil. ii. 9-11, "Wherefore God also hath highly exalted Him, and given Him the name that is above every name, that in the name of Jesus every knee should bow . . . and that every tongue should confess that Jesus Christ is Lord"; and Col. i. 19, 20 (a true parallel), "It pleased the Father that in Him should all fulness dwell; and having made peace through the blood of His cross, by Him to reconcile all things unto Himself." The apostle, it seems to us, is quite clear as to the universal scope of the Divine purpose of mercy. But he realises also that there are proud and perverse wills which steadfastly refuse to bow to that purpose.[1]

Just as little is any such theory to be found in those paragraphs of the Epistles which are usually quoted for it. Let us consider 1 Cor. xv. 21, 22, in the first instance, as here he is specially occupied

[1] See, *e.g.*, Ménégoz, *Le Péché et la Rédemption d'après St Paul*, pp. 131-133, 143, 144.

with the experience of death and a future life: "For seeing that by man (came) death, by man also the resurrection of the dead. For as in Adam all die, so also in Christ all shall be made alive." These verses must on no account be isolated from their context. Solitary proof-texts have wrought more havoc in theology than all the heresies. St Paul has just declared that Christ is the first-fruits of them that have fallen asleep (verse 20). He never applies κοιμᾶσθαι to any but believers. Here he states that Christ, as risen, is the first and choicest sheaf reaped of that which is to be a glorious harvest of risen souls. And then he turns to his favourite contrast of the first and second heads of the race. He was evidently versed in that Adam-theology which seems to have been current in the Rabbinic schools of the day, and more than once it supplies the framework of his discussions.[1] The comparison must obviously be taken in the widest sense. "Through man, death; through man, resurrection of the dead." In these words there is no question as to the *range* embraced by the contrasted experiences. But when he adds, "For as in Adam (τῷ 'Αδάμ, the head of the genus) all die," a fact which is universally admitted, he does not feel any necessity for qualifying the "all" whom he has in view in the antithetical clause by such additions as *οἱ πιστεύσαντες* or *οἱ δικαιωθέντες* (*δεδικαιωμένοι*). As a matter of fact, the words of

[1] "As the sentences which Paul utters concerning the fall of Adam and its meaning in Rom. v. 11, are on precisely the same lines as those of 4 Ezra, Baruch, and the later Talmudic anthropology, we must affirm that already in the first half of the first Christian century, the Adam-theology was circulating in Rabbinic circles" (Bousset, *Religion d. Judenthums*, p. 389). See also Bacher, *op. cit.*, i. p. 36.

the clause are themselves sufficiently clear to prevent misunderstanding. All his readers knew well enough what to be ἐν τῷ Χριστῷ meant for the apostle. That is the central note of his theology, the pivot on which everything hinges. And even if this were not sufficient proof, there is abundance of further evidence in the verb ζωοποιηθήσονται. For this term only applies to those who have received the gift of the πνεῦμα, those who in this present have become "new creatures" (see 1 Cor. xv. 36, 45, Rom. viii. 11, where the ζωοποιεῖν is entirely dependent on the πνεῦμα ἐνοικοῦν ἐν ὑμῖν. *Cf.* Charles, *Eschatology*, p. 391.) "In Adam," we may paraphrase the words, "all who belong to Adam's family must die. Similarly, in Christ, all who belong to Christ shall be made alive." The passage in Romans is almost an exact parallel to this. Here, again, the two heads and the two families are before his mind. On Adam's side, transgression, condemnation, death; on the side of Christ, free gift of grace, justification, life. The closest similarity is to be found in v. 19, "For as through the disobedience of the one man the many were constituted sinners, so also by the obedience of the one shall the many be constituted righteous." It is evident that he is not employing terms with any strictness, or he would have substituted πάντες (as in verse 12) for πολλοί in the first clause. As it is, he uses πολλοί to correspond to the second πολλοί, whom he already has in view. The same usage appears in verse 5, where he only affirms that *οἱ πολλοὶ ἀπέθανον,* to bring the clause into sharp contrast with "the many" who have enjoyed the free gift of God's grace, although a sentence or two before, in verse 10, he has deliberately affirmed, *εἰς πάντας ἀνθρώπους ὁ θάνατος διῆλθεν.* But over and above these most valid considerations, it happens that St Paul himself has supplied the materials for the limitation which we are defending. For, in verse 17, the future victorious life is restricted to *οἱ τὴν περισσείαν τῆς χάριτος καὶ τῆς δωρεᾶς τῆς δικαιοσύνης λαμβάνοντες*, "those receiving the superabundance of grace and of the gift of righteousness," where the participle shows that he has in view those whom he elsewhere designates *οἱ σωζόμενοι.* It is safe to conclude that no definite and unmistakable traces of a universalistic doctrine are to be found in the Pauline letters, while the whole content of his soteriology, as well as many distinct affirmations, points the other way.[1]

There is a strange disproportion between St Paul's treatment of the future destiny of *unbelievers* and that accorded to it in modern times. And, looking at the matter from the largest point of view, the advantage lies on the side of the apostle. He was not possessed by any painful curiosity. He knew that he had found eternal life in Christ Jesus. That fact gave its decisive basis to his Eschatology. The influence upon his heart and mind of the crucified and risen Messiah fixed for ever the point of emphasis in his outlook upon the future. He was able to ignore many aspects of the Last Things on which Jewish and Christian Apocalyptic had set great importance. To go to Christ, to be with Christ, overshadowed all the accompaniments of the End. He knew that nothing could separate His followers from the love of Christ in time or in eternity.[2] Of what use, then,

[1] *Cf.* Wernle, *Anfänge*, pp. 174, 175.

[2] See this fact well brought by Bornemann in his introductory

or profit could it be for him to speculate on the fate of those who had rejected the choicest gift which had ever been offered them? What possible value could accrue to the Christian communities whom he addressed in his Epistles from any discussion of the penalties which awaited the stubborn and disobedient? Doubtless he would sympathise with the words of 4 Ezra ix. 13, "Enquire not further how the ungodly are to be tormented, but rather investigate the manner in which the righteous are to be saved." One may even question whether in his missionary preaching he laid strong emphasis on the doom of the impenitent in comparison with that on the bliss of the redeemed. So much dearer were the positive aspects of the Christian faith at all times to this man than the negative.[1]

Whatever be the precise reason, there is extraordinarily scanty material in the writings of St Paul on which to build up anything like a detailed theory on this most awe-inspiring of all subjects. Yet we cannot but believe that he has said enough to permit of our drawing clear inferences of a more or less general kind. The terms he employs to denote the fate of the unbelieving are: ὄλεθρος (1 Thess. v. 3; 2 Thess. i. 9), θάνατος (*e.g.*, Rom. vi. 23, viii. 6), φθορά (Gal. vi. 8), ἀπώλεια, ἀπόλλυσθαι (1 Cor. i. 18, x. 9, xv. 18; 2 Cor. ii. 15-16, iv. 3; Rom. ii. 12; Phil. i. 28, iii. 18), ὀργή (*e.g.*, 1 Thess. v. 9; Rom. ii.

remarks on the section, 1 Thess. iv. 17-v. 10. "Felicity in the heaven of Mazdeism consists above all in being with the Lord; 'yes, in truth, in the worlds where dwells the Lord'" (Yasna lxiii. 3), (Söderblom, *op. cit.* p. 101).

[1] See Reuss, *Histoire de la Théol. Chrét.* ii. p. 237. In the sacred books of Persia, also, a far deeper interest is shown in the journey of the pious soul from earth to heaven than in the contrasted fate of the impious (see Söderblom, *op. cit.*, p. 86).

5, 9, v. 9). The last-named term applies strictly to the visitation of sinners at the Day of Judgment. It expresses the reaction of God against persistent sin. Necessarily it is an idea common to the other descriptions of doom which have to be examined. These combine to form a group of conceptions which have the one idea of "destruction" linking them together. In one instance (2 Thess. i. 9), the much-debated adjective αἰώνιος is joined to ὄλεθρος. In another (Phil. iii. 18), St Paul speaks with tears (κλαίων) of some "whose end (τέλος) is destruction" (ἀπώλεια; *cf.* Rom. vi. 21, τὸ γὰρ τέλος ἐκείνων θάνατος).

The two questions which have bulked most largely in modern discussions of the problem before us are: (1) the nature, (2) the duration, of that experience which the apostle habitually views as "destruction." In a preceding chapter, in dealing with St Paul's conception of death, we endeavoured to show that this was an experience which he never attempted to analyse. He looked at the fact synthetically, and the thought of it filled him with horror. He felt no need of further inquiry into the *nature* of death, as it visited those who did not possess the life-giving (ζωοποιοῦν) Spirit of the living Lord. Their death could only be regarded as sheer doom and disaster. Distinctions, such as "physical" and "spiritual" in the sphere of death, possessed, as we saw, no significance for the apostle. In a previous investigation, also, we sought to guard against unwarranted deductions which might be drawn from his use of the terms ἀπώλεια, ἀπόλλυσθαι (and cognates such as ὄλεθρος and φθορά). Destruction, like death, means for St Paul *paralysis of life*: its negation, its undoing. For him it is not a question of *existence*—that is to say, not a physical or even a metaphysical problem. The problem belongs altogether to the religious sphere. The use of *ἀπώλεια* (and its related terms) in the LXX. (which is of primary importance in an inquiry like the present), or in ordinary Greek literature, by no means connotes such ideas as that of annihilation or the extinction of consciousness. Such speculations would have appeared meaningless to the apostle. For him, as for Hebrews and Greeks alike, there would probably always remain in the background the notion of a dreary, wretched existence, removed by the whole infinitude of God from that which he designated "Life." Hence, if we proceed to ask how St Paul understood what is commonly termed the "punishment" of the impenitent, it is sufficient to reply that he could conceive no more awful doom than that of separation from God, that exclusion from the bliss of the heavenly Kingdom, called by our Lord, *τὸ σκότος τὸ ἐξώτερον,* "the darkness outside," in contrast to the joy and brightness of the marriage-festival of the King (*cf.* Ps. Sol. xiv. 6, "their inheritance is Hades and darkness and destruction" [see Volz, pp. 284-285], and "the obscure world," which is a designation of hell in the Avesta, Vendîdâd 5, 62 [Söderblom, *op. cit.*, p. 104]), which was involved in *ἀπώλεια,* and made the condition of such persons one of hopeless ruin.[1] It is because the modern mind has failed rightly to estimate the mean-

[1] Contrast the "wise Agnosticism" (the phrase is Dr Orr's in discussing the teaching of Scripture on eternal punishment) of St Paul with the attempted theories of the Synagogue-theologians (see Weber, pp. 327-330, 373-380). Philo's teaching as to the bliss of the righteous and the condemnation of the wicked is tersely summed up by Volz, *op. cit.*, pp. 143, 144.

ing of "life" and "death," for the first Christians, and especially for St Paul, that it has exhausted its energies in striving to extract from the New Testament a decisive verdict as to the *nature* and *conditions* of future punishment.

We have noted that there are only two passages which explicitly shed any light on the apostle's idea of the *duration* of doom. In one, he speaks of a "destruction" (ὄλεθρος) which is αἰώνιος (2 Thess. i. 9). In the other, he describes a class of persons "whose end is destruction" (ἀπώλεια, Phil. iii. 18). A large number of expositors, of whom Farrar and Cox may be cited as leading representatives, have expended a vast amount of ingenuity in the attempt to rid the adjective αἰώνιος of its natural, and apart from this controversy, invariably accepted sense, "eternal," in the writings of the New Testament. These discussions reveal with striking clearness the difference between the early Christian and the modern standpoint. Yet, in our judgment, the evidence, both detailed and general, tells completely against the modern hypothesis. We know, for example, that in the metaphysical arguments of Plato, αἰώνιος is synonymous with our term "eternal" (see, *e.g.*, Timæ. 38 D, ἡ μὲν οὖν τοῦ ζώου φύσις ἐτύγχανεν οὖσα αἰώνιος; Legg. 904 A, ἀνώλεθρον δὲ ὂν γενόμενον, ἀλλ' οὐκ αἰώνιον, ψυχὴν καὶ σῶμα). Aristotle, *De Cælo*, i. 9, 15, gives an interesting and important definition of αἰών: "The limit (τὸ τέλος) which embraces the time of each man's life, outside of which there is nothing by nature, is named each man's epoch (αἰών). Similarly, the limit of the whole heaven, and that which embraces all times and infinity (τὴν ἀπειρίαν) is αἰών, taking its name from ἀεὶ εἶναι" (*sic*). We have referred to the philosophical usage, since this is so frequently appealed to in exegetical discussions, although for our own part we believe that such an appeal often confuses the issues, inasmuch as the apostolic writers used the popular terminology of their day. Accordingly. when we turn to the LXX., which reflects the colloquial language, we find the phrase, εἰς τὸν αἰῶνα (or, εἰς τοὺς αἰῶνας), employed as the equivalent of the idea which we express by the English collocation, "for ever." Now we quite readily admit that αἰών and αἰώνιος may be used to express, not merely endless time, but longer periods or epochs, as we commonly designate them. Thus, as Heinrici (on 1 Cor. x. 11) observes, αἰών can be joined, *e.g.*, with γενεά, generation (see Col. i. 26). In this aspect it passes over into the sense of κόσμος, world; *cf.* Heb. i. 2, "By whom also He made τοὺς αἰῶνας," virtually, "the worlds"; xi. 3, "By faith we discern that τοὺς αἰῶνας ('the worlds') were framed by the word of God."[1] This phase of the meaning of αἰών has been laid hold of, and upon its basis has been framed the adjective "æonial" (= "age-lasting"), a translation which has been rashly supposed to solve the problem for the New Testament writers. But such an interpretation in no sense alters the situation as we find it in St Paul. For him, as for all his Jewish and Christian contemporaries (see, *e.g.*, Volz, p. 270), the whole providential order of things is divided into two great epochs, ὁ αἰὼν οὗτος, co-extensive with the present world, and evil, as not yet subordinated to the Divine dominion (see, *e.g.*, Rom. xii. 2, 1 Cor. i. 20, 2 Cor. iv. 4, Gal. i. 4, etc.; οἱ αἰῶνες in 1 Cor. x. 11,

[1] See also Beet, *Last Things*, pp. 118-123.

probably from the idea of the present epoch being made up of a number of smaller subdivisions of time), and *ὁ αἰὼν ὁ μέλλων*, the coming age, the era of the sway of God, attained through the mediation of Christ. The actual phrase is only found in St Paul's writings in Eph. i. 21, and the parallel, *οἱ αἰῶνες οἱ ἐπερχόμενοι*, in Eph. ii. 7. He has preferred to substitute for it such phrases as *ἡ βασιλεία τοῦ θεοῦ* (see Dalman, *Worte Jesu*, p. 120), or, what is almost an equivalent, "eternal life." We need not linger here over the various and conflicting opinions which prevailed in Jewish thought as to the point of time at which the *αἰὼν μέλλων* (עוֹלָם הַבָּא) should begin. An admirable account of these, terse and yet adequate, may be found in Marti, *Geschichte d. Israelit. Religion*, pp. 295-299. The one epoch, in St Paul's view, is drawing on towards its close. The ends of the age (*τῶν αἰώνων*, 1 Cor. x. 11) have overtaken them. The new era, in which the rule of God shall be established, is soon to set in. That era, however, from the very nature of the case, has no termination. So strictly is this true, that at length the adjective *αἰώνιος*, in many Johannine passages, seems to lose the time-notion, and rather to express the qualitative idea of "supra-earthly," becoming virtually equivalent to "transcendent, perfect."[1] The age of God's dominion is necessarily final. If St Paul does not describe it as "eternal," in so many words, it is because the conception is self-evident to his readers. "The things

[1] See Haupt, *Eschat. Aussagen Jesu*, pp. 83-85. Haupt shows that in the third section of Enoch this same usage appears. The examples in Volz, pp. 286, 287, 328, 368, 369, clearly prove that in Jewish books the eternity of bliss and woe was the normal doctrine.

which are seen are temporal; the things which are unseen (τὰ μὴ βλεπόμενα, primarily, the future epoch of blessedness and transfigured life) are eternal" (2 Cor. iv. 18). The other passage which was quoted (Phil. iii. 18), occurring in one of the latest of his writings, bears out our conclusion to the full. If the apostle affirms ἀπώλεια to be the "end" (τέλος) of a certain group of persons, it is plain that he thinks of something decisive and final. And it is important to observe that τέλος means far more than "termination." It denotes the issue as expressing and manifesting the goal of the whole course. It is parallel to his utterance in Gal. vi. 8, "He that soweth to his own flesh, shall of the flesh reap destruction" (φθοράν). It is also in strict accord with the general tenor of his teaching. To the one group of his hearers, the knowledge of Christ which he proclaims in the Gospel is a "savour from life unto life"; to the other (οἱ ἀπολλύμενοι), "a savour from death unto death." The result is one which may well overawe the reflective mind, and the apostle, it is clear, feels its terrific pressure, for he adds, "And who is sufficient for these things?" (2 Cor. ii. 15, 16).

But it is time to turn from that part of St Paul's thought which deals with the future destinies of individuals, and to reach some conception of the manner in which he pictured to his mind the actual consummation of all things. At this point we are confronted by one or two perplexing problems, problems which mainly arise from the brevity of his descriptions, and his habit of throwing out isolated hints rather than of entering into detailed statements. It is perhaps most convenient to begin with the important paragraph in 1 Cor. xv. 22-28: "For as in Adam all die, so also in Christ shall all be made alive. But each (ἕκαστος) in his own order (τάγμα): the first-fruits Christ, thereafter those who belong to Christ at His Parousia ; then (εἶτα) the end, when He shall have handed over the kingdom (βασιλείαν) to His God and Father, when He shall have abolished every rule and every authority and power. For it is needful for Him to reign until He shall have put all his enemies under His feet. As the last enemy is abolished death (ὁ θάνατος): for all things He (*i.e.* God) subordinated under His (*i.e.* Christ's) feet. But when it is said (εἴπῃ, a quotation from Ps. viii. 7, πάντα ὑπέταξας ὑποκάτω τῶν ποδῶν αὐτοῦ) that all things have been subordinated, it is evident that He (*i.e.* God) is left out who subordinated all things to Him (*i.e.* Christ). But when all things shall have been subordinated to Him (*i.e.* Christ), then the Son Himself also shall be subordinated to Him (*i.e.* God) who subordinated all things to Him (*i.e.* the Son) that God may be all in all." With this passage we may combine the difficult statement of Eph. i. 9, 10: "(God) having made known to us the mystery (μυστήριον = "secret now revealed," see Hatch, *Essays in Biblical Greek*, pp. 58, 59) of His will, according to His good pleasure which he purposed in Him (*i.e.* Christ) with a view to a dispensation (οἰκονομίαν, lit. "arranging" or "ordering") of the fulness of the times (this, in Judaistic literature, is the time of Messiah's entrance to restore Israel politically and spiritually, see Marti, *op. cit.*, p. 295), to sum up (ἀνακεφαλαιώσασθαι) all things in Christ, the things in heaven and the things on earth (*cf.* verses 20-22, "Having raised Him from the dead, and seated Him at His right hand in the heavenly places, high above every rule, and authority, and power, and lordship, and every name that is named not only in this age but also in that to come; and subordinated all things beneath His feet, and gave Him as Head over all things to the Church").

The verses quoted from 1 Corinthians supplement those conceptions of St Paul concerning the Last Things which have already been the subject of our consideration. These we followed up to their climax along certain lines in the case of individuals, both believers and unbelievers. Now we have to keep before us a larger development. The paragraph starts with the resurrection of deceased believers and the transformation of the living. "In Christ all shall be made alive" (ζωοποιηθήσονται). The word τάγμα in the next sentence, translated "order" in our version, means more strictly "division," "troop," or "group." In the LXX. (also in Aquila, Theodotion, and Symmachus) it is the rendering of the Heb. דֶּגֶל, lit. "banner," "ensign": hence, like Latin *vexillum*, the troop or company marshalled under the same colours (see Dillmann on Num. ii. 2). Thus Polybius uses τάγμα as the equivalent of the Latin *manipulus*, a subdivision of the legion, *e.g. Hist.* ii. 69, 5: κατ' ἄνδρα καὶ κατὰ τάγμα ἁμιλλᾶσθαι. Possibly the introduction of τάγμα may be due to a difficulty the Corinthians may have felt because their dead Christian friends did not rise on the third day, or soon after death, like their Lord. But more probably the apostle employs the conception because he recognises two "groups" of the risen.[1] The one contains none but

[1] There is a curious parallel in the Persian Eschatology. According to Bundehesh xxx. 7, men will rise in a determined order: first, Gaya Maretan, the original man, then Mastya and Mastyana, then the rest of mankind. Böklen, in quoting this

Christ Himself: He stands solitary and unique: He is the First-begotten from the dead, the First-fruits (ἀπαρχή) of those that have fallen asleep. Thereafter (ἔπειτα) the other group appears, and it is composed of those who belong to Christ at His Parousia. Evidently the παρουσία defines the point of time as ἔπειτα.

It is at this stage that perplexities have been dragged into the discussion. Grimm (*Z. w. Th.*, 1873, pp. 399 ff.), Kabisch (*op. cit.*, pp. 259, 260), Teichmann (p. 108), and others have put forward the hypothesis that between the ἔπειτα (defined as above) and the following εἶτα, an intervening period must be assumed, of indefinite duration, in which Christ rules over His kingdom, and gradually subdues all His enemies. This period is made equivalent to the Millenium of the Apocalypse. Students of Paulinism are not in a position to determine whether the apostle did or did not hold this conception. But on the basis set before us in our present passage, we have no hesitation in asserting that it would be most precarious and unwarranted to build up any such theory.[1] Here, again, there is a danger of being misled through ignoring St Paul's standpoint. We are accustomed to think of Christ's conquest of the opposing forces of evil as a long and gradual process. That is the appearance of things as it presents itself in the fortunes of the Kingdom in this world. But St Paul, in the words we are reviewing, has before his mind a different series of events altogether. We might

statement, refers to Vita Adæ et Evæ xlii., and Apoc. Mosis xiii. 41, which affirm that Adam shall first be raised, then his posterity (*op. cit.*, p. 109).

[1] So also Titius, pp. 47, 48; Charles, *Eschatology*, pp. 389, 390; Reuss, *Histoire de la Théol. Chrét.* ii. p. 227 *et al.*

almost say that for him these unique experiences of the End are timeless. After speaking of the Resurrection in the clause beginning with ἔπειτα, he goes on to describe the final culmination of the history of redemption in the sentence which opens with εἶτα. Numerous examples in the New Testament demonstrate that εἶτα by no means presupposes an interval of any duration between the preceding clause and that which it introduces. See, *e.g.*, John xiii. 4, 5, "Taking a towel, He girded Himself, then (εἶτα) He puts water into the basin"; xix. 26, 27, "He saith to His mother, Woman, behold thy son. Then (εἶτα) saith He to His disciple, Behold thy mother." In this same chapter of 1 Corinthians, there are some very instructive instances of the usage in connection with the various appearances of the risen Jesus to His disciples, *e.g.* verse 5, "He appeared to Cephas, then (εἶτα, a few hours intervening at most) to the twelve; verse 6, "Thereafter (ἔπειτα) He appeared to above five hundred brethren at once. . .; (verse 7) thereafter (ἔπειτα) He appeared to James, then (εἶτα) to all the apostles" (these various events being all embraced within a few days). But apart from linguistic considerations, which evidently do not favour the theory, our position is corroborated by the actual statements made here by St Paul. The end (τὸ τέλος),[1] the final consummation, the

[1] Although we always hesitate to differ from Heinrici, we can by no means agree with his interpretation of τὸ τέλος in this passage as "the point of time in which . . . this Age ceases, and all that must happen before the entrance of the complete rule of God is accomplished." It is rather the culmination of the events which usher in the new Æon. For a concise summary of Rabbinic teaching as to the relation between the Messianic period and the coming Æon, see Volz, *op. cit.*, . 63.

perfect realisation of the Divine aim, is made possible "when He shall have abolished every rule (ἀρχήν) and every authority (ἐξουσίαν) and power" (δύναμιν). This might appear to justify the notion that in St Paul's view He has still to wage a conflict with many authorities and powers. But how does the case actually stand? In Col. ii. 15, he boldly declares of Christ: "Having hurled aside (ἀπεκδυσάμενος, lit. stripped off Himself) the rules (τὰς ἀρχάς) and the authorities (τὰς ἐξουσίας), He made a show of them openly (or boldly, ἐν παρρησίᾳ), triumphing over them in it" (*i.e.* the Cross). That province of His dominion, therefore, has been attained. He has baffled, defeated, defied all "the spiritual hosts of wickedness in the heavenly places" (Eph. vi. 12).

It would lead us too far aside from the main course of this investigation to examine with care St Paul's conception of those mysterious, spiritual forces, antagonistic to the Divine dominion, which, in the passage before us, he names ἀρχαί, ἐξουσίαι, and δυνάμεις. To these he adds κυριότητες in Eph. i. 21 (*cf.* ἀρχαί and ἐξουσίαι in Eph. iii. 10), and in vi. 12 the group consists of ἀρχαί, ἐξουσίαι, κοσμοκράτορες τοῦ σκότους τούτου, τὰ πνευματικὰ τῆς πονηρίας ἐν τοῖς ἐπουρανίοις. In Col. i. 16, he speaks of θρόνοι, κυριότητες, ἀρχαί, and ἐξουσίαι, while the latter two classes appear in ii. 10, 15. We may associate with these the strange figure of Eph. ii. 2, ὁ ἄρχων τῆς ἐξουσίας τοῦ ἀερός, τοῦ πνεύματος τοῦ νῦν ἐνεργοῦντος ἐν τοῖς υἱοῖς τῆς ἀπειθείας. Probably in most of these passages, the recurring terms describe invisible powers of evil. As God has His hosts, those ministers of His that do His pleasure, so the apostle pictures a hierarchy of wickedness, waiting on the bidding of the "prince of the power of the air." But this can scarcely be held of Col. i. 16, and perhaps not of Col. ii. 10. Possibly we have a parallel to these mysterious powers in the four angels of Rev. vii. 2, "to whom it was appointed to hurt the earth and the sea." So, in Rev. xiv. 18, we read of an angel "who had power over fire." But this is uncertain (*cf.* the observations of Volz as to the two-fold view of the stars in Jewish dogmatic, on the one hand as examples of obedience, on the other as demonic forces opposed to God, p. 298). In any case, we find many points of contact between this world of ideas and the Jewish apocalyptic writings. Thus, in Enoch lxi. 10, 11, it is said of the Messiah, "He shall summon the whole army of heaven, all the holy ones on high, the army of God, the Cherubim, Seraphim, and Ophanim, all the angels of the authority (ἐξουσία), all the angels of the lordships (κυριότητες), the elect ones, and the other powers (δυνάμεις) which are upon *terra firma* and above the water, and they shall raise one voice." Slav. Enoch xx. 1 tells how Enoch was brought to the seventh heaven, "and I saw there a very great light, and all the fiery hosts of great archangels, and incorporeal powers, and lordships, and principalities, and powers; Cherubim and Seraphim, and the watchfulness of many eyes." In Jub. ii. 2 there is a description of the creation of the various spirits which serve before God: "The angels of the Presence . . . the angels of the spirit of the wind, the angels of the clouds of darkness and of the snow and of the hail and of the frost, and the angels of the sounds and of the thunderbolt and of the lightning, and the angels of the spirits of cold and heat and winter . . . and of all the spirits of His works in the heavens and on earth, and in all the abysses of the deep and of darkness and of evening," etc., etc. And Enoch lxxxii. 10 ff. gives an elaborate catalogue of the "leaders" (ἄρχοντες) of the stars, who rule the progress of the seasons. Parallels to these strange lists are to be found in later writings, both Jewish and Christian. Thus, in the Syriac Apocalypse of Adam,[1] a classification of angels is given, corresponding to the seven heavens, according to which ἄγγελοι rule over men, ἀρχάγγελοι over beasts, ἀρχαί over clouds, snow, and rain, ἐξουσίαι over the heavenly bodies, δυνάμεις are the guardians against demons, κυριότητες have the sway over kingdoms, while θρόνοι do service before the throne of Messiah. No doubt in a book like this, the direct influence of the New Testament might be suspected. But the tradition apparently belongs to Judaism. For in a quaint mediæval treatise of magic, of Jewish origin, the *Schemhamphorasch Salomonis Regis*,[2] the same classification is adjusted to the gods of the Roman Pantheon. Saturn is identified with θρόνος, Jupiter with κυριότης, Mars with ἐξουσία, Sol with δύναμις, Venus with ἀρχή, Mercury with ἀρχάγγελος, and Luna with ἄγγελος. Evidently we have here a curious angelology, apparently unknown to the Old Testament, although a hint of it appears in Dan. x. 13, where the "prince" (LXX. ἄρχων) of the kingdom of Persia, that is, the angel who is set over the kingdom, is mentioned, and as his antagonist, Michael, "one of the chief princes,"

[1] Published by Renan, *Journal Asiatique*, Sér. V. tome ii. p. 458 f., qu. by Bousset, *Archiv f. Religionswiss.* iv. H. 3, p. 269.

[2] Horst's *Zauberbibliothek*, iii. pp. 134 ff. (qu. by Bousset, *loc. cit.*).

named in Jude 9, "the archangel," ἀρχάγγελος, and described in Rev. xii. 7 as warring against the dragon. And again, in Dan. xii. 1, he is designated "the great prince" (ὁ ἄρχων ὁ μέγας), the guardian angel of Israel (ὁ ἑστηκὼς ἐπὶ τοὺς υἱοὺς τοῦ λαοῦ σου). In the apocalyptic literature of which Daniel is the prototype, the conception of the hierarchies of spirits is enormously developed, no doubt incorporating many elements of popular tradition, until it finds a permanent place in late Jewish theology.[1] In all likelihood the prominence of these groups of intermediate spiritual beings in the apocalyptic period is mainly due to the feeling of the remoteness of God. His transcendence, as we have seen, was a characteristic belief of later Judaism. In their craving to have some access to God, the apocalyptic writers fill in the gulf that lies between earth and heaven with a multitude of mediating supra-earthly existences. The New Testament only affords us the rarest glimpses into this strange realm, for the spiritual peerlessness of Jesus Christ banishes these dim figures of the invisible world into the darkness, whence they emerge again in the writings of the heretical sects, more especially of Gnosticism. In the Jewish tradition, they seem, for the most part, to be in the service of the Most High, exemplifying the description of Heb. i. 14, "ministering spirits"

[1] It is possible that Persian influence has contributed to this development. See Stave, *Parsismus*, pp. 175, 196 f., 203; Bousset, *Religion d. Judenthums*, pp. 472, 473; Moulton, art. "Zoroastrianism," in *H.D.B.* On St Paul's conceptions in this province of thought as a whole, see Everling, *Die paulinische Angelologie und Dämonologie*. It contains many exaggerated statements, but gives a fair survey of the field. Of importance for the subject in general is *Michael*, by W. Lueken, Gött., 1898.

(λειτουργικὰ πνεύματα); *cf.* Ps. ciii. 21. St Paul appears not to have wholly departed from it, for his language in Col. i. 16 at least is neutral. This may be due to the special circumstances of the Colossian Church, where Jewish influences were probably shaping a kind of incipient Gnosticism (*cf.* ii. 18 ff.). But in any case, several of the instances we have quoted from the Epistles are unmistakable, notably Eph. vi. 12, "our conflict is not with flesh and blood, but with rules (ἀρχάς), with authorities (ἐξουσίας), with the world-governors of this darkness, with spiritual powers of wickedness in the heavenly places," and the passage which we are considering. It is conceivable that the apostle, feeling no need of the mediation of angels between God and the world, once the supreme revelation in Christ, the Head of all things, has been given, applies the terms which were originally used in a good or a colourless sense (personifications of powers of nature) to those unseen forces of wickedness which strive against the complete establishment of the Divine Kingdom. The question cannot be decided on the basis of our evidence. But it is altogether groundless to rear on this foundation the theory of a cosmic dualism in St Paul. He does not think of the present world as being, from its very essence, under the control of Satan, in contrast to the future era when God shall be supreme. For him the Old Testament principle is authoritative, that the world is God's world, as created by Him and destined ultimately to fulfil His purpose. The passages we have already discussed, bearing on the cosmic significance of Christ, are sufficient evidence of this. But necessarily, on the foundation of his own experience, he is conscious of the existence of opposing forces, which have to be subdued before God's right to His own can be fully vindicated.[1] In 1 Cor. xv. 24, therefore, when read in the light of Col. ii. 15, he takes for granted that a great part of the victory has been already won by the triumphant Saviour, won in principle (*cf.* Chrysost. on θάνατος in this passage: τῇ μὲν οὖν δυνάμει καὶ νῦν κατήργηται, τῇ δὲ ἐνεργείᾳ τότε), that is to say, like His victory over sin, won for all who are willing to shelter themselves in the great Victor. The "rules" and "authorities" and "powers" have been reduced to impotence against those who will arm themselves with the panoply of God (see Volz, pp. 270, 271). But Christ must still reign until all His enemies have been subdued. This reign, according to St Paul's view, is not one which begins after the Parousia. He has left behind him the Messianic Hope of Judaism. The rule of Christ has begun with His exaltation as κύριος, Lord; He already sits on the throne, and His advent at the last is simply the culmination of His sway (so also Charles, *Eschatology*, p. 390). Are there any foes which still hold out? The apostle has one supreme Power in his mind, which apparently continues to defy the royal supremacy of Christ. That Power is Death. His expression, ὁ θάνατος, almost personifies it. "As the last enemy, death is abolished." When "he" has been vanquished, Christ's dominion

[1] See also Titius, p. 247. Undoubtedly such a dualism is common in Judaistic literature, and reveals the "immense prostration of post-exilic Judaism" (J. Weiss). Perhaps the forms in which it clothes itself are related to Persian influence; see Stave, *Einfluss des Parsismus auf d. Judenthum*, p. 196, and Porter, art. "Revelation," *H.D.B.* iv. p. 246. Certainly one of its results was to inspire a more transcendental view of salvation.

is complete.[1] Obviously, this final destruction of death is revealed by the event of the Resurrection, when the redeemed of the Lord prove by their rising that they also are stronger than death—that the indwelling might of the πνεῦμα of Christ has vanquished the darkness of the grave. Thus, in our judgment, the argument to be drawn from St Paul's own words is decisive against a protracted struggle between Christ and His adversaries after the Parousia. But even had it been impossible to appeal to definite statements, we could not associate with the thought of the revelation of the returning Lord a further process of conflict with human conditions. This would be utterly alien to the apostle's standpoint. Take, as an instance of his point of view, his description of the fate of the "lawless one," "whom the Lord Jesus shall destroy by the breath of His mouth, and abolish by the manifestation of His coming" (2 Thess. ii. 8); or, recall the pictures of judgment in 2 Thess. i. 7-10, and Rom. ii. 5-10. These passages make it indubitably clear that, in the apostle's idea of it, the crowning revelation of the exalted Christ is one which overwhelms and renders powerless all opposing forces, whether human or diabolic.[2]

[1] We may compare Isa. xxv. 8, "He will swallow up death in victory"; Hos. xiii. 14, "O death, I will be thy plague; O grave, I will be thy destruction"; 4 Ezra viii. 53, "The germ of sin is sealed up from you, sickness is taken away, death is hidden, Hades has disappeared"; Rev. xx. 14, "Death and Hades were cast into the lake of fire." Bousset finds in this conquest of death an aspect of the final conflict between God and the Devil, who is lord of death (*Religion d. Judenthums*, pp. 241, 242). There may be some ground for the hypothesis, but it was quite natural to personify Death vaguely, and exult over his downfall.

[2] See Volz, p. 302. A remarkable parallel is found in the Persian doctrine of the final conflict of good and evil. After

Probably this is the stage in God's redemptive purpose which is before St Paul's mind, when, in Eph. i. 10, he speaks of the Divine intention "to sum up (ἀνακεφαλαιώσασθαι) all things in Christ, the things in heaven and the things on earth." The expression is difficult, and there is no parallel to it in the New Testament.[1] Gunkel (on 4 Ezra xii. 25, in *Kautzsch*) holds that ἀνακεφαλαιοῦν is "certainly an apocalyptic term; at the end of the world-history all the evil that is diffused and isolated, and in the same way also the good, shall be summed up." There may possibly be traces of this conception lying in the background of the apostle's thought. In any case, it seems to us that the idea is virtually equivalent for him to the statement in 1 Cor. xv. 28, "When all things shall have been subordinated to Him" (*i.e.* Christ). No doubt it includes more than the subordination, for the idea of summing-up seems to be related to his conception of Christ as the root-principle of all creation. "He is before all things, and in Him all things consist" (συνέστηκεν, Col. i. 17; the whole passage, Col. i. 15-19, is the best commentary on the thought).

lasting throughout the course of the world, it is ended by the annihilation of evil on the Last Day. Ahura Mazda, the Amshaspands, the true Word, and Sraosha on the one hand, struggle with Angra Mainyu, the Anti-Amshaspands, the Word of Lies, and Aêshma, on the other side—*Bundehesh* xxx. 29 ff. (See Böklen, *op. cit.*, p. 125; Hübschmann, *Jahrb. f. prot. Theol.* 1879, pp. 225, 226; Söderblom, *op. cit.*, pp. 267, 268.)

[1] The phrase in Acts iii. 21, ἄχρι χρόνων ἀποκαταστάσεως πάντων ὧν ἐλάλησεν ὁ θεός, is no true parallel, and only appears so because of the misleading translation in A.V., "until the times of restitution of all things, which God hath spoken." There should be no comma after "things," and, as Dalman shows, the Syriac version gives the correct sense, "until the fulfilling of the times of all that God hath said," etc. (*Worte Jesu*, pp. 145, 146).

The development and final issue must correspond to the original intention of the Creator. The world-plan is a unity. This unity is realised in the Eternal Son, who became incarnate, accomplished redemption, conquered sin and death (to the apostle's mind the great forces of disturbance in the Divine order), and has been exalted at God's right hand to claim that universal adoration which is His due (Phil. ii. 9, 10). In His Incarnation, He has become the type and pattern for humanity; in His atonement for sin, He has reconciled men to God; in His resurrection and glorified life, He reveals that splendid vista which is the consummation of perfected human nature. "As the inferior stages of existence are summed up in man, who stands at the head of earthly creation, and forms a first link between the natural and the spiritual, so are all stages of humanity summed up in Christ, who in His person as God-man, links the creation absolutely with God" (Orr, *Christian View*, p. 284).[1] Bearing in mind that it involves this aspect, we may note that intimate connection with the idea of *subordination* to which reference has already been made. Now, when this subordination is viewed in the light of its context, it means that evil has been finally vanquished, so that it can no more raise up its head in defiance of the exalted Lord. The continuous *existence* of impenitent sinners, which might seem to conflict with that victory as affecting the completion of the divine purpose, is a question which lies outside the apostle's horizon. He is only concerned with the antithesis of *life* and the loss of it. It means that redeemed humanity has now reached its full assimilation to its Lord and Head. His Divine σῶμα (τοῦ σώματος, τῆς ἐκκλησίας, Col. i. 18)

[1] See also Weizsäcker, *Apost. Zeitalter*, p. 120.

has reached its maturity. There is no dissension between the Head (*ἡ κεφαλή*, Eph. i. 22) and His members (*τὰ μέλη*). His life circulates through them in unimpeded richness. They have now attained "to the measure of the stature of the fulness of Christ" (Eph. iv. 13). They, the *ἐκκλησία*, make up "the fulness of Him that filleth all in all" (*τὸ πλήρωμα τοῦ τὰ πάντα ἐν πάσιν πληρουμένου*, Eph. i. 23). God's aim is secured, the aim of "reconciling through Him (*i.e.* Christ) all things unto Himself, having made peace through the blood of His cross, whether the things on earth or the things in heaven" (Col. i. 20). Thus Christ is "all and in all" (*πάντα καὶ ἐν πᾶσιν*, Col. iii. 11). The summing-up and the subordination each describes the crowning of the Father's purpose in His exalted Son.

It is comparatively easy to understand the application of St Paul's words to "the things that are in heaven." We are not so ready to give its full force to his equally emphatic declaration about "the things on earth." He takes a large view of creation. For him the whole universe is animated by the breath of the Divine life.[1] The moral and spiritual order extends to the material world. Existence as a whole is connected in one process. There is "one spiritual life," as Dr E. Caird expresses it, "which flows out from God to the Creation, and which flows back to Him again through man, the highest of all the creatures" (*Evolution of Religion*, ii. p. 125). The being of the material world has been affected by that sin which human self-will has introduced into the

[1] *Cf.* Wisd. i. 14: *ἔκτισεν γὰρ εἰς τὸ εἶναι τὰ πάντα καὶ σωτήριοι αἱ γενέσεις τοῦ κόσμου, καὶ οὐκ ἔστιν ἐν αὐτοῖς φάρμακον ὀλέθρου, οὔτε ᾅδου βασίλειον ἐπὶ γῆς.*

universe. It has been subjected to futility, to vain striving (τῇ γὰρ ματαιότητι ἡ κτίσις ὑπετάγη, Rom. viii. 20). We may compare 4 Ezra vii. 11: "For your sakes, indeed, I created the Æon; but when Adam transgressed my commandments, the creation was judged."[1] It is under the sway of φθορά, decay. The very process which is the pathos and doom of human life is the law of the universe also. And the sensitive heart of the apostle overhears the complaint of creation. It becomes animate to his mind, as the offspring of God's creative will, and its sigh for permanence, for the realisation of purpose, for perfection, catches the ear of his soul (Rom. viii. 19-22), and echoes in sympathy with his own craving for complete, victorious *life*. Now if there is to be a redemption (ἀπολύτρωσις) of the material body, a rescue of it from the bondage of decay, an inspiration of it with an immortal existence, a prospect which for St Paul is a glorious certainty, why may not the redemption go further: why may not it extend to that entire creation which as it left His shaping hand, the Creator pronounced to be very good? The thought had appeared already in the Old Testament: *e.g.*, Isa. lxv. 17, "Behold, I create new heavens and a new earth"; Isa. lxvi. 22, "As the new heavens and the new earth which I will make, shall remain before me, saith the Lord, so shall your seed and your name remain" (*cf.* Ps. cii. 26). It finds frequent expression

[1] See Gunkel (*ad loc.*), who calls the conception of a Fall of creation "a compromise between the old optimistic view of the world, which is only recognised for the primitive age, and the modern pessimistic view of Judaism, which holds good for the present." But the growth of such an idea is quite conceivable without any such explanation.

in apocalyptic literature: *e.g.*, Enoch xlv. 4, 5, "I will transform heaven and make it an everlasting blessing and light. I will transform the earth and make it a blessing, and cause mine elect to dwell upon it"; Jub. i. 29, "And the angel of the Presence . . . took the tables of the division of the years . . . from the day of the new creation onwards, when heaven and earth and all its creatures are to be renewed"; Apoc. Bar. xxxii. 6, "Greater than both these tribulations shall be the conflict, when the Almighty will renew His creation."[1] For St Paul, the expectation is confirmed by the future experience of believers as he conceives it. The material universe stands there as the realm of man's earthly activity. It is the sphere assigned him for the present realisation of his relation to God. May it not be that, when the spiritual reaches its full development, completely conquer-

[1] "As the sin and death of the First Adam, the Old Man (אדם הראשון, אדם הקדמוני [*cf.* Levy, *Neuhebr. Wörterbuch*, *s.v.*, אדם and קדמוני] ὁ πρῶτος Ἀδάμ, ὁ ἔσχατος Ἀδάμ, 1 Cor. xv. 45; ὁ πρῶτος ἄνθρωπος, 1 Cor. xv. 47; ὁ παλαιὸς ἄνθρωπος, Col. iii. 4 ff.), were decisive for the earlier epoch, so will the righteousness of life of the New Man, the Second Adam, be for the Second" (Gunkel, *Schöpfung und Chaos*, p. 368). The same idea is expressed by the παλινγενεσία of Matt. xix. 28; *cf.* Rev. xxi. 1. See also the admirable statement of Dr Davidson, which lays bare the basis of St Paul's thought: "The great conception of the Old Testament is, that the world is a moral constitution. Behind the physical world is God, a free, conscious, moral being; on this side of it and over it, is man, another free, moral being. The world is but the means of their intercourse. It is this moral character of its whole constitution, which explains how the external world is always drawn into the relations of God and man, and reflects these relations according as they are normal and disturbed, rejoicing and blossoming like the rose in man's redemption, and falling into desolation in man's destruction under God's wrath" (*Old Testament Prophecy*, p. 209).

ing and controlling the material in the person of redeemed man, there shall still be a province for this new, glorified life, consisting in a transformed and glorified universe in which that which has been imperfect shall be done away?[1] Perhaps there is a hint of this prospect in 1 Cor. vii. 31: "The fashion (σχῆμα) of this world (κόσμος) passeth away." There is more than a hint in Rom. viii. 19-21. The creation looks with eager longing for the manifestation (ἀποκάλυψιν) of the sons of God, which is to be a manifestation of glory (verse 18). That manifestation must have a direct bearing on its own future, for the outlook which lies before it is deliverance from the bondage to decay, and an entrance upon the liberty of the glory of the children of God. Such is the splendid vision which opens to the apostle's ardent soul.[2] Is

[1] *Cf.* Ducasse, *Revue de Théol.*, July 1882 (summarised by Orr, *op. cit.*, p. 447): "Does not a new kingdom appear in man? . . . He is the bond of union between the world of nature and the Divine world. Why then should it not have been precisely his vocation to spiritualise matter, and lead it up to the conquest of new attributes?" It is stating the facts in too speculative a fashion to say with Dr E. Caird, that in Rom. viii. 19 f., "St Paul combines the idea of the *spirituality* of God, which was characteristic of monotheism, with the idea of the *immanence* of God, which was characteristic of pantheism, uniting both in one conception by the aid of the idea of evolution" (*Evolution of Religion*, ii. p. 125). What we find in the passage is rather the poetry of the religious imagination.

[2] A remarkable parallel is found in the Persian conception of the new world. "The dearest dream of Mazdean piety," says Söderblom, "was that of life eternal in a purified, incorruptible body, upon a new earth delivered from all that which as yet mars it. . . . Men, having the appearance of people of forty and fifty years, live immortal, without needs, free from every evil. The end of 'the progress' is attained, 'the world is made

it not in harmony with the profoundest intuitions of those who have

> "The sense sublime
> Of something far more deeply interfused,
> Whose dwelling is the light of setting suns
> And the round ocean and the living air
> And the blue sky, and in the mind of man:
> A motion and a spirit, that impels
> All thinking things, all objects of all thought,
> And rolls through all things."[1]

There still remains one stage to be considered in St Paul's conception of the consummation of the Kingdom of God. He introduces it in the paragraph which we have been examining, at first, without any qualification. "Then the end, when He shall have delivered up (παραδιδοῖ) the Kingdom to His God and Father" (τῷ θεῷ καὶ πατρί). Some further light is thrown upon this momentous statement by verses 27,

progressive (*frasem*) according to its desire' (Yast xix. 89). . . . The ideal world of Mazdeism implies not merely the extinction of Hell, but there is no longer any difference between Heaven and Earth. 'The earth extends to the sphere of the stars' . . . Men can exist in heaven with their bodies" (*op. cit.*, pp. 269, 270). See also Moulton, art. "Zoroastrianism," in *H.D.B.*

[1] It is of curious interest to compare with this forecast one which is thrown out by an evolutionary philosopher like Herbert Spencer. "Confining ourselves to the proximate and not necessarily insoluble question," he says, "we find reason for thinking that after the completion of the various equilibriums which bring to a close all the forms of Evolution we have contemplated, there must continue an equilibrium of a far wider kind. When that integration everywhere in progress throughout our Solar System has reached its climax, there will remain to be effected the immeasurably greater integration of our Solar System with other such systems" (*First Principles*, p. 536.) His conclusion appears to be a succession of evolutions, "ever the same in principle, but never the same in concrete result."

28. In verse 27, quoting Ps. viii. 7 (*cf.* Ps. cx. 1, which our Lord Himself quotes in support of His Messianic Kingship), he assigns the subordination of all things under Christ to the direct power of God. Still keeping this fact in the forefront, he draws the inference that one Power or Authority lies outside this universal subordination. For manifestly He, by whose operation the subordination is brought about, cannot Himself be included in it. Not only so; he takes a further step. There cannot remain two co-equal authorities in the Kingdom of redemption. For "when all things have been subordinated to Him (Christ), then the Son Himself also shall be subordinated to Him (God), who subordinated all things to Him (Christ), in order that God may be all in all" (πάντα ἐν πᾶσιν). It is of importance to inquire whether there are other passages in St Paul's writings which illustrate or elucidate this remarkable conception. The inquiry is a delicate one, for we know that the apostle attributed divinity, in its full and essential sense, to Jesus Christ. Various suggestive utterances may be found which help us to understand his view in the words before us. We are familiar with such passages as Rom. viii. 11: "If the Spirit of Him who raised Jesus from the dead dwell in you, He that raised from the dead Christ Jesus, shall quicken also your mortal bodies." Here, and in its parallels, the potency of the new spiritual life is directly referred to God the Father, even as regards Christ Himself (cf., *e.g.*, 1 Thess. iv. 14, "So also them that sleep through Jesus will God bring with Him"). But the apostle looks upon this power as mediated by the Son. Thus, in 1 Cor. xv. 57, he ascribes thanks "to God who giveth us the victory through (διά) our Lord Jesus

Christ." In 2 Cor. v. 18, we meet his favourite thought of God as "reconciling us to Himself through Christ." It is needless to quote instances of this conception, as they occur on every second page of the Pauline Epistles. But repeatedly we find St Paul emphasising the fact that God, as the Father, is both the primal source and the ultimate goal of all things. Hence he makes such affirmations as that of Rom. xi. 36, "For from (ἐκ) Him, and through (διά) Him, and unto (εἰς, with a view to) Him, are all things"; Eph. iv. 6, where, after enumerating the binding ties of the Christian brotherhood, "one Lord, one faith, one baptism," he names "one God and Father of all, who is over (ἐπί) all and through (διά) all, and in (ἐν) all"; 1 Cor. viii. 6, "For us there is one God the Father, from (ἐκ) whom are all things, and we unto (εἰς) Him, and one Lord Jesus Christ, through (διά) whom are all things, and we through Him"; and we may add Col. i. 19, 20, "It was the good pleasure (of the Father) that the whole fulness should dwell in Him (Christ), and through (διά) Him, to reconcile all things unto (εἰς) Himself (God)." Plainly, from the above passages, a ruling thought with St Paul is that of God as the final aim of all redemptive activity.[1] All things, indeed, are summed up in Christ, in whom dwells the complete fulness of the Divine nature in organised form (σωματικῶς, Col. ii. 9). But Christ Himself carries forward the Divine purpose to its fulfilment. As the Son, He performs His mediatorial function; as the Son, in the deepest reciprocal relation of love with the Father, His life is "with God,

[1] *Cf.* the suggestive statement of Titius (p. 25): "As with Jesus, so with Paul, in this new view of God (*i.e.* as Father), the source of the *whole of salvation* is given" (the italics are ours).

for God, in God." The Divine consummation is attained when "God is all and in all."[1] The process by which such a climax of the highest development of life is reached, may be felt to be suggested by the statement of 1 Cor. iii. 22, 23, "All things belong to you, and you belong to Christ, and Christ belongs to God." This relationship is expressed even more definitely in 1 Cor. xi. 3, "Now I desire you to know that of every man, the Head is Christ. But the Head of Christ is God." Here is an ascending scale, as in the preceding passage, in which God, as it were, gives unity and complete realisation to the whole series of spiritual relations. It is from the same point of view that St Paul, in dealing with the supreme glory of the risen Christ (Phil. ii. 9-11), declares that "God hath highly exalted Him, and given Him the name which is above every name (*i.e.*, the name κύριος, virtually equivalent to the Old Testament *Jehovah*); that in the name of Jesus (often erroneously taken as τὸ ὄνομα τὸ ὑπὲρ πᾶν ὄνομα) every knee should bow, of things in heaven and things on earth, and things under the earth, and every tongue should confess that Jesus Christ is *Lord*, to the *glory of God the Father*." The supreme dignity of the risen Christ, that is to say, points beyond Him to God the Father. Even the

[1] It is perhaps needless to point out that πάντα and ἐν πᾶσιν (which is equivalent to πάντα), in the apostle's view, have no reference save to the redeemed Kingdom of God. This is evident, if we remember that St Paul is here occupied with a discussion of the relation of the Resurrection of Christ to that of believers. He is only concerned with those who, through Christ, have been subordinated to the sway of God. Everything beyond the scope of the direct development of the Kingdom of God lies outside his range. (See also an excellent note of Heinrici, *ad loc.*)

most daring human thought can go no further than the culmination of all things in God.

It would be useless to speculate on the *manner* in which St Paul conceived this great consummation to be fulfilled. Unquestionably he would have regarded all philosophical categories as inapplicable to his momentous theme. For his mind, its interest and importance are wholly religious. He could not realise a more glorious issue for the wondrous process which germinated for humanity with the Incarnation, blossomed in the atoning Passion, and came to full maturity in the Exaltation, than a re-entrance of the glorified Lord into the depths of the Godhead, so that His own words should receive their profoundest significance, "I and my Father are one." In that crowning end, the Consummation of the Kingdom of God is accomplished.

ADDITIONAL NOTE TO CHAPTER II

THE PAULINE ESCHATOLOGY AND HELLENISM

AMONG those influences which in some form or other have contributed to the shaping of St Paul's Conceptions of the Last Things, various competent theologians have included that of Hellenism. And there is nothing in the nature of the situation to preclude such a possibility. The century in which St Paul wrote was one famous for the popularising of philosophical doctrines. In all the chief centres of civilisation throughout the Roman empire, the philosophical lecturer was a familiar figure. His knowledge was often superficial enough, but it became a fashion to attend his prelections, and if he proved a lively and elegant speaker he might count on a large audience. Hence the favourite ideas of Platonism, of the Stoa, of Epicurus, were in circulation widely. At least, every person who pretended to be educated must have had a superficial acquaintance with them. It might be imagined, no doubt, that this condition of popular thought would not affect the Jews, the members of the Diaspora, found in every province of the imperial dominions. They were famed for their exclusiveness. Their one bond of union as a people was their attachment to the religion of their fathers. They prided themselves on their isolation. But their cosmopolitan experience began to tell on their nationalistic prejudices. Even around their own Synagogues, the focus of their life and worship, a fringe of Gentiles had gathered, attracted by the Jewish Monotheism, which met a strong craving of that age, and eager to learn more of that purer morality which stood in so sharp a contrast to their own social environment. Through special circumstances such as these, and the more vague and general influence of the *Zeit-Geist*, they were compelled, however reluctantly,[1] to enlarge their horizon, and admit into their thought speculations which had sprung from a foreign source.

But there were thinkers here and there who showed no such reluctance, who yielded themselves cordially to this growing Hellenic influence, who assimilated the doctrines of Plato and the Stoics so far as loyal Jews could assimilate them, and in their own fashion bridged the cleft between Judaism and Hellenism. These writers mainly belonged to the famous school of Alexandria, a stronghold of Jewish life and influence; their best known representatives are Philo and the author of the Book of Wisdom. It is impossible for us here to examine Philo's Eschatology. But, speaking broadly, it is genuinely Greek in character, assimilating Platonic influences in the most conspicuous fashion, departing wholly, for example, from the expectation of a quickening of the complete personality in a future life. This latter deviation rests on his belief that the

[1] See, *e.g.*, Menzel, *Der griech. Einfluss auf Prediger u. Weisheit Salomos*, 1889.

body is entirely antagonistic to the soul. But this antagonism he ascribes, not to the fact that the body is material, but that it is merely phenomenal, and so transient, in contrast to the "world of eternal ideas amid which reason lives."[1] "It is not possible," he says, "while dwelling in the body and the mortal *genus*, to hold communion with God" (*Leg. Alleg.* iii. 14). As might be expected, he spiritualises all the common eschatological ideas. "The true Hades is the life of the wicked man exposed to vengeance with uncleansed guilt, obnoxious to every curse" (*Congr. Erud. Gr.* 11). The death which is his wages is "to live always dying, and to endure, as it were, death deathless and unending." It is "to be haunted with unmingled grief and fear" (*Praem. et Poen.* 12). The virtuous, on the other hand, shall leave behind them the strife and necessity and corruption of the lower world, and come to the Unbegotten and Eternal, the city of God, the mystical Jerusalem which signifies the vision of peace (*Somn.* ii. 38; *Quis rer. div. her.* 58).[2] These extracts suffice to show how completely the spirit of Hellenic philosophy has penetrated this remarkable Jewish thinker. The same influences assert themselves, although less prominently, in the Wisdom of Solomon.[3] Several of the stable elements in Jewish

[1] See Drummond, *Philo*, ii. p. 297.

[2] We take the translations from Drummond's invaluable work (ii. pp. 322, 323).

[3] Its close connection with the Wisdom-literature of the Old Testament has not been sufficiently recognised in current discussions. For a similar contact between Judaism and Greek philosophy, see the marked traces of Stoic influence in the discourse on the Devout Reason as Mistress of the Desires, in 4 Maccabees.

Eschatology remain side by side with those which are purely Hellenistic, and so irreconcilable positions are held simultaneously. Thus there appears, *e.g.*, the notion of a Day of Judgment; but how this is combined with the unquestionable teaching of the book, that the souls of the righteous, immediately after death, appear in the presence of God and enter perfect blessedness, there is no indication. In any case, the conception of immortality is wholly spiritual.

This book is of special interest for our discussion, inasmuch as an intimate relationship has been assumed between it and St Paul. Indeed, it may be said that the Hellenistic Judaism of Alexandria has usually been regarded as the main instrument in bringing the apostle into contact with Hellenism, for we may leave out of account the far-fetched theory of Teichmann that St Paul became acquainted with Greek ideas by means of the apocalyptic literature. If this close connection can be established, it would be reasonable to expect further traces of the effect of Greek speculation on the apostle's thinking. An interesting monograph has been written on the subject by Prof. E. Grafe in *Abhandlungen . . . C. von Weizsäcker gewidmet.* Grafe finds proofs of St Paul's dependence on Wisdom, not merely in thought, but even in language. In 1 Cor. ii., for example, in agreement with Pfleiderer (*Urchristentum*, pp. 161, 257), he compares verses 8, 10, 11 with Wisd. ix. 7, ii. 9 with vii. 28, ii. 10 with vii. 27, ii. 14 with ix. 14, ii. 15 with ix. 11, ii. 16 with ix. 13 (p. 278). It appears to us, that unless one came to the passages prepared to find parallels, the correspondences would scarcely appeal to him. Take, *e.g.*, the famous statement of 1 Cor. ii. 14: ψυχικὸς δὲ ἄνθρωπος οὐ *δέχεται τὰ τοῦ πνεύματος τοῦ θεοῦ· μωρία γὰρ αὐτῷ ἐστιν, καὶ οὐ δύναται γνῶναι, ὅτι πνευματικῶς ἀνακρίνεται.* Its companion passage runs thus: *λογισμοὶ γὰρ θνητῶν δειλοί, καὶ ἐπισφαλεῖς αἱ ἐπίνοιαι ἡμῶν*, Wisd. ix. 14. It is hard to see wherein the kinship lies. St Paul's words refer to a great principle of the spiritual life: the Wisdom-passage is one of those general maxims with which the Book of Proverbs has made us familiar. Grafe finds corroboration for the parallelism in the repeated occurrence of *σοφία* in 1 Cor. ii. and in chaps. vii. and ix. of Wisdom, with which the comparison is made. But the apostle's introduction of *σοφία* is entirely due to its antithesis, *μωρία*, "folly," the term by which the cultivated Greeks described the preaching of the Cross. They demand a Gospel which shall be *σοφία*, suiting their intellectual presuppositions. St Paul has a *σοφία* to preach, namely, God's wonderful redemptive purpose, whose profound depths can be set before those who are mature. The *σοφία* of Wisd. vii. and ix. is identical with that of Prov. viii., the auxiliary of God in creation, that genuine knowledge, that moral insight personified, which forms the basis of all true life. The Book of Proverbs would supply an equally relevant parallelism. Grafe identifies the *σοφία* of St Paul with the *πνεῦμα ἅγιον* which occasionally occurs in Wisdom (p. 278). There is certainly much force in this equation, but the remarkable conception of Prov. viii. seems, in our judgment, to approach even nearer the Pauline idea of the *πνεῦμα*. In any case, the intimate relation between *σοφία* and the Divine *πνεῦμα* has its roots entirely in the Old Testament, where the Spirit of God is the principle of all the highest phenomena of moral and intellectual life. Grafe further points out that the idea of the body as a σκῆνος, tent, for the soul (2 Cor. v. 1, Wisd. ix. 15), "is a fundamental thought of Alexandrian philosophy." But our exposition of the Pauline passage reveals the essential contrast of thought underlying their respective uses of the term. It is strange to find so careful a student of St Paul as Prof. Grafe asserting (p. 276) that for the belief in *immediate* fellowship with Christ after death, "the apostle has found a conception which helps him in the spiritualistic hope of the Alexandrians" (he compares Phil. i. 23 with Wisd. iii. 1-3, vi. 20). To begin with, the passage quoted says nothing about *immediate* fellowship with Christ after death:[1] if it did, the apostle, in accordance with his central conception of the Resurrection and its accompaniments, must have conceived it on totally different lines from the "spiritualistic hopes of the Alexandrians."

But the feature in Paulinism which is supposed to reveal most plainly the influence of Hellenic thought is his conception of the antithesis between σάρξ and πνεῦμα. The significance of the antithesis, as our chapter on the Resurrection shows, lies at the very basis of the profoundest portion of his Eschatology. If the apostle has shaped his ideas under the guidance of Greek speculation at this point, it must be admitted that a foreign element has penetrated deep into his thinking. The question is, Does St Paul hold a dualistic conception of human nature? Does he believe that matter, flesh (σάρξ) is essentially evil, that the human consciousness is defiled for the very reason that it is clothed in a material form? This is asserted, among others, by Holsten,

[1] See chap. v. pp. 272-273.

who finds in St Paul the contrast between the wholly sensual nature of mortal flesh and the pure essence of the eternal Spirit (see, *e.g.*, *Paulin. Theol.* pp. 80-84); by Holtzmann, who, however, supplies a hint towards the true understanding of the problem when he says: "*Like his ethic*,[1] this new (*i.e.* pneumatic) Eschatology is built upon the Hellenistic antithesis of flesh and spirit" (*N.T. Theol.* ii. p. 195); and by Prof. Percy Gardner, "Put in the form in which it appears in Romans, the doctrine of the evil flesh is one familiar to students of ancient religion as one of the main tenets of the mysteries in later Greece" (*Historic View*, p. 224). What are the facts? To begin with, St Paul was no metaphysician. We never find in him any attempt at a theoretical solution of the great problems of the world. True to his Old Testament basis, his statements about flesh and spirit must be understood wholly in *the light of his own practical relation to God.* When we examine them from that standpoint, it is easy to discover that they are for him matters of religious experience. His meaning is made plain by such a statement as that of Rom. viii. 7: "The mind of the flesh is hostile to God, for it is not subjected to the law of God, nor can it be. They that are in the flesh (ἐν σαρκί) cannot please God. But ye are not in the flesh but in the Spirit, inasmuch as (εἴπερ) the Spirit of God dwelleth in you." This is not metaphysics. This is a contrast between the actual condition of human nature, untouched by the Divine power, and that nature as directly influenced from above. It is the bodily nature, as he has discovered it in himself, continually biassed

[1] The italics are ours.

towards sin, which he places in antithesis to that Divine, supernatural might, which alone is able to rescue it from the thraldom of evil. How little ground there is for attributing to St Paul the metaphysical theory that the flesh is inherently evil, is evident from such an affirmation as that of Gal. ii. 20, "No longer do I live, but Christ lives in me; but what I at present live in the flesh (ἐν σαρκί), I live by faith, faith in the Son of God," etc. The fact of the matter is that σάρξ may be translated "body" as correctly as "flesh." It was used in that sense, even in Greek philosophical circles, at the time when St Paul wrote (see Zeller, *Theol. Jahrbücher*, 1852, pp. 293-297). But in the case of the apostle, for whom the relation of life *to God* was the supreme interest, it was wholly natural, when he thought of man as distinguished from God, to describe him as "flesh," in contrast to "spirit." And thus the distinction easily passed into an opposition; for man, as he had discovered in his personal experience, was under the sway of sin and could not break its yoke, apart from the aid of the Spirit who is the Divine, supernatural Agent. Plainly, therefore, the antagonism of which the apostle is conscious between σάρξ and πνεῦμα is a moral and not a metaphysical antagonism, and it is one discovered, not by the path of speculation, but from the humiliating experiences of actual life.[1] Siebeck, writing

[1] It is worth observing, in passing, that St Paul recognises the presence of evil in spirits, who have no share in the flesh at all (*cf.* Eph. ii. 2), while Christ, who was sent "in the likeness of the flesh of sin" (*i.e.* in the likeness of human flesh, human nature, which, as a fact of experience, is sinful), was without sin (see Müller, *Doct. of Sin*, i. pp. 346-348).

as a historian of psychology, well expresses the facts when he says: "In no passage do the Pauline psychological views deny their Hebrew origin. . . . As in Plato, the circumstance that God's being was conceived ethically had the consequence that its dialectic antithesis, matter, receded into the position of 'evil,' so also in Paul the flesh becomes, on the ground of that natural antithesis to the moral contrasted pole of the Divine Spirit, the bearer of sin and weakness" (*Geschichte d. Psychol.* 1ter Th. 2te Abth., p. 311). If any further evidence were needed, it might be found in St Paul's central conception of the Resurrection, in which all his arguments are directed to the establishing, not of a break between the present and the future life, but of "an organic link between the temporal and the eternal," that link whose existence has been demonstrated for him by his own experience of the risen Christ, in whom the human and the divine are perfectly united in the σῶμα τῆς δόξης αὐτοῦ (Phil. iii. 21).

But while firmly controverting the presence of any philosophical dualism, the result of Hellenic or Hellenistic influence, in the foundations of St Paul's eschatological thought, we would by no means deny the appearance in his writings of many spiritual tendencies which associate him with the deepest currents of contemporary Greek philosophy. Yet it is, in most cases, a kinship independently reached. If they agree in a lofty conception of God, which sets in bold relief the imperfections of human life; if they are both conscious of a conflict between good and evil in the human soul, which can nevertheless be surmounted by a communion of man with the Divine; if they are at one in exalting the spiritual life as that alone worth living, because it is the pathway to the true goal of existence,[1]—their agreement should not be traced to any direct interchange of ideas. The fulness of the time had come. The most earnest minds of ancient Hellenism were groping towards the same vision which for the Christian apostle had made all things new.

[1] See an admirable paragraph in Titius, pp. 286, 287.

INDEX.

I.—SUBJECTS.

II.—AUTHORS.

III.—REFERENCES.

1. OLD TESTAMENT.

2. New Testament.

3. Judaistic Writings.